ENGLISH FOR THE TELECOMMUNICATIONS INDUSTRY

Jeremy Comfort
Rod Revell
Ian Simpson
Trish Stott
Derek Utley

Oxford University Press

Oxford University Press
Walton Street, Oxford OX2 6DP

Oxford New York
Athens Auckland Bangkok Bombay
Calcutta Cape Town Dar es Salaam Delhi
Florence Hong Kong Istanbul Karachi
Kuala Lumpur Madras Madrid Melbourne
Mexico City Nairobi Paris Singapore
Taipei Tokyo Toronto

and associated companies in
Berlin Ibadan

ISBN 0 19 437643 5

First published 1986
Fourth impression 1994

Phototypeset by Promenade Graphics Ltd

Printed in Hong Kong

Contents

Acknowledgements

The authors and publishers would particularly like to thank the following individuals and organizations for their help in providing source material, technical advice, and opportunities to pilot the material:

Ecole Nationale Supérieure des Télécommunications (Bretagne), France
Swedish Telecom
British Telecom (in particular the York area)
Norwegian Telecommunications Administration
York Language Training Ltd
Horst Lamers, Telecommunications Engineer at **ADB**

The following organizations and publications have kindly given permission to use source material:

The Book Publishing Company; British Telecom; Electrical and Electronic Press Ltd; FutureComm Publications Inc; Guardian Newspapers Ltd; ITU Telecommunications Journal; New Science Publications; Nottingham Building Society; Pitman Publishing Ltd; Prentice-Hall Inc Publishing; Siemens AG; Telecom Users Association; Times Newspapers Ltd; VNU Business Publications.

The publishers have been unable to trace the copyright holders for the adaptation of the following material in Unit 15: the second reading passage, the second listening passage, and the chart for discussion. The publishers would be pleased to hear from them.

Teacher's notes

1 Aims of the course

English for the Telecommunications Industry is designed to improve the job-specific English of non-native speakers of the language who are working, or being trained for subsequent careers, in the telecommunications industry. These include managers, engineers and technicians working or training for Telecommunications Administrations (PTTs); equipment manufacturers; government departments; international agencies; international consultancies; data communications departments of user companies; technical/vocational training colleges.
English for the Telecommunications Industry aims to practise the four skills of listening, reading, speaking and writing through the use of varied and authentic activities.

Duration of the course

The course represents about one year's institutional use (3/4 hours per week). Each unit should take about 5/6 hours of classroom time.

Entry level

The course starts at a pre-intermediate level of English and is designed to upgrade a student's level to post-intermediate on completion.
The course is suitable for learners at a higher entry level who have not used their English for some years or who wish to revise their knowledge.
From a technical point of view, the course presupposes a basic knowledge of, or a strong interest in, telecommunications.

Methods of use

The course is designed either for use in a class setting with a teacher or for individual learners without access to a teacher.
It is designed so that it can be used sequentially from Unit 1 to 15. However, each unit stands on its own so students and teachers can use it selectively.

Parts of the course

The course consists of this book and two C90 cassettes containing material for the listening activities in the course.

2 Structure of the course

The course consists of 15 main units and 3 revision units (for detailed unit by unit breakdown, see contents grid).
There are three sections to the book:

Section A Consolidation

Units 1–5 These units provide an opportunity for students to be introduced to or revise basic language structures, functions, telecommunication concepts and terminology. They concentrate on description of components, systems and techniques.
Revision Unit A This revises the language introduced above and introduces a telecoms case-study based on an imaginary country (continued in Revision Units B and C).

Section B Exploitation

Units 6–10 These units exploit the technical information presented in the previous section. The activities involve interpretation of technical information and application to problem-solving.
Revision Unit B This unit revises the language of Units 1 to 10. It continues the case-study presented in Revision Unit A.

Section C Extension

Units 11–15 The final five units use the technical input of the previous ten units in management-related contexts. The units look at telecoms in four countries (France, Britain, India and Sweden) from the Telecom Administration's, supplier's and user's points of view. The final unit looks at the growth of telecoms internationally.
Revision Unit C The final revision unit revises language skills developed in the previous 15 units and forms the last part of the case-study.

Key/ Tapescripts

At the back of the book, there is a comprehensive key providing answers or solutions to all questions and problems set during the course. This is followed by tapescripts of the listening passages.

3 Unit structure

The main units are divided into the following sections:

Reading 1

Each unit begins with a textual extract which introduces the theme of the unit. There are usually two types of comprehension task associated with the extract:

i) An 'as you read' task often involving transfer of information to chart or table.
ii) Follow-up comprehension questions or task involving extraction of more detailed information from the text.

As the course progresses, these texts are less and less edited so that, at the end, they appear unchanged from the original.

Listening 1

The reading activity is always followed directly by a listening passage recorded on the cassette. These are scripted mono-, dia- or polylogues which recreate 'authentic' situations such as seminar lectures, committee meetings, conference presentations and informal discussions. Again there are two types of comprehension task: an 'as you listen' transfer of information and follow-up comprehension questions or task.

Language practice

In the first ten units, there are always three language exercises which practise structures and functions the students have read or heard in the previous two sections. The final language exercise is usually based on the listening section and concentrates on spoken language.
In the final five units, there are two language exercises per unit which concentrate more on vocabulary learning and extension.

Reading 2/ Listening 2

The language practice is followed by a further reading or listening passage which extends the theme of the unit and is often used as a basis for a follow-up activity or the writing exercise in the next section. In the final five units, there is both a Reading 2 and Listening 2.

Writing

In this section the students use their knowledge gained in the unit to write: technical descriptions, instructions, telexes, letters and reports. In the last five units, there is no separate writing section. Writing tasks are set in conjunction with the listening and reading passages.
Note that the writing tasks very often have more than one right answer. Therefore the key only provides model versions of the telexes, letters, reports etc. A useful technique here is to get students working individually or in small groups of 3 or 4 to provide their version on transparency. This can then be displayed using an overhead projector for the rest of the class and teacher to compare with other versions, comment and correct.

Discussion/ Role-play

Each unit raises some important issues in the field of telecoms. This section provides an opportunity for students to give their opinions, based on their existing knowledge and that gained from the unit. Usually, there are three or four discussion topics to choose from. In some cases, a role-play is suggested.
Your students will probably be best qualified to choose one of the suggested topics or suggest an alternative, if none appeal. Also try using the visuals (photos, charts and graphs) which have appeared in the unit as a springboard for discussion.

Word List

This is designed as both a reference for students working on reading and listening passages and as a source of important productive vocabulary when discussing the topics above.

Self-study guide

For students using the course without a teacher.

Who is the course for?

This is a course for managers, engineers and technicians working in or training for the telecommunications industry. If you already have some English (2 or 3 years at school), but want to improve your English for your job, this course will give you practice in all four skills—*listening*, *reading*, *speaking* and *writing*. It will also teach you the technical and commercial vocabulary related to the telecoms industry.

How long does it last?

There are fifteen main units and three revision units. Working on your own, you will find that each unit takes about four hours, slightly less for the revision units.

What level do I need to be?

Language: You need to have a good basic understanding of English grammar. If you have studied English for several years, you may find the first few units easy but work through them as they will help you to revise your knowledge.
Technical: You need to have a basic knowledge of telecoms technology. If you work or are training for the administration/ management side, you will find the first five units provide a good background in the technology and terminology. If you are on the technical side, you will find the last five units more management-related but including some technical content.

How can I use this course?

The course consists of this coursebook and two cassettes. It is best if you work through the course from Unit 1 to Unit 15. If you don't have time, use the Contents grid (pp. 6–9) to select units or part of units which interest you. The instructions below tell you what to do in each unit.
Note that the key (pp. 216–236) sometimes provides 'right' answers (there is only one answer), sometimes a model answer (more than one answer is possible). Also note that there is a word list at the end of each unit. Use this when you meet difficult words or expressions in the Reading and Listening passages.

Section	Instructions
Reading 1	1. Make sure you understand what you have to do 'as you read'. 2. Read the text and complete the 'as you read' task. 3. Check your answers in the key. 4. Read the text again and answer the comprehension questions which follow the text. 5. Check your answers with the key.
Listening 1	1. Make sure you understand what you have to do 'as you listen'. 2. Listen once and complete the task. 3. Listen again, if necessary. 4. Check your answers in the key. 5. Listen a third time. Stop the cassette in order to answer the comprehension questions. 6. If, after listening 2 or 3 times, you can't answer the questions, look at the tapescript in the key.
Language practice	1. Look carefully at the examples/explanations at the beginning of each language practice exercise. 2. Do the exercise. 3. Check your answers in the key. Note that the third Language practice exercise often involves replaying the Listening 1 passage.
Reading 2/ Listening 2	Follow the instructions as for Reading 1 or Listening 1.
Writing	1. Read the instructions/model carefully. 2. Do the writing exercise. 3. Check your answers in the key. Note that you will often find a model version. Your version may be different but also right.
Discussion	You cannot do this section by yourself!
Word list	Use this when you meet difficult words or expressions in the listening passages. Try not to use it too much. You will find you can often guess the meaning of a word from the context.

Detailed contents grid

	THEME	READING 1	LISTENING 1
1	**Networks (1)** Description of telephone & data networks	Description of local, junction & trunk networks	Seminar on extension of local network
2	**Transmission (1)** Description of transmission systems	Description of basic transmission means	Training session on PCM transmission
3	**Switching (1)** Development of switching systems	Historical account of development of switching	Telephone call about PABX
4	**Computer communications (1)** Developments in data processing & telecommunications	Speech about trends in computer communications	Telephone call about word processors
5	**Radio communications (1)** Forms of radio communications	Description of types of radio communications	Radio telephone call giving directions
REV A	**Case-study: Stage 1** Meeting the customer	1. Reniat: multinational company organization 2. Costerutsi: description of developing country 3. Telecoms Administration: developments in Costerutsi	
6	**Networks (2)** Local Area Networks	Comparison of LANs & PABXs	Seminar on LANs
7	**Transmission (2)** Modern transmission techniques	Article about common channel signalling	Meeting about call diversion facilities
8	**Switching (2)** Development of electronic switching & telematics	Comparison of space division vs. time division switching	Discussion about French E 10 exchange system
9	**Computer communications (2)** Telecommunications & data processing	Article about evolution of Prestel	Presentation on international developments
10	**Radio communications (2)** Role of communications satellites	Historical description of types of satellites	Interview about European communications satellites
REV B	**Case-study: Stage 2** Defining needs	1. Communication needs 2. Available services 3. Meeting the needs	

LANGUAGE PRACTICE	READING 2/ LISTENING 2	WRITING/ LISTENING 2	DISCUSSION
Classification; use of active & passive; clarification & interruption	Description of Public Data Network	Writing description of an SPC system	Digitalization; maintaining existing analogue networks
Process description; explaining relationships; asking for & giving explanations	Description of optical fibres	Writing description of an FDM system	Optical fibres; satellites; transmission speed & quality
Comparison; present perfect/simple past; giving & asking for instructions	Description of electronic exchanges	Writing instructions: how to call transfer	Changeover to digital exchanges in developing countries; future of operator staff
Forecasting; telephoning; definition	Description of electronic telex machine	Writing a telex: reply to enquiry about word processor	Integrated Service Networks; the office of the future
Quantity & amount; prepositions of location; asking questions	Description of mobile telephone system	Writing a letter; replying to a telex	Radio-paging; mobile telephone services
Classification, process description; active to passive Description, prepositions, comparison; past to present perfect Listening, note-taking, discussion			
Present continuous; modal verbs; expressing opinions	Discussion about optical fibre LAN in Biarritz	Writing a letter arranging a visit	LANs in the office; LANs vs. PABXs; the Biarritz network
Future & conditions; past continuous; polite responses	Meeting about teleconferencing	Writing minutes of meeting about teleconferencing	Subscriber complaints; leased lines vs. PSTN; teleconferencing vs. videophone
Combining sentences; expressions of frequency; question tags	Teleshop discussion about telematics	Writing a systems description; applications of telematics	TDS systems; applications of telematics; effects of telecommunications and data processing on society
Contrast & difference; adjectives & adverbs; giving presentations	Enquiries about home-banking: Homelink	Writing a report: decision on Homelink	Videotex & the media; the informed & the uninformed; effects of home computer services on local communities
Reason & result; plans & intentions; dealing with difficult questions	Sales talk about small home earth stations	Writing a report; reporting speech	Uses of satellites; the influence of satellites & home earth stations; space-shuttle
Ordering a report Writing a reply Role-play or writing up minutes of a meeting			

Detailed contents grid

	THEME	READING 1	LISTENING 1
11	**Telecoms in France** Dealing with growth	Background: Vélizy project (Télétel)	Presentation on history of growth
12	**Telecoms in Britain** Privatization/deregulation	Background: trade union vs. management views	Radio discussion about privatization & the suppliers
13	**Telecoms in India** Developing country	Background: telephone industry & distribution	Interview about recruitment & training
14	**Telecoms in Sweden** Organization & efficiency	Background: organization of telecoms administration	Visit to ELLEMTEL research labs.
15	**International Telecoms** Dealing with growth	Historical overview; future prospects	Discussion about optical fibre developments
REV C	**Case-study: Stage 3** Growing pains	1. C.T.A. in perspective 2. Trouble shooting 3. Press launch	

LANGUAGE PRACTICE	READING 2/ LISTENING 2	WRITING/ LISTENING 2	DISCUSSION
Degree; describing change	Technical description of Télétel systems	Listening to discussion of results of Vélizy experiment	Society & videotex
Word study: derivatives; trends & developments	Article about B.T. meeting the competition	Listening to presentation of MERCURY network	Issues of monopoly & privatization
Word study: derivatives; written & spoken language	Article about research & development	Listening to discussion about technology transfer	Issues of development
Describing an organigram; dealing with visitors	Text about reasons for success	Listening to discussion about international management training	Reasons for efficiency
Immediate past & immediate future; countries, nationalities & languages	Article about world market for suppliers	Listening to discussion about development of user networks	Impact of growth of telecommunications

Listening and note-taking
Negotiating and report-writing
Reading and planning

Unit 1 **Networks 1**

This first unit presents and practises technical descriptions of telephone and data networks.

1.1 **Reading 1**

1.1.1

Read the following description of a national network. As you read, complete the labelling of Figures 1a, 1b, and 1c.

The **UK national network** comprises:

a) the local network
- the lines between the subscriber and the local exchange.

b) the junction network
- the circuits between a local exchange and another local exchange.
- the circuits between a local exchange and a primary centre, sometimes termed a tandem exchange.
- the circuits between a local exchange and a secondary centre, sometimes called a Group Switching Centre (GSC).

c) the main/trunk network
- the circuits between GSCs.
- the circuits between GSCs and tertiary centres, known in the UK as District and Main Switching Centres (DSCs and MSCs).

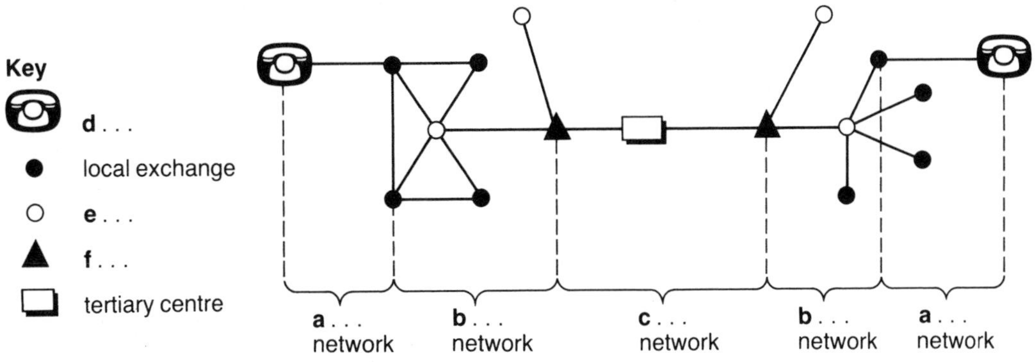

Fig 1a The national network

In the **local network,** each subscriber is connected to a local exchange. To reduce the number of cables, the local network is usually divided into three parts:

a) **the subscriber circuit:** this consists of the telephone set, in the customer's premises, and a cable pair, often an open-wire line, which is connected to a distribution point (DP).
b) **the secondary circuit:** this is made up of a number of pairs (a multi-pair cable) connected over- or underground to a cabinet, sometimes called a cross connection point (CCP).
c) **the primary circuit:** this is composed of a number of multi-pair cables (a multi-unit cable) connected in ducts or in a cable tunnel to the main distribution frame in a local exchange.

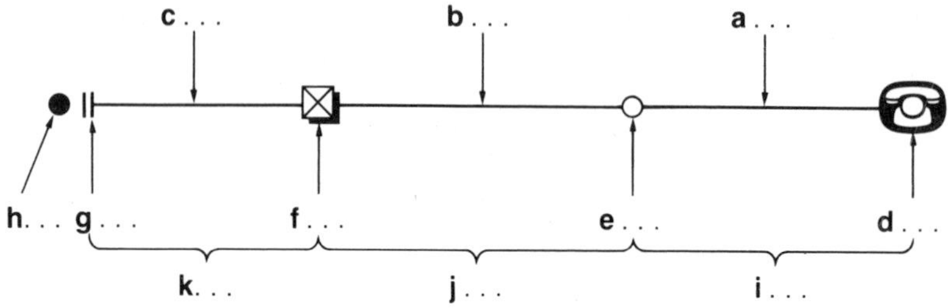

Fig 1b The local network

In the **trunk network**, all non-local calls are set up via a GSC and the main network. In the UK, 70% of all traffic is routed direct to another GSC, 24% via one other GSC. The traffic which cannot be handled by these direct routings is carried by a new network, called the Transit Network. This network, which also carries overseas traffic to the International Gateway Exchanges, comprises 11 MSCs and 26 DSCs, known collectively as Transit Switching Centres (TSCs). Transmission on this network can be by coaxial cable or radio link.

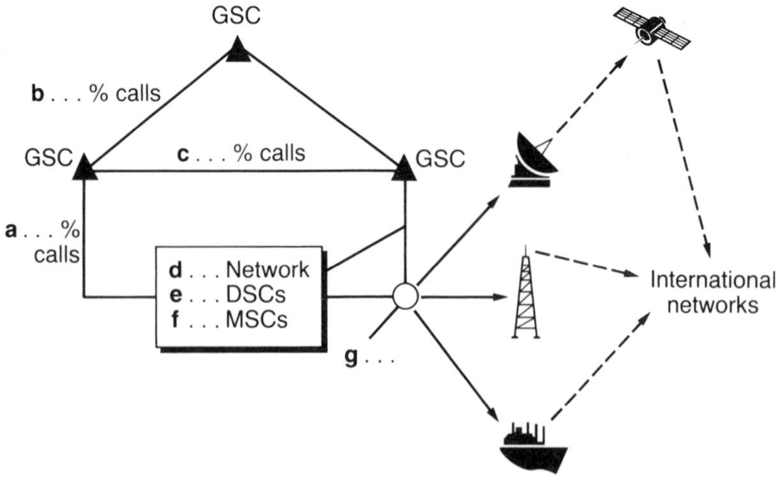

Fig 1c The analogue trunk network

1.1.2 Comprehension

Answer the following questions:

What do the following abbreviations stand for?

a GSC ...
b DSC ...
c MSC ...
d DP ...
e CCP ...
f TSC ...

What is another term for?

g the main network ...
h a primary centre ...
i a secondary centre ...
j a tertiary centre ...
k a cabinet ...

What other means of transmission are mentioned in the passage?

an open wire line

l ...
m ...
n ...
o ...
p ...

What types of traffic does the transit network carry?

q ...
r ...

1.2 Listening

1.2.1

Listen to the following extract from a training seminar about the extension of a local network. As you listen, label the figures below with the correct reference number and title. Also complete the keys where necessary.

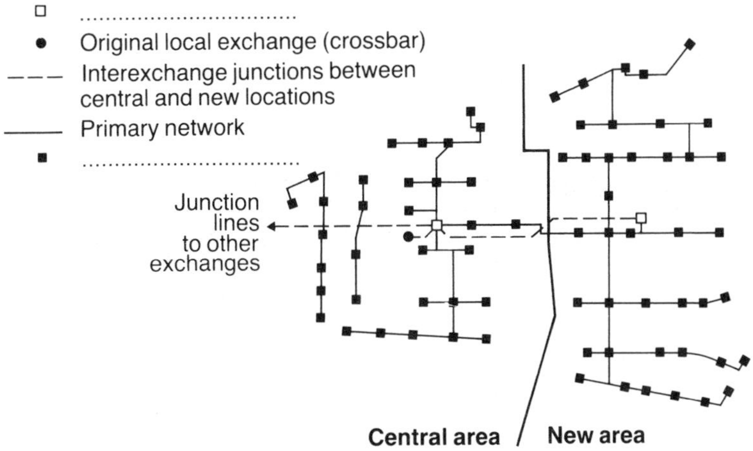

Fig ...

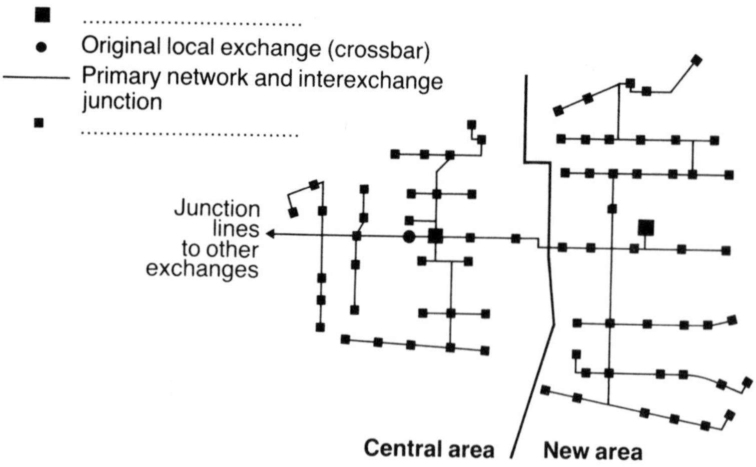

Fig . . .

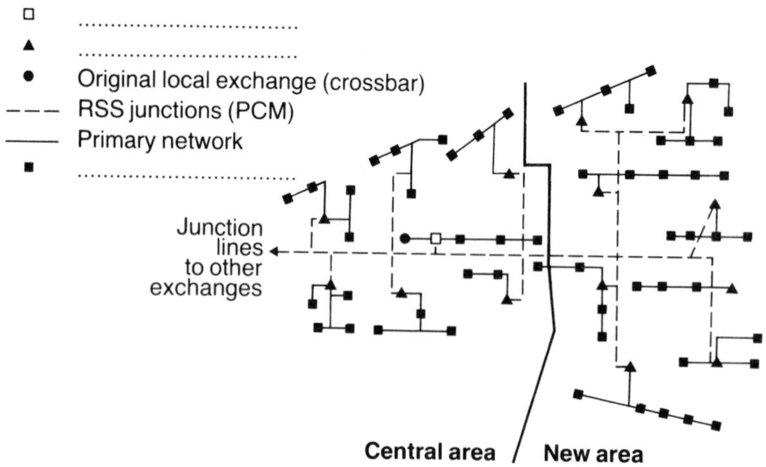

Fig . . .

1.2.2 Comprehension

Listen again and answer the following questions:

a What is the aim in this case-study?
b Which part of the local network is considered in this case-study?
c What type of transmission is used in the first solution?
d What types of exchange are used in the first solution?
e What are the purposes of the two new exchanges in the second solution?
i) . . . ii) . . .
f Where, in the Central Area, is one of the new exchanges located?
g Which part of the network uses digital transmission in the second solution?
h How many exchanges are used in the third solution?
i Do the Remote Subscriber Switches replace the cabinets?
j Which part of the network in Solution 3 uses analogue transmission?

1.3 Language practice

1.3.1 Classification

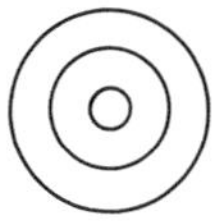

The network	is composed of	3 parts.
	consists of	
	comprises	
	is made up of	

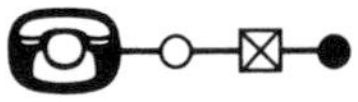

The local network	can be/is divided into	3 parts.
	can be/is broken down into	
	can be/is separated into	

[A] + [B]

There are **two** exchanges. **Both** are traditional electromechanical exchanges.

[A] , [B]

Two SPC exchanges are installed; **one** to extend the central area, **the other** to serve the new area.

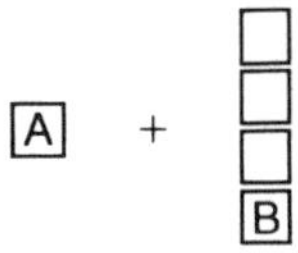

70% of traffic is routed direct from **one** GSC to **another** GSC.

Use the map to complete the sentences below:

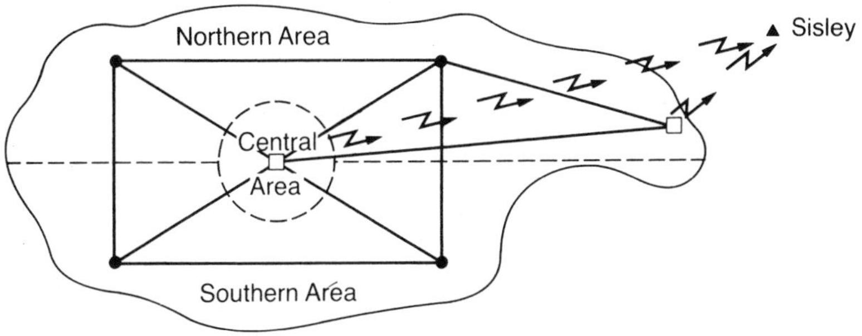

Fig 1g The Newtown local telephone area

a The Newtown telephone network . . . . . . 2 secondary centres and . . . .

b The Area . . . . . . into 3 sub-areas; North, ...

c There . . . . . . secondary centres. . . . . . . are connected to the DSC in Sisley by radio link.

d There . . . . . . junction routes between the secondary centres: . . . . . . direct, ... via a local exchange.

e Routing from . . . . . . local exchange to . . . . . . can be direct or via . . . . . . exchanges.

f . . . . . . Northern and Southern areas are served by . . . . . . local exchanges.

1.3.2 Description use of active and passive

Look at these two sentences:

A International traffic **is carried** by the Transit Network.
B The Transit Network **carries** international traffic.

Both A and B are correct. The choice (A or B) depends on what you want to emphasize: 'International traffic' (sentence A) or 'The Transit Network' (sentence B).

Now look at these two sentences:

C Additional cables **are laid**.
D They **lay** additional cables.

C is much better than D. The personal subject 'they' in D does not add any information. In fact, it makes the important information more difficult to see.

Make sentences from the table below. In some cases, you can make both an active and a passive sentence.

	Agent	Action	Object	Adverbial
a	You	expand	the central exchange	
b	The junction circuits	use	PCM	mainly
c	SPC exchanges	serve	both areas	
d	They	install	cabinets	in the local area
e	We	route	traffic	direct to a GSC
f	An open-wire line	connect	the subscriber	to the DP
g	We	set up	all non-local calls	via a GSC
h	A machine	dig up	the road	in order to lay a cable
i	We	site	the exchange	near the old exchange
j	The RSS	switch	the call	to the designated cabinet

1.3.3 Clarification and interruption

The expressions below are very important in two situations:
1 When you do not understand a speaker.
2 When you want to clarify something or make sure your listener understands you.

Interrupting
Sorry to interrupt
Excuse me

→

Asking for clarification
What do you mean by . . . ?
I'm not sure I understand.
So that means that . . . ?

Giving clarification
What I meant was . . .
Let me put it another way . . .
In other words . . .

→

Checking understanding
Is that clear?
Do you follow me?

Now listen again to section 1.2. Pick out the times you hear the above phrases or similar ones.

Then, listen once more. Work in pairs. Stop the tape to interrupt when you don't understand something. Ask your partner to clarify.

1.4 Reading 2

1.4.1

Read the following passage about **data networks**. As you read complete Figure 1h.

Public Data Networks are designed for data transmission only. They therefore avoid the limitations of speed etc. of transmission over the switched public telephone or telex network. The Nordic Public Data Network is a circuit-switched type of digital network and its basic purpose is to provide a means of synchronous data transmission.

The network consists of a number of components which are interconnected as shown in Figure 1h.

The data switching exchange (DSE) controls the set-up and clear-down of data calls, and monitors the connections and functions of the network. This exchange, which is capable of handling 100 calls per second, may be supplemented at a later date with a special service centre (SSC) for the introduction of certain new facilities. The DSE is connected to a data circuit concentrator (DCC). The purpose of the concentrator is to collect traffic from a number of individual subscriber circuits. This traffic is passed via time division multiplexed high-speed links (TDM) to the exchange. These TDMs, which consist of time division multiplexed streams (64 Kbps), also transfer traffic between the DCC and one of the multiplexors (RMX). The multiplexors (RMX and DMX) connect several subscriber lines either directly to the DSE or to the DCC which passes traffic to the DSE. Between the RMX and the DMX and the data terminal equipment (DTE), the data circuit terminating equipment (DCE) is located in the subscriber's premises. It primarily provides the standardized interface between the DTE and the network. Lastly, the DTE, which consists of a printing or alphanumeric visual display terminal or a computer, provides the subscriber with the data reception facilities.

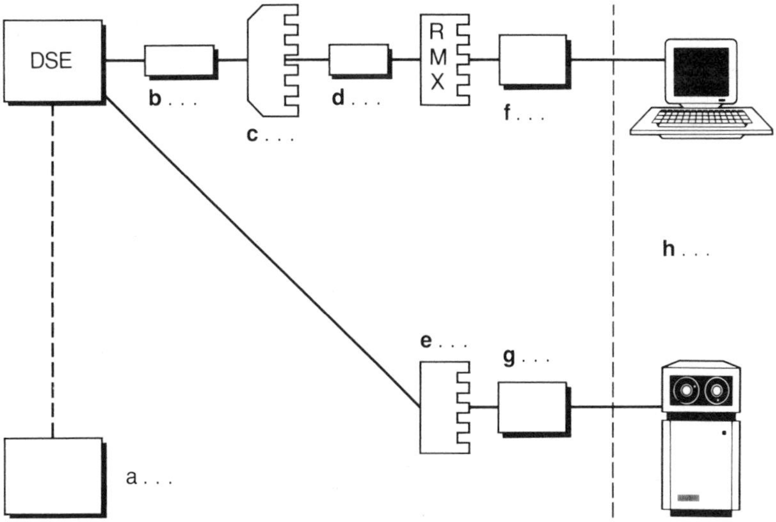

Fig 1h The Nordic Data Network

1.4.2 Comprehension

Answer the following questions:

a Match the components with their appropriate functions. (NB Some components have more than one function).

Components	Functions
1 DCC	**a** introduction of new facilities
2 RMX/DMX	**b** provision of data reception facilities
3 DSE	**c** collection of traffic from subscriber circuits
4 DCE	**d** connection of subscriber lines
5 SSC	**e** transfer of traffic
6 TDM	**f** control of set-up and clear-down
7 DTE	**g** provision of interface between DTE and network
	h monitoring of network connections and functions

b What is the advantage of data networks compared with data transmission over the telephone?

c What is the capability of the DSE?

d What does the data terminal equipment consist of?

1.4.3 Activity

a Below are some of the facilities a subscriber in the Nordic Public Data Network can have. Match them with the appropriate description.

Facilities	Description
1 Abbreviated address call	**a** On dialling, the subscriber is always connected to a pre-determined number.
2 Direct call	**b** The same number is used for several equivalent terminals. The connection is made to a free terminal.
3 Closed user group	**c** A number of subscribers are protected against calls from subscribers outside the group.
4 Outgoing calls barred	**d** The subscriber cannot call other subscribers.
5 Group number	**e** The subscriber uses only 2-digit numbers for a limited number of other subscribers.
6 Connect when free	**f** The subscriber is informed of the cost of a call on completion of a call.
7 Charge advice	**g** A call to an engaged connection is put in a queue and established when it becomes free.

b Discuss in what situations and for which user groups the above facilities would be useful. For example, 'Would an abbreviated address call facility be useful to small companies such as travel agents?'

1.5 **Writing**

Use the simplified block diagram of a Stored Programme Control system (SPC) to complete the description below.

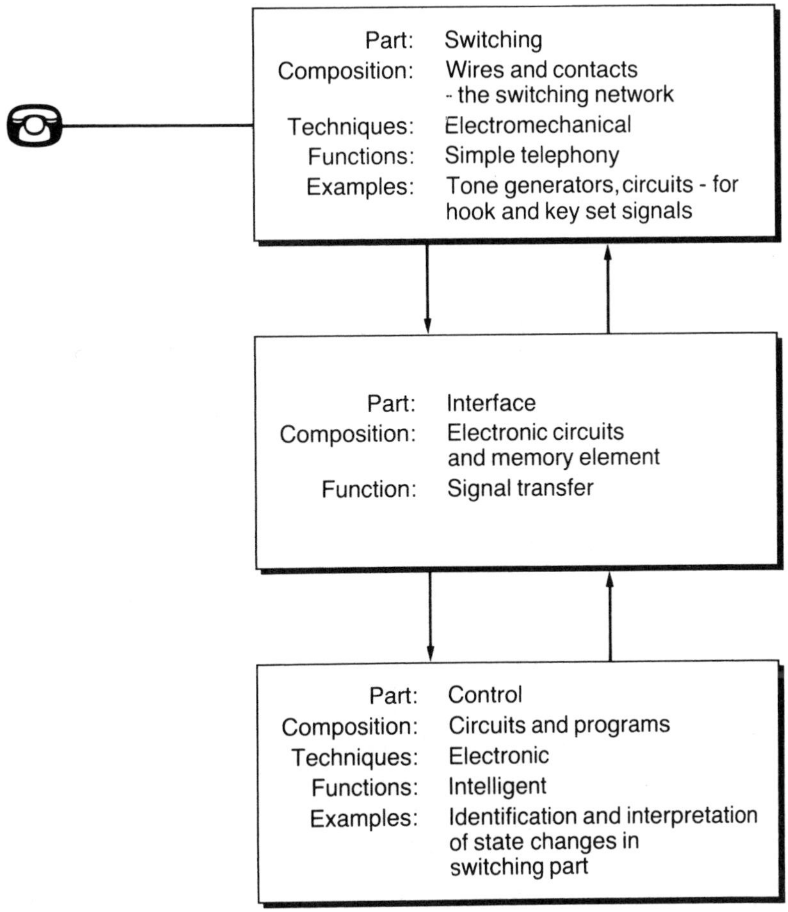

Fig 1i The SPC System

The subscribers . . . . . . a switching part. This . . . . . . wires and contacts over which signals and speech connections are established . . . . . . the switching network. It also . . . . . . circuits for simple telephoning functions . . . . . . tone generators and circuits for hook and key set signals. The control part is . . . . . . circuits and programs which take care of the more intelligent functions in the exchange . . . . . . identification and interpretation of state changes in the switching part. The techniques . . . . . . in the switching part are mainly electromechanical . . . . . ., in the control part, they are electronic. This difference in technique . . . . . . that there must be an interface part in . . . . . . that the switching part can communicate with the control part. The interface part . . . . . . electronic circuits whose function is . . . . . . signal transfer.

1.6 Discussion

Choose one of the following for discussion:

a Should modernization/digitalization of the telephone network be a priority for national investment in a developing country?
b What are the problems of maintaining existing analogue networks during the gradual process of modernization of the network?
c Do you think the whole of the local network (primary, secondary and subscriber circuits) will be digitalized in the near future? What problems will be encountered in digitalizing the secondary and subscriber circuits?

1.7 Word list

The meaning of the words below is normally clear from the context (page reference for first appearance is given. T = Tapescript.). Where the meaning is not clear, a short explanation is given.

Networks

local . . . p. 11
junction . . . p. 11
trunk/main . . . p. 11
transit . . . p. 12

Distribution

cabinet/CCP p. 12
distribution point p. 12
remote subscriber switch p. 198(T)

Exchanges

local . . . p. 11
primary centre/tandem exchange p. 11
secondary centre/GSC p. 11
tertiary centre/DSC/MSC/TSC p. 11
main distribution frame p. 12 point of termination of external cables in an exchange.
electromechanical switching p. 19 a system of switching using part electrical components and part mechanical components.
electronic switching p. 19 a system using electronic components.
Stored Programme Control/SPC p. 198(T) a mainly electronic form of switching.
Crossbar . . . p. 198(T) an electromechanical switching system.
International (Gateway) Exchange p. 12

Transmission

pair p. 12 two wires.
open-wire line p. 12 an uninsulated overhead wire.
multi-pair cable p. 12
multi-unit cable p. 12
duct p. 12 an underground pipe in which cables may be laid.
cable tunnel p. 12 a large underground hole for carrying cables.
coaxial cable p. 12 a cable consisting of a number of tubes each with a central copper wire and a shield. Each pair of tubes carries a number of speech channels (usually 120–2700).
to lay a cable p. 198(T)
circuit-switched p. 17 when a circuit is connected, it is used for the entire duration of the call.
radio link p. 12 transmission by means of sound waves.
synchronous p. 17 transmission is carried out in both directions at the same time.

Miscellaneous

subscriber p. 11 individual or organization which rents

equipment or services from a Telecoms Administration.

to set up p. 12 to establish a call/ connect.

to clear down p. 17 to disconnect a call.

traffic p. 12 the aggregate of calls in a network or part of a network.

multiplexor p. 17 the device for combining a number of signals so that they can share a common transmission medium.

Unit 2 **Transmission 1**

This unit introduces and describes basic transmission systems in the telephone network.

2.1 **Reading 1**

2.1.1

Read the following description of transmission systems. As you read, label Figures 2a, 2b, 2c, 2d and 2e.

Many different transmission systems are used in telecommunications technology. Transmission on open-wire lines was the earliest method used for telephone traffic, and this method is still used in the local networks of many countries. Nowadays, due to the demands on operating reliability, local networks are built up using aerial or underground cable.

Fig 2a . . .

Fig 2b . . .

Between the subscriber and the local exchange two-wire circuits are used, often placed in symmetric cable pairs. Between the local and transit exchanges either two- or four-wire circuits are used. On longer routes, it may be advantageous to use PCM on coaxial cable. These cables are also used for FDM systems transmitting up to 10 800 telephone channels. At regular intervals along the coaxial line, line amplifiers are provided; these are mounted in underground housings and are called 'intermediate repeaters'. In principle, the greater the number of channels transmitted, the larger the number of repeaters required.

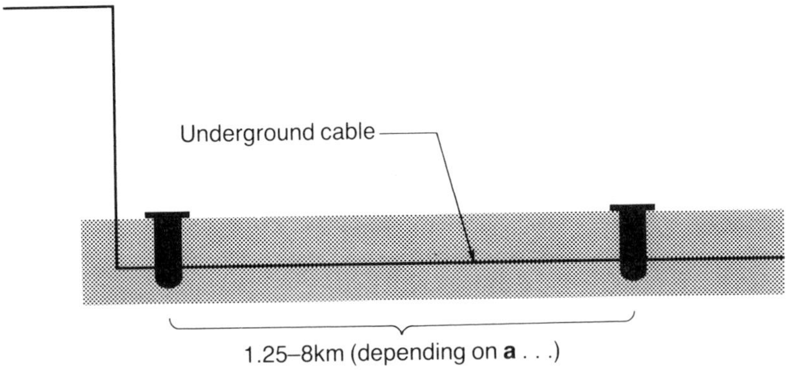

Fig 2c **b** . . .

Since 1965, satellites have become increasingly important for long distance communication, especially across the oceans. In principle, the satellite operates as an intermediate repeater; signals are received, amplified and transmitted to the ground station on the receive side. Satellites use the same frequency band as radio relay systems.

Radio relay links operate with line of sight between the send and receive stations. In principle, the greater the diameter of the parabola in relation to the wavelength, the higher the degree of directivity.

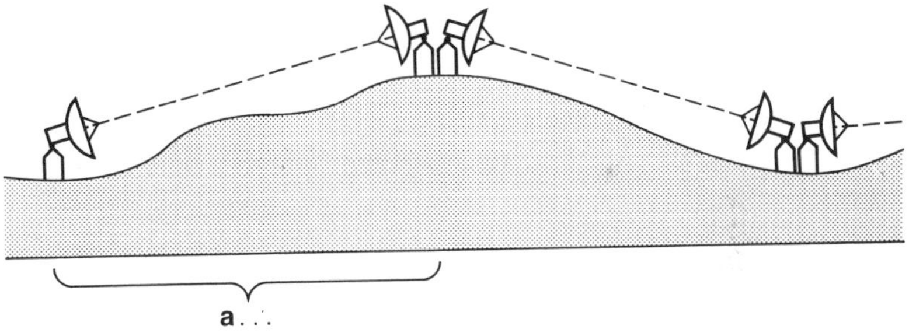

Fig 2d **b** . . .

In terminal repeater stations, situated in ground stations and transit exchanges, speech signals are modulated and combined before transmission. Each separate conversation is shifted to a significantly higher frequency range. This is done in a number of steps. First, by selecting suitable modulation frequencies, the conversations can be placed next to each other along the frequency axis. Then, they are transmitted as a group to the receive side where a similar station demodulates the signals and extracts the various conversations before they are transmitted in two- or four-wire circuits to another transit exchange.

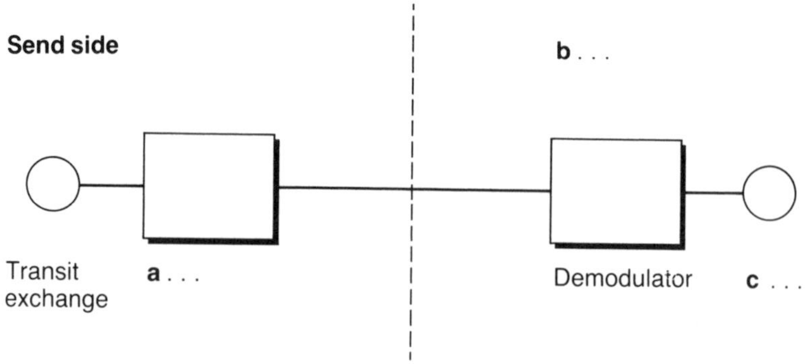

Fig 2e

2.1.2 Comprehension

Answer the following questions:

a Why are local networks built up using cable rather than open wire?
b What type of cables are used for systems which transmit up to 10,800 telephone channels?
c What is another term for 'intermediate repeaters'?
d What are the three functions of a satellite?
e What is the directivity of a radio relay system proportional to?

Complete the following simple process description of the function of a terminal repeater station:
– selection of modulation frequency
– placing of signal on frequency axis

f – . . .
g – . . .
h – . . .
i – . . .

j Complete the following tree diagram:

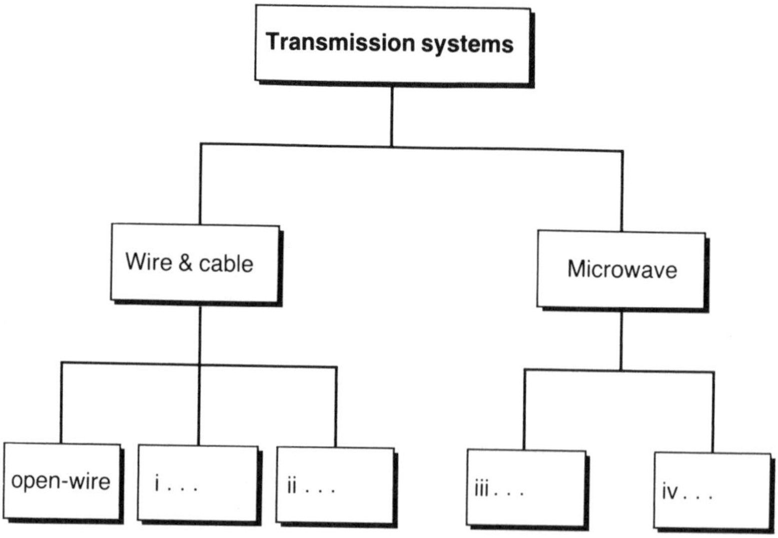

Fig 2f

2.2 Listening

2.2.1

Listen to the following extract from a training session in which an instructor is being asked about PCM. As you listen, label and complete the graphs below in the order they are mentioned.

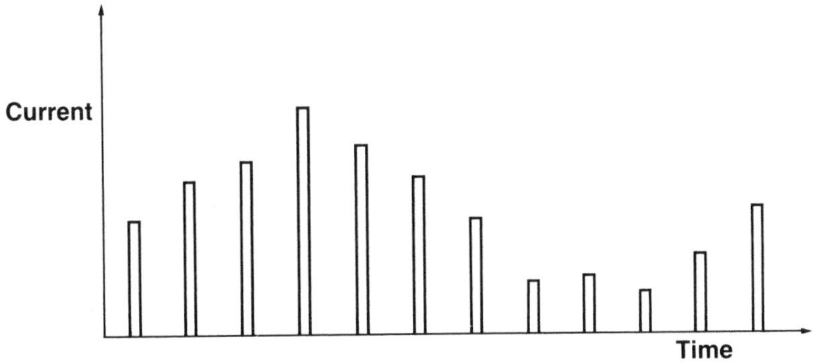

Fig . . .

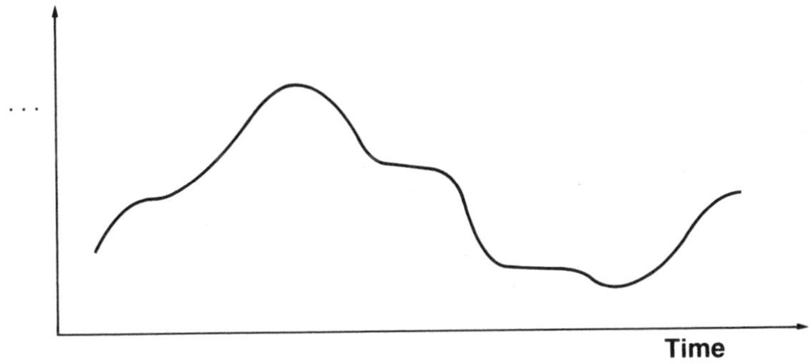

Fig . . .

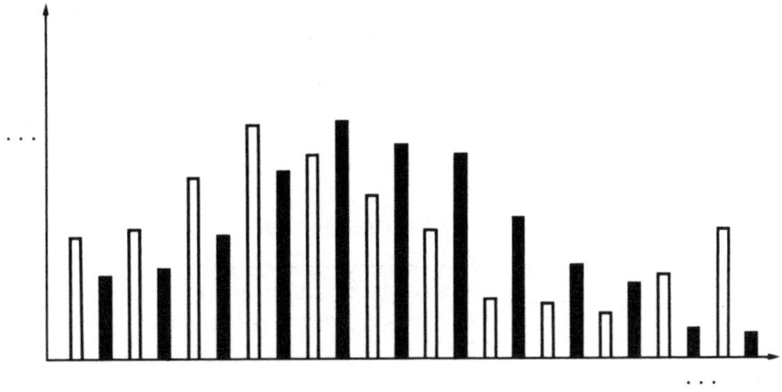

Fig . . .

2.2.2 Comprehension

Listen again and answer the following questions:

a What type of energy is speech in its raw state?
b What type of energy is speech converted into for transmission?
c What is the best definition of the word 'analogue'?
   i) the form of waves
   ii) something similar to something else
   iii) something that can be analysed.
d If the highest frequency is 4 800 Hz, what should the sampling rate be?
   i) 4 800 samples per second
   ii) 10 000 samples per second
   iii) 7 200 samples per second.
e Is 24 the highest number of channels which can be carried?
f Why are PAM pulses not transmitted directly?
g What is the best definition of 'quantization'?
   i) the process of sampling and coding sound waves
   ii) the process of measuring the height of a waveform
   iii) the process of measuring the height and giving it a coded level.

2.3 Language practice

2.3.1 Process description

Look at the following short descriptions of processes:

- The height of the pulse is measured
- and (it is) given a binary code.
- Each code is then transmitted as a train of pulses.
- First, by selecting suitable modulation frequencies
- the conversations can be placed next to each other.
- Then, they are transmitted as a group to the receive side
- where a similar station demodulates the signals
- and extracts the various conversations,
- before they are transmitted to another exchange.

Notice two features:
 i) The use of the **present simple** (active or passive)
  e.g. **is measured**, **are transmitted**, **extracts**
 ii) The use of **sequence markers**
  e.g. **First**, **then**, **before** etc.

Describe the following processes in a similar way:

a
- subscriber A/lift/the handset
- wait for/the dialling tone
- dial/the number
- hear/the ringing tone
- subscriber B/pick up/the receiver
- conversation/take place
- the two subscribers/replace/the handsets

b ▶ the handset/lift
▶ a signal/send/the exchange
▶ the exchange/send/a dialling tone
▶ the number/dial
▶ subscriber B number/select/in the exchange
▶ subscriber A number/connect/subscriber B number
▶ conversation/take place
▶ handsets/replace
▶ connection/break

c Now describe other processes, such as: laying a cable, installing a phone etc.

2.3.2 Explaining relationships

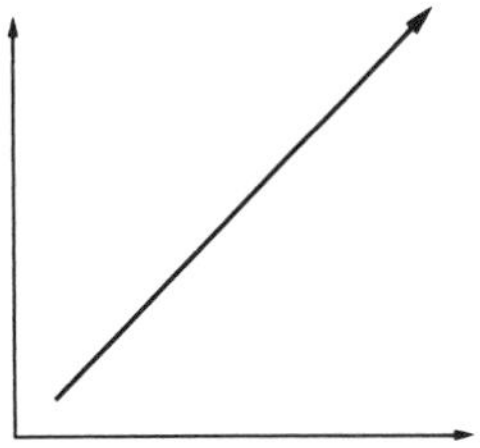

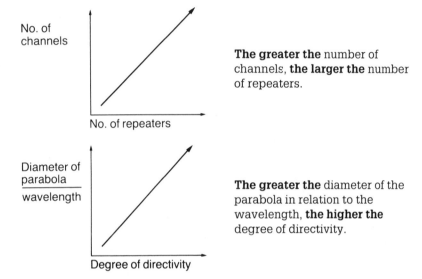

The greater the number of channels, **the larger the** number of repeaters.

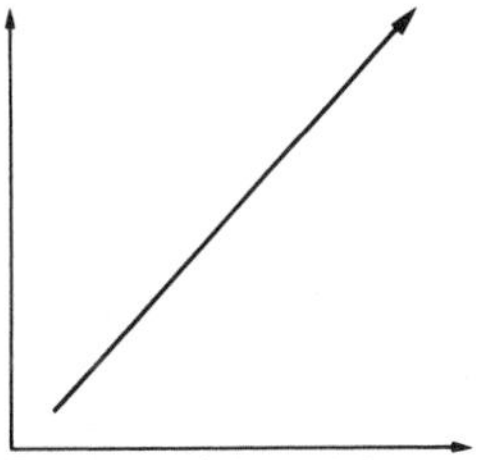

The greater the diameter of the parabola in relation to the wavelength, **the higher the** degree of directivity.

Note that when talking about 'degree' or 'frequency' we normally use 'higher' or 'lower'. Now make similar sentences for the following relationships:

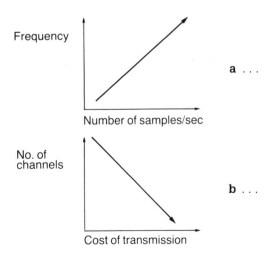

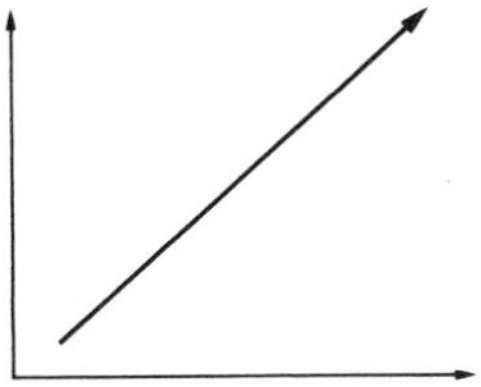

a . . .

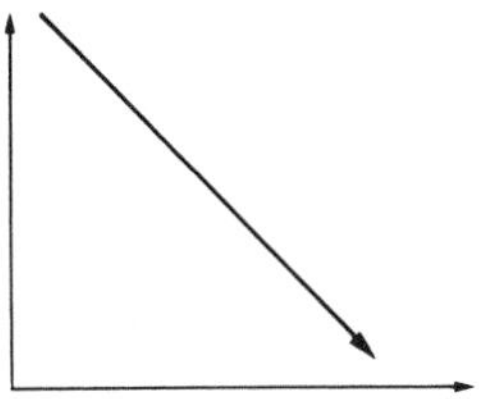

b . . .

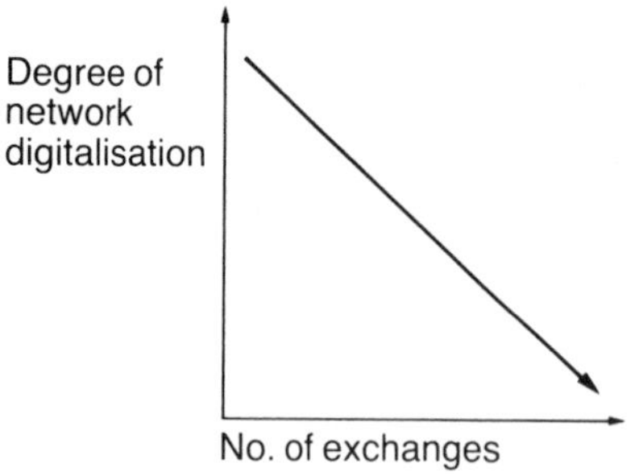

c . . .

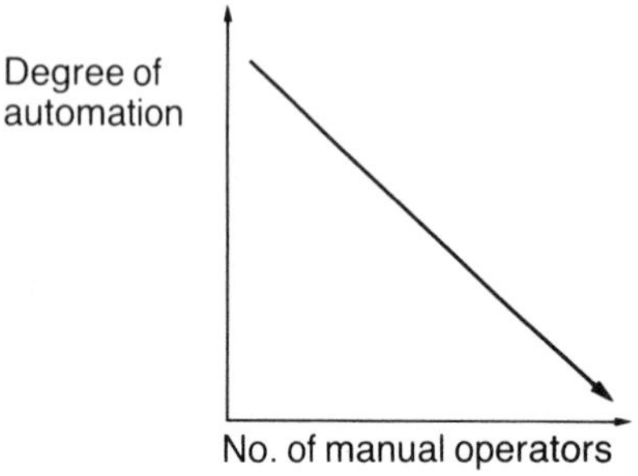

d . . .

Now look at how we can explain a more precise relationship:

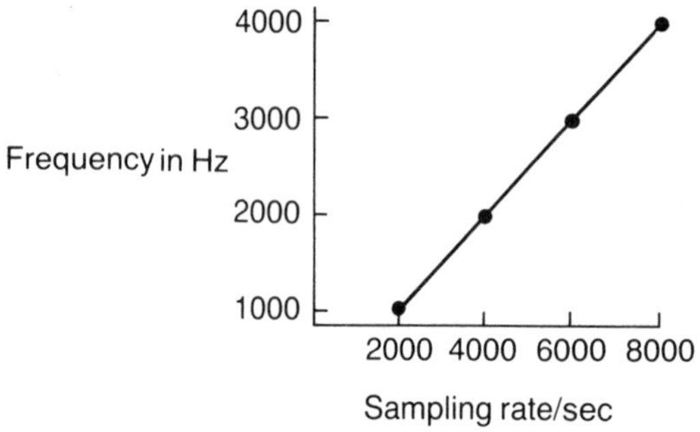

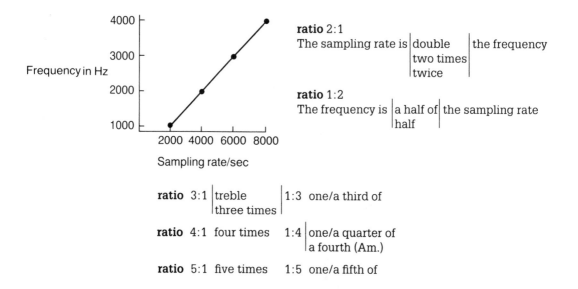

ratio 2:1
The sampling rate is | double / two times / twice | the frequency

ratio 1:2
The frequency is | a half of / half | the sampling rate

ratio	3:1	treble three times	1:3	one/a third of
ratio	4:1	four times	1:4	one/a quarter of a fourth (Am.)
ratio	5:1	five times	1:5	one/a fifth of

Now make similar sentences for the following relationships:

e Return on investment £2,000: original investment £500
f New system 48 channels: old system 24 channels
g Cable costs 1985 £500 per kilometre: cable costs 1980 £125 per kilometre
h New distance between repeaters 2 km: old distance between repeaters 6 km
i The pulse rate 8,000 per second: the capacity 16,000 per second.

2.3.3 Asking for and giving explanations

Questions for information
Could you give me some (background) information about . . . ?
How often does it need to be sampled?

Questions for explanation
What do you mean by . . . ?
What's the difference between . . . and . . . ?

Responses
Of course. As you know . . .
Well, . . .
(That's a) good question.
I was just coming to that.

Giving explanations
In other words . . .
As you can see . . .
Let's look at this graph.
You'll notice . . . shown in black . . .
} Using an illustration to help explain something

Showing understanding
I see.
So, that's what PCM is.
Thank you, that's a lot clearer.

Now listen again to section 2.2. Notice the use of the above phrases or similar ones.
Then, listen once more. Stop the tape to interrupt and ask for explanation from your partner.

2.4 Reading 2

2.4.1

Read the following article about optical fibres. As you read, label Figures 2j, 2k and 2l.

Why optical fibres are useful and how they work
Fibre-optic communications, in which electrical signals are converted into pulses of light that are squirted along very thin glass pipes, have several advantages over conventional copper cables:

- The signal fades (attenuates) less so repeaters can be more widely spaced.
- Fibres can carry a lot of information.
- Most fibres are made from silica, which is very cheap. At present a kilometre costs £1,000 or more but when they are produced in bulk, this figure should come down to as little as £25.
- Fibres are immune to interference and crosstalk.
- The material is lightweight and flexible. A 500 m fibre weighs about 25 kg; a coaxial cable of the same length weighs 5 tons.

Although ordinary glass can only support effective light transmission for a few tens of metres, optical fibres, which are made of pure glass, can carry light signals for up to 50 km without amplification. Silica glass fibre has two components—the highly transparent 'core' at the centre and the opaque surrounding called 'cladding'. Three main types of fibre are possible: stepped-index monomode, stepped-index multimode and graded-index multimode (see figures below). Stepped-index fibres proceed from transparency to opaqueness in straight, defined bands while graded-index fibres go progressively from transparency to opaqueness. Monomode fibre has a very narrow core—such a fibre can support just one 'guided electromagnetic mode'. In a multimode fibre, up to 500 light rays, each of slightly different wavelengths, pass through.

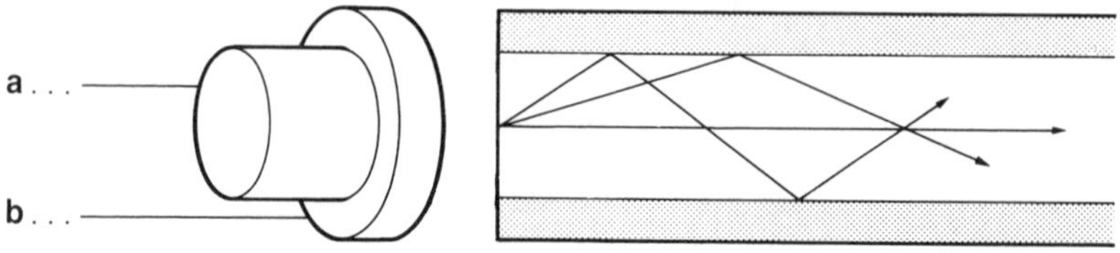

Fig 2j . . .

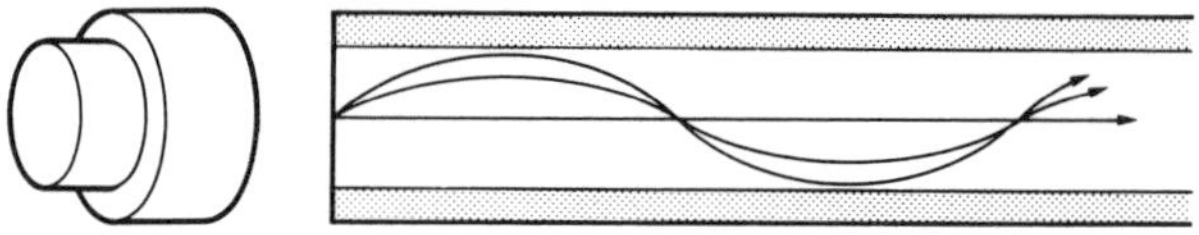

Fig 2k . . .

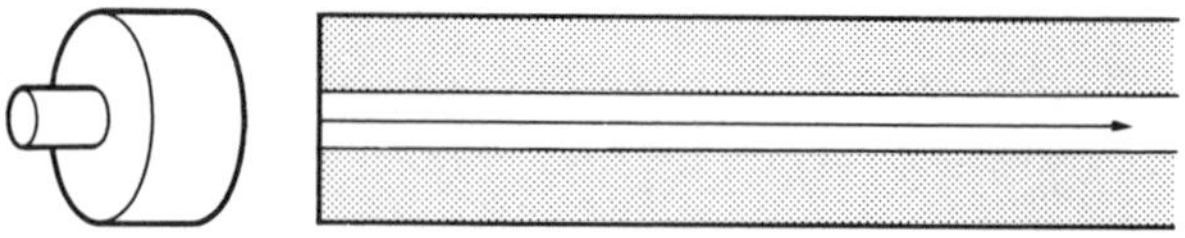

Fig 2l . . .

Telecommunication engineers want to keep reflections in the core to a minimum so that pulses of light do not overlap and make messages unintelligible. In the early days of fibres, engineers used graded-index multimode fibre, rather than stepped-index, to keep overlapping to a minimum. But it is more satisfactory to use monomode fibre, in which pulse spreading does not occur.

Light sources can be either light-emitting diodes (LEDs) or lasers. The first give less powerful signals but are considerably cheaper and last longer. Lasers, however, produce light of a closely-defined wavelength and so are suitable for monomode fibres.

There are also two types of photodetectors—the silicon pin photodiode and the silicon avalanche photodiode. The avalanche devices are generally more sensitive but they are also more expensive.

2.4.2 Comprehension

Complete the following tables:

	Composition	Types	Main features	Quality
Glass fibre	**a** . . .	Stepped-index multimode	overlapping	*
	b . . .	**c** . . .	**d** . . .	**e** . . .
		f . . .	**g** . . .	**h** . . .

In 'Quality' *** is better than ** and ** is better than *.

Table 2a

	Types	Features	Applications
Light sources	**a** . . .	**b** . . .	Multimode and monomode
	c . . .	**d** . . .	**e** . . .

Table 2b

	Types	Features
Photodetectors	**a** . . .	**b** . . .
	c . . .	**d** . . .

Table 2c

2.4.3 Activity

a Below are the advantages of optical fibres. Match them with an appropriate explanation.

Advantages

1 Potentially low material cost **2** High immunity to interference and crosstalk **3** Very large information bandwidth **4** Small and light cable **5** Complete electrical isolation.

Explanations

a This means that they are suitable for crossing places which contain lots of electrical apparatus that give off stray signals. A fibre-optic link is also difficult to 'tap'.

b This means that the signal fades less so that repeaters can be more widely spaced.

c This means that fibres can carry a lot of information, 8,000 or more telephone conversations.

d This means that when manufacturers start to produce fibre in large quantities, the price will be relatively low.

e This means that the cables can easily be laid and that they will not occupy much duct space.

b Discuss the importance of the above advantages in using optical fibre in public telephone networks. Try to rank the above advantages in order of importance.

2.5 Writing

a Use Figure 2m to order the sentences below to form a text describing a simple FDM system.

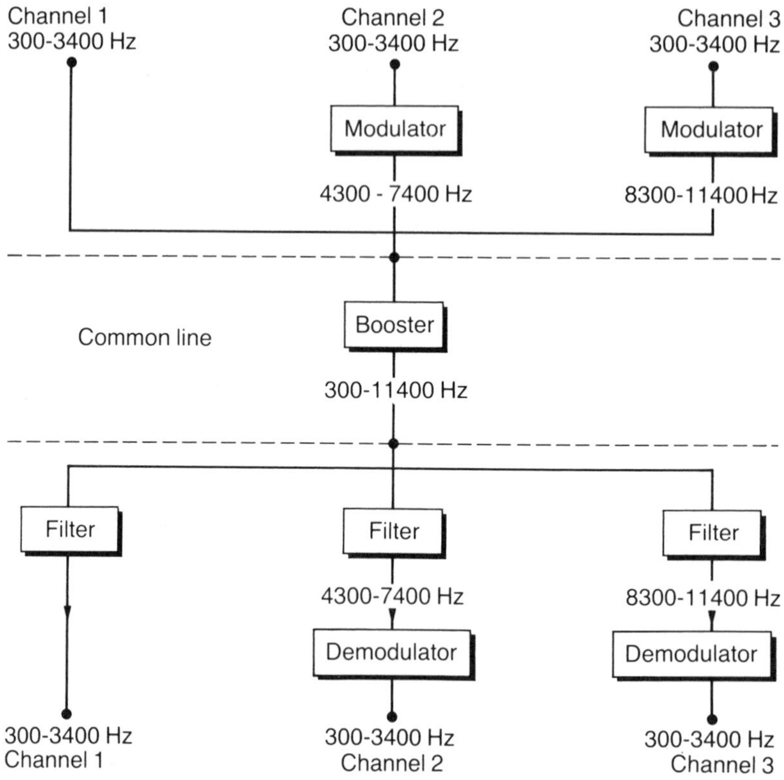

Fig 2m An FDM system

A The second and third channels cannot be transmitted directly over the line.

B At the receiving end, filters separate the three channels and finally demodulators restore channels 2 and 3 to their original frequency position.

C To illustrate the principle of a frequency division multiplex (FDM) system, consider the simple case of transmission of 3 telephone channels, of bandwidth 300–3400 Hz, over a common line.

D Now, the three channels can be passed over the common line, boosted at intervals as necessary.

E First, they are passed through a modulator which frequency-shifts them to frequency bands 4300 to 7400 Hz and 8300 to 11400 Hz respectively.

F The first of these channels can be transmitted directly over the common line and occupies the bandwidth 300–3400 Hz.

b Now use the above description of an FDM system as a model to write a description of a TDM system, using Figure 2n as a basis.

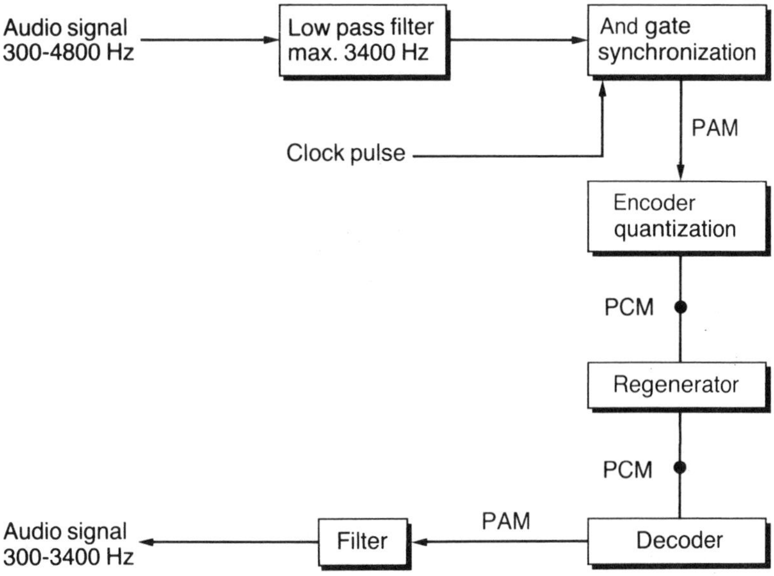

Fig 2n A TDM system

2.6 Discussion

Choose one of the following for discussion:

a Do you think telecoms administrations should start introducing optical fibres on trunk and local networks despite the present high material costs?
b Do you think optical fibres are a complement or a competitor for satellite transmission?
c Are major increases in transmission speed and quality such important factors for the national network in a developing country?

2.7 Word list

Transmission

aerial/underground cable p. 22
circuit p. 22 a link between 2 or more communication points.
symmetric cable pairs p. 22 equally dimensioned two-wire circuits.
channel p. 22 a path for carrying telephone calls.

Amplification

a line amplifier/an intermediate repeater p. 23
to amplify p. 23
to boost p. 32 to amplify.

Frequencies

frequency band/bandwidth p. 23 a continuous range of frequencies e.g. 300–3400 Hz.

wavelength p. 23

to shift p. 23 to change, to move up or down.

Microwave transmission

a ground station p. 23 a transmission or reception facility at one end of a radio relay line.

satellite p. 23

radio relay station p. 23

parabola p. 23 a dish antenna.

directivity p. 23 radiation density in a particular direction.

De/modulation

to modulate—modulation p. 23

to demodulate—demodulation p. 23

to extract/to separate p. 23 to take out and split up separate conversations.

Pulse Code Modulation

to sample—a sample p. 198(T)

to reconstitute p. 198(T) to change back to.

to insert p. 198(T) to place between.

a binary code p. 198(T) a coding system using binary digits 0 and 1.

a train of pulses/a pulse train p. 198(T) a series of pulses having similar characteristics.

a time slot p. 198(T) a period of time used for sampling.

quantization p. 33

to restore p. 32 to change back to.

encoder p. 33

decoder p. 33

regenerator p. 33 a device which accepts distorted pulses and produces well-formed pulses.

Transmission problems

to fade/to attenuate p. 29 to be reduced in strength (opp. *to amplify*).

interference p. 30 the presence of unwanted signals.

crosstalk p. 30 the unwanted transfer of energy from one circuit to another.

to distort p. 198(T) to change to an unwanted waveform.

to overlap p. 30

pulse-spreading p. 30 dispersion and therefore fading of strength of pulse.

General telephony

handset/receiver p. 26

dialling/ringing tone p. 26

to dial p. 26

to pick up p. 26

to replace p. 26

Miscellaneous

to squirt p. 29 to shoot out a thin line of liquid.

in bulk p. 29 in large quantities.

transparent p. 30 light can pass through.

opaque p. 30 light cannot pass through.

to tap p. 31 to listen in to a private telephone conversation.

duct p. 31 an underground pipe in which cables are installed.

Unit 3 Switching 1

This unit provides a brief description of the main stages in the development of telephone exchanges (US: switching centers or central offices).

3.1 Reading 1

3.1.1

Read the following text. As you read, complete Figure 3a.

On March 10th 1876, in Boston USA, Alexander Graham Bell spoke the first recognizable words over what was certainly his most famous invention, the telephone. "Mr Watson, come here. I want you," he called out to an astonished assistant.

It quickly became necessary to link up people using the new invention. This was done through the telephone exchange. In the first simple exchanges, all calls were handled manually by the operator. Using the switchboard in front of her, she plugged the line of the subscriber calling her into the line of the subscriber being asked for.

The idea of an automatic exchange was soon suggested. In 1892, three years after patenting his ideas, Almon B. Strowger saw his system installed at La Porte, Indiana. Strowger, an undertaker from Kansas City, found his business was becoming less and less profitable because the operator always connected calls intended for him to other undertakers.

Strowger's automatic exchange underwent several modifications over the next fifty years, but the principle has remained the same ever since. It is known as the 'step-by-step' system and there are still thousands of Strowger exchanges in service throughout the world today.

The next generation of exchanges was first developed in Sweden. Crossbar exchanges, as they are called, consist of a series of vertically and horizontally crossed bars. For the first time a common control system was used. This made crossbar exchanges cheaper than Strowger, for each selector could now carry up to ten calls. They were not as noisy as Strowger, either. These exchanges are electro-mechanically operated, using electromagnets.

In 1948, the invention of the transistor at Bell Telephone Laboratories led to a revolution in electronics and to the creation of semi-electronic telephone exchanges.

The old mechanical and electromechanical exchanges have now begun to disappear, and since the 1970s they have started to be replaced by exchanges built around electronic components. The latest digital switching centres have several advantages over other types of exchange, for they provide: a substantial reduction in equipment cost; a large reduction in equipment size; shorter procurement times; shorter installation and commissioning times; greater reliability and reduced running costs; new services for the customer; and new facilities for the administration.

1880 . . . System	1892 . . . System	1940s . . . System	1948 . . . System	1970s . . . System

Main characteristics of the systems

First, simple exchanges. Connections manually established	. . .	. . .	. . .	. . .

Fig 3a

3.1.2 Comprehension

Answer the following questions:

a What do Americans call a telephone exchange?
b Who invented the telephone? When and where?
c What did the first operators do?
d Why did Strowger invent the automatic telephone exchange?
e What is a 'crossbar' system?
f What advantages does crossbar offer over Strowger?
g What important development took place in 1948?
h What are mechanical and electromechanical exchanges being replaced by?

3.2 Listening

3.2.1

Listen to the following conversation about a call connect system, or PABX (Private Automatic Branch Exchange). The conversation is between Tim Allison, a sales representative, and John Gibbs, manager of a company in the south of England. As you listen, complete Fig 3b.

Indicate which of the following sentences are true (T) or false (F).

e For internal calls, you can dial the extension number immediately. T/F
f You push button 2 to get an outside line. T/F
g An operator isn't necessary with such a PABX. T/F
h You will hear two different dial tones when you transfer your number to another extension. T/F
i To transfer calls back to your own office, you dial 8 and then your extension number. T/F
j If your correspondent's line is engaged, you can press button 4. Your phone and his phone will then ring simultaneously when he hangs up. T/F

	Functions		Instructions
a	Internal calls	i ii iii	Pick up the handset . . . Dial the four digits of the extension
b	External calls	i ii iii iv v	Pick up the handset . . . Push button 2 . . . . . .
c	Transferring calls	i ii iii iv v	Pick up the handset Wait for the internal dial-tone . . . .
d	Automatic call-back	i ii iii iv	Dial your internal correspondent . . . Push button 4 . . .

Fig 3b

3.3 Language practice

3.3.1 Comparison

The comparative and superlative of one-syllable adjectives and adjectives ending in 'y' are formed like this:

Adjective	**Comparative**	**Superlative**
great	greater	the greatest
noisy	noisier	the noisiest

With most adjectives of two or more syllables, we use **more** and **most**:

profitable	more profitable	the most profitable

Note the following important irregular comparatives and superlatives:

good	better	the best
bad	worse	the worst
far	further	the furthest
little	less	the least
many/much	more	the most

Note, too, how we use **as . . . as**:

He's not as stupid as he looks. We have as much time as we need.

Now fill in the blanks in the following sentences.

a In my opinion, Bell is . . . inventor of all time. (great)
b A Strowger exchange is . . . a crossbar central office. (noisy)
c A Strowger exchange is not . . . crossbar. (reliable)
d Your English accent is . . . hers. (bad)
e Bell made a lot of inventions, but the telephone was . . . . (important)
f After inventing the automatic exchange, Strowger found that his business became . . . . (profitable)
g A digital exchange works . . . a crossbar one. (fast)
h He speaks English . . . his brother. (good)

3.3.2 **Description:** using the present perfect and the simple past tenses

Strowger's automatic exchange **underwent** several modifications.

The action is situated in the past and is now finished. Here we use the simple past.

The principle **has remained** the same **ever since**.

'Ever since' links the past to the present in this case. Here we use the present perfect.

Now put the verb in brackets into the correct tense. In some cases, both the simple past and the present perfect are possible.

a Bell . . . the first word on the telephone in 1876. (speak)
b Over the last few years, electromechanical exchanges . . . to disappear. (begin)
c It soon . . . necessary to find a way to link up subscribers. (become)
d He . . . here all his life. (live)
e In the early exchanges, all calls . . . through the operator. (go)
f He . . . in that office for two years. (work)
g With digital techniques, telephone exchanges . . . another great change. (just + undergo)
h Strowger . . . his idea in 1889. (patent)
i I . . . that film about Bell. (already + see)
j The operators always . . . calls for Strowger to other undertakers. (connect)

3.3.3 **Giving and asking for instructions**

Asking for information
Could you tell me where . . .?
Could you tell me how to . . .?
In what way does the PABX help the operator?
Would you mind explaining how . . .?
Perhaps you would let me know what . . .?

Giving instructions
Pick up the handset.
Wait for instructions.
You should pick up the handset.
You dial the outside number.
Push button number 8.
Do make sure you . . .
Let's make sure you . . .
Don't forget to dial number 8.

Now listen again to 3.2. Pick out the times you hear the above phrases or similar ones.
Then, listen once more. Stop the tape to interrupt and ask for explanation from your partner.

3.4 Reading 2

3.4.1 Read the following passage about electronic exchanges. As you read, complete Figure 3c.

Classification	**Electromechanical exchange**	**Digital exchange**
Transmission type	Analogue transmission	Digital transmission and switching
Installation	**a** . . .	**b** . . .
Maintenance	High maintenance cost **c** . . .	Lower maintenance cost **d** . . .
Technical comments	crossed lines **e** . . . rigidity of design wrong numbers **f** . . .	**g** . . . **h** . . . **i** . . . **j** . . . **k** . . . higher evolutionary potential **l** . . .

Fig 3c

Most of the world's telephone traffic is still handled by exchanges of electromechanical design, each with thousands of wear-prone exposed moving parts. Analogue exchanges of this type are costly to install and maintain, and are subject to familiar faults such as crossed lines, noise and wrong numbers.

Many of the world's telecommunications administrations have explored other, digital, solutions. They are designing networks that offer: a much higher quality of service than before, using the latest microchip technology with few or no moving parts; less interference than previously; lower installation and maintenance costs; and much faster connection speed for calls and fewer wrong numbers than in the past.

The main characteristics of a digital exchange are:

1 Integrated Digital Transmission and Switching
Speech and other signals are digitally encoded and a common method of time division multiplexing is used in both transmission and switching equipment. The main advantage of this system is that the transmission loss encountered by speech becomes more or less independent of both distance and the number of exchanges through which a call is routed.

2 Stored Program Control (SPC) is the application of data processing and computer techniques to an exchange, thus providing a powerful, flexible method of controlling the operation of the exchange.

3 Common Channel Signalling (CCS) uses just one (go and return) pair of signalling channels, not directly associated with the traffic circuits, for performing all the signalling functions of an entire route which may contain several hundred traffic circuits.
4 Microelectronics technology is the application of solid-state semi-conductor technology to provide components which range in function from a single active element (e.g. a transistor) to large scale integrated circuits. Use of this technology offers small physical size and reliability, together with automated design, manufacture and testing. The components are fixed onto printed circuit boards, and if there is a fault, the defective printed circuit board can be taken out and replaced by another in a matter of seconds.

3.4.2 Comprehension

a Match each of the headings with one set of functions:

1 Stored Program Control
2 Common Channel Signalling
3 Integrated Digital Transmission and Switching
4 Microelectronics Technology

a The application of solid-state semi-conductors to provide greater reliability, smaller size and automated design.
b The application of data-programming techniques to an exchange, providing greater control and flexibility in the operative of an exchange.
c The use of one pair of channels not directly associated with the traffic circuits, to perform all signalling functions on a complete route.
d Speech and other signals are digitally encoded and a common method of time-division multiplexing is used.

b What are the advantages of using (large-scale) integrated circuits in an exchange?

3.4.3 Activity

a Match the following terms with a suitable explanation:

1 an electromechanical exchange
2 a digital exchange
3 a wrong number
4 a crossed line
5 analogue transmission
6 call charges

a a call is incorrectly routed
b a system in which a varying electrical current transmits the caller's voice pattern
c an exchange which uses microchip technology
d the cost of a telephone call
e during a telephone conversation, you hear another conversation at the same time
f a switching centre, the design of which is based on thousands of moving parts

b Describe the advantages and/or disadvantages of the terms 1–5 in Activity **a** in a given situation.

3.5 Writing

Teacher Read out the extra piece of dialogue in the Answer Key on page 220.
Student Listen to this dialogue and complete the instructions for transferring a call, Figure 3e.

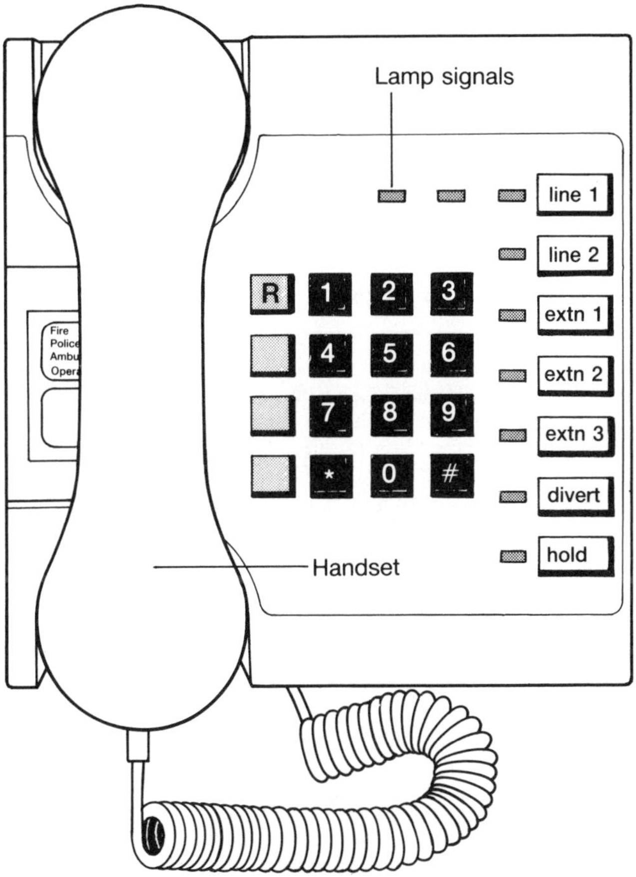

Fig 3d

Instructions for call transfer

1.	Lift handset when phone rings
2.	. . .
3.	. . .
4. a	. . .
OR	
b	. . .
i	. . .
ii	. . .

Fig 3e

3.6 Discussion

Choose one of the following for discussion:

a Discuss the present state of the national network in your country (exchanges, equipment).

b What problems for the developing countries do you foresee in installing digital exchanges in place of old, mechanical switching centres?

c What future do you think operator personnel have in either public exchanges or private branch exchanges?

3.7 Word list

Using the phone

extension p. 199(T)
correspondent p. 199(T)
engaged tone p. 199(T)
internal call p. 199(T)
external call p. 199(T)
wrong number p. 39
crossed line p. 39
call charge p. 40
to transfer a call p. 199(T)
to call back p. 199(T)
to push/press a button p. 199(T)
to switch/connect p. 199(T)
local/regional/international codes p. 199(T)

Exchange equipment

selector p. 35 a switching device with one inlet and many outlets, or vice versa.

Dealing with exchange equipment

wear-prone moving parts p. 39 parts that often become weak through frequent use.
transmission loss p. 39 reduction in power between two points in a transmission system.
fault p. 40 a failure.
defective p. 40 not perfect.
to maintain p. 39
to modify p. 35 to change a little.
to undergo modifications p. 35 to be changed.

Comparative characteristics of exchanges

flexible (ity) p. 39 will bend easily.
rigid (ity) p. 39 not flexible.
reliable (ity) p. 35 dependable, can be trusted.
profitable (ity) p. 35 makes more money than it costs.
procurement time p. 35 the time it takes to obtain something.
commissioning time p. 35 the time it takes to get something done.
running costs p. 35 operating costs.

Microelectronics technology

components p. 40 individual parts.
integrated circuit p. 40
large scale integrated circuit p. 40
printed circuit board p. 40

Miscellaneous

exposed p. 39 not covered.
invention p. 35
to invent p. 38
to patent p. 35 to obtain protection for an invention.

Unit 4 Computer communications 1

This unit presents the background to future developments in the parallel fields of data processing and telecommunications.

4.1 Reading 1

4.1.1

Read the following extract from a speech about 'Trends in Computer Communications'. As you read complete Figure 4c on page 46.

The present status of telecommunications is a result of a long evolution through more than a hundred years. It is interesting to note that the old telegraph system used digital transmission. When, many years later, telephony was introduced, analogue transmission was used. Telex, on the other hand, worked with a digital technique while video transmission in principle uses analogue transmission. Data communication is digital and a transition is now taking place where all services, voice, text, data and picture—will be integrated in a basic digital network. This digital network will be an ideal carrier of data communications and will promote the growth of such communications.

The development of data communications depends, to a great extent, on the development of data processing. So far, all the signs indicate a trend towards remote data processing which means a greater usage of data communications services. Indeed, a 'marriage' of telecommunications and data processing will be the result. This 'marriage' will hopefully result in a number of useful products. Already a range of specialized services is foreseen—in particular in the text and picture communication field.

A number of new text services have been, or will be, introduced shortly:
Firstly, a lot of interest has been shown in **Teletex** which is already being introduced in some countries. Teletex is an international service enabling subscribers to exchange correspondence on an automatic memory to memory basis, via telecommunications networks. As a successor to telex, it will use specially adapted word processors and electronic typewriters and enable a 3-page A4 letter to be sent almost instantaneously from one end of the country to the other. In Britain, estimates vary of when teletex will be forthcoming, but meanwhile, Germany and Sweden already have systems in operation and teletex launches are planned in France, Spain, Belgium and Canada before long.

The **Telefacsimile** service is well established, though faster and more advanced systems (Group 4 types) will be introduced shortly. This service provides for the transmission and reproduction of still pictures and printed matter. Telefax has its biggest market in Japan where the complexity of Japanese script makes this an ideal medium of transmission.

Videotex, called viewdata in the UK, has passed through an experimental and testing stage and is now available in many countries. Videotex is a service enabling a subscriber to obtain information over the public switched telecoms network (PSTN) for presentation in alphanumeric and/or graphic form on a VDU—usually a specially adapted TV receiver. This service is marketed under different names in different countries. Prestel in the UK, Bildschirmtext in FRD and Telidon in Canada. Videotex subscribers may choose to have an additional service—**electronic mailbox** enabling them to send messages directly and instantaneously to one another. The UK viewdata system, which is an interactive service, should not be confused with **Teletext**, a one-way information service which TV companies broadcast. (In the UK two systems are available—Ceefax and Oracle.)

Technically it will be possible to integrate various types of telecommunications networks (private and public, data and telephony) to form an Integrated Services Digital Network (ISDN). In Germany the BIGFON experiment has recently been launched. BIGFON is a wide-band integrated services local communications system, offering the subscriber the complete spectrum of telecommunications services, including a new video telephone service as well as radio and TV broadcasts, all transmitted via optical fibre cables. (See Figure 4b.)

Despite this development towards ISDN, a number of specialized networks will have to live side by side for many years to come. From the customer's point of view, it is therefore essential that networks and services are compatible. It should be possible to use one and the same terminal for different services and to send traffic over different networks. The question is how can this be realized? Could an integrated network be developed? (See Figure 4a.)

Concept of a possible "intelligent" network

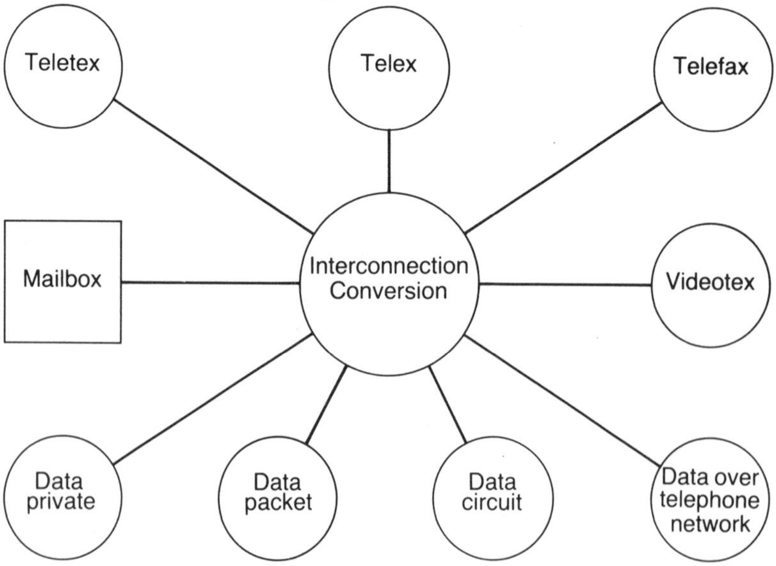

Fig 4a

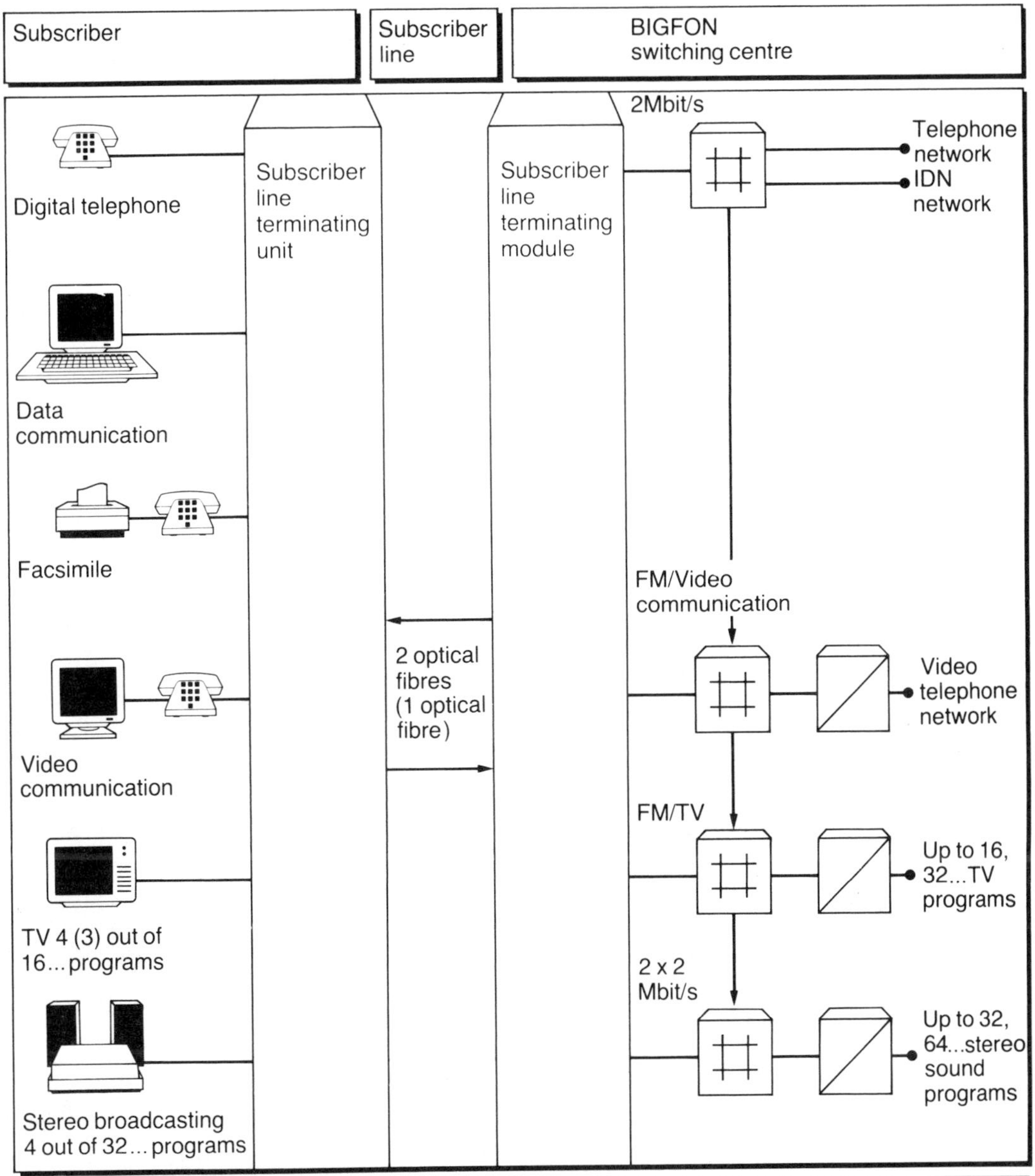

Voice communication
- Telephone service
- Repertory dialing
- Repetitive dialing
- Consultation hold
- Call transfer
- Call pick-up
  Call forwarding
  Transfer of ringing
- Call waiting
- Visual displays
- Monitoring
- Hands-free speaking

Video communication
- Video telephone service (colour) optional picture switch
- Video transmission of documents
- Interactive videotex
- Remote control
  Hands-free speaking
  Self view, etc

Text services
- Teletex
- Facsimile
- Data transmission

Distribution services
- TV
- Broadcast videotex
- Stereo sound programs

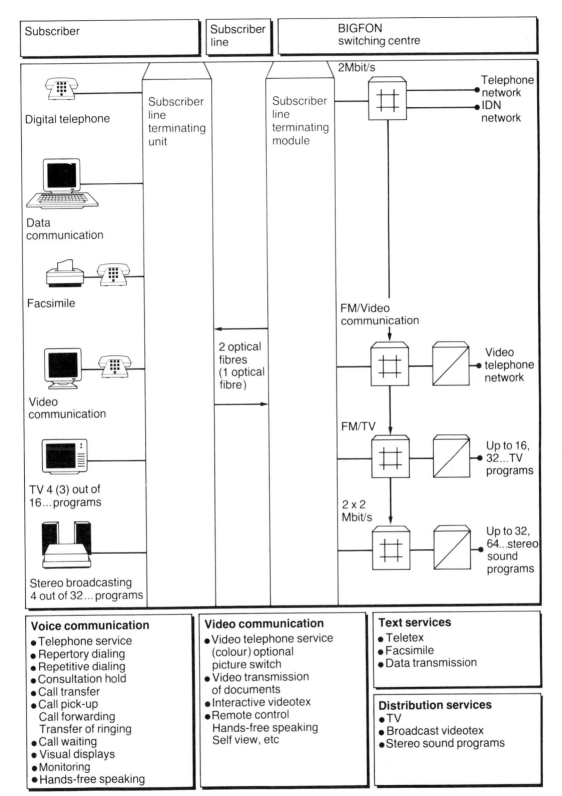

Fig 4b

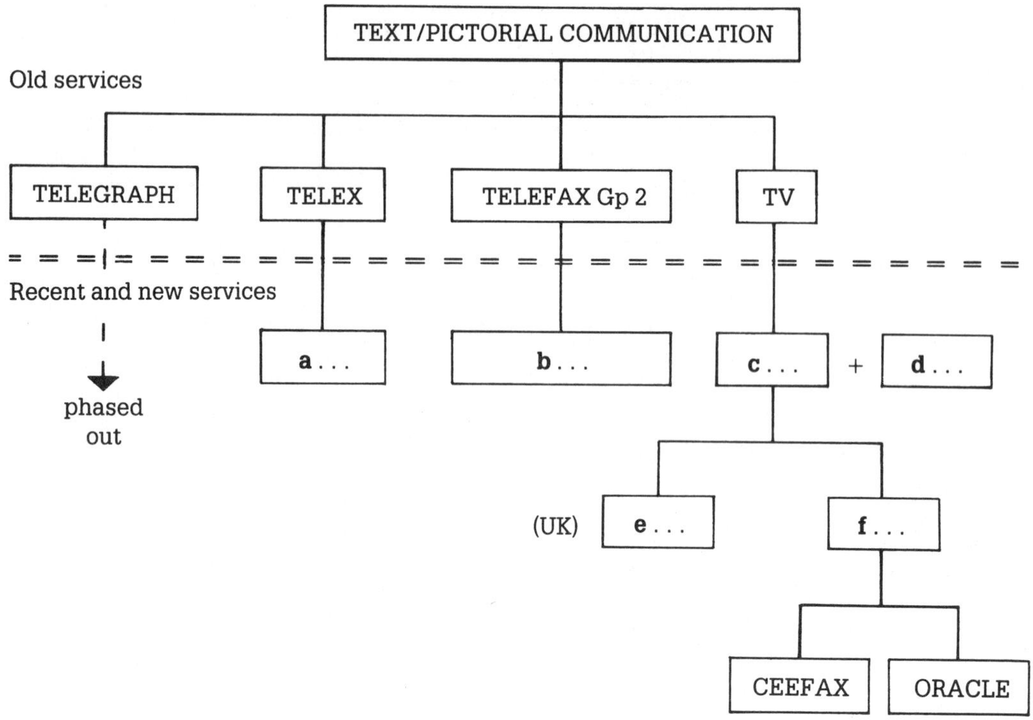

Fig 4c

4.1.2 Comprehension

Answer the following questions:

a Classify the following services under Digital (D) or Analogue (A) transmission:
telegraphy . . .   telephony . . .   telex . . .
video . . .   data . . .

b What does 'remote data processing' mean?
  i) data processing is carried out in one central place
  ii) the processing of different types of data
  iii) data processing is carried out in different geographical locations.

c What two features which distinguish teletex from telex are mentioned?
  i) . . . ii) . . .

d Why is Japan such a big market for Telefax?
e What is the main difference between Viewdata and Teletext?
f Why is it necessary for networks and services to be compatible?

4.2 Listening

4.2.1

Listen to the following telephone conversation between a prospective customer and supplier representative. The customer is enquiring about B.T.'s new word processing system. As you listen complete as much of Figure 4d as possible.

PROSPECT CALL FORM: (completed by (a)...........................)

Name: (b)..

Company: (c)....................................

Address: (d).....................................

Telephone: (e).................................

Product interested in: (f)..

Add-on facilities: (g)...

Intended use: (h)...

Existing equipment (i)..

Software (j)..

Terms of sale: (k)..

Action: Demonstration [(l) ...] arrangements (n)...............

....

Visit to exhibition [(m) ...] ....

Fig 4d

4.2.2
Comprehension

Answer the following questions:

a What is the likely cost of replacing his existing telex with an electronic PUMA?

b Which of the following telecommunications facilities are available with the M3300? Please tick (√) or cross (×).

electronic telex	☐
teletex	☐
videotex	☐
telefax	☐
access to data banks	☐

c What are the delivery times for the following?
screen . . .
keyboard . . .
electronic telex . . .
printer . . .

d How could the client speed up the process of inserting data (customer names and addresses) into the word processor data store?

e Why can't Mr Dale attend the Harrogate Business Systems Exhibition?

4.3 Language practice

4.3.1 Forecasting

When we talk about the future, we indicate the relative probability of events happening as follows:

Certainty

More advanced systems **will** be introduced.
It **won't** (will not) work out more than the existing telex.
You **will** be getting a lot of new facilities.

Probability

All the signs indicate that . . .
It **should** be possible . . .
The cost **is likely to** be . . .
We **ought to** be able to install . . .
It'**ll probably** be 4 or 5 weeks . . .

Possibility

You **might** be interested . . .
That **could** be useful . . .

Now use the table below to complete sentences **d** to **j**; **a** to **c** have been done for you as examples.

Installation Schedule for Extension Telephones

Type of telephone	**Special fast-rate** (£15 extra fee)	**Business customers**	**Residential customers**
DIAVOX	3–5 days *	2–4 weeks	5–10 weeks
AMBASSADOR	3–5 days	3–5 weeks	4–6 weeks
MICKEY MOUSE	10–15 days	———	10–12 weeks
REGENCY	3–5 days	4–6 weeks	5–7 weeks

*In all cases: first figure (3) represents a **minimum** waiting time for installation
last figure (5) represents a **maximum** waiting time for installation

Possibility

a If you need one in a hurry, we **could** deliver a Diavox **in 3 days**, but you will have to pay £15 extra.

Probability

b For a business customer we **should/ought** to be able to deliver an Ambassador **in 4 weeks**.

Certainty

c For a residential customer, we **will** install a Mickey Mouse extension phone **in 12 weeks**.

d If you need an Ambassador soon, we . . . deliver one in 5 days.

e For a business customer, we . . . deliver a Regency extension in 4 weeks.
f It's . . . be 6 weeks before we can install a Regency extension for a residential subscriber.
g We . . . be able to deliver a Mickey Mouse extension set before 10 weeks.
h All . . . that delivery time will be around 7 or 8 weeks for the Diavox if you are a residential subscriber.
i We . . . be able to install the Mickey Mouse in your house in 11 weeks time.
j You . . . receive the new Ambassador before 4 weeks if you are a residential customer.

4.3.2 Telephoning

The expressions below are useful in making a telephone call.

Identifying yourself	Mr Binns speaking. This is Mr Binns.
Identifying your caller	Who's speaking, please?
Getting connected	Could you put me through to . . . ? Could I have extension 283?
Waiting	Hold on a moment, please. Would you mind holding? I'll hold on.
Taking a message	I'm afraid Mr X is out at the moment. Can I take a message?
Leaving a message	Could you give him a message? Could you ask him to call me back on York 20042 (two, double Oh, four, two). Could you tell him I'll call again later?
Reason for phoning	I'm phoning about . . . because . . .
Communication problems	I'm sorry, I didn't catch that/your number/your name. Could you spell that, please? It's a bad line, I'll call you back. Could you/repeat that?/speak up? (a little louder)/speak more slowly?
Signing off	Thanks, goodbye. Bye. (more informal)

Put the following jumbled telephone conversation in the correct order. Start with 6A: 'Amway International. Can I help you?'

1 B: Hello, Mr Barker, this is Mr Jakeson. How are you?
2 C: Of course, I'll ring you as soon as my secretary gets back from lunch. Can I have your number?
3 B: It's Mr Jakeson of Rushfords.
4 C: How do you spell Eindhoven?
5 B: Yes, but can you make it before 5?
6 A: Amway International. Can I help you?
7 B: Good. Goodbye.
8 C: M for Michael?
9 B: E, I, N . . .

10 C: Fine, thanks. How can I help you?
11 B: Well, I'm phoning about our order no. 541.
12 A: Hold on a moment Mr Jakeson. I'll put you through.
13 C: Just a moment, I'll find the file . . . I can't seem to find it. Can I call you back?
14 B: double O, two.
15 C: Eindhoven 4, 8, 3 . . .?
16 A: Who's speaking, please?
17 C: Bye.
18 B: Yes, could you put me through to Mr Barker, please?
19 C: Thank you. I'll call you within the next hour or so.
20 B: Yes, it's Eindhoven 483002.
21 C: Barker speaking.
22 B: No, N for Nicholas, D, H, O, V, E, N.

4.3.3 Definition

Look at the way we can put together a definition of a product or service.

Name	Classification	Characteristics/Function
Teletex	International service	It enables subscribers to exchange correspondence on an automatic memory to memory basis.

Teletex is an international service enabling subscribers to exchange correspondence on an automatic memory to memory basis.

Use the table below to put together similar definitions:

Name	Classification	Characteristics/Function
a Videotex	Means of transmission	It provides a means of synchronous data transmission.
b Lasers	Service	It uses one pair for performing all signalling functions of one route.
c PCM	Circuit switched network	It involves the sampling and coding of analogue signals.
d Electronic mail	New service	They enable PCM transmission to be used further out in the local network.
e Telefax	Method of signalling	They produce light of a closely defined wavelength.
f CCS	Packet switched network	It enables a subscriber to obtain alphanumeric and/ or graphic information over the PSTN.
g SPC	Electronic system	It uses data processing and computer techniques for switching.

Name	Classification	Characteristics/Function
h Datex	Light sources	It enables videotex subscribers to send messages directly and instantaneously to one another.
i Remote concentrators	New service	It provides a means of asynchronous data transmission.
j Nordic Public Data network	Remote part of an exchange	It provides for the transmission and reproduction of still pictures and printed matter.

4.4 **Reading 2**

4.4.1

Read the brochure about the Puma Telex Terminal on page 53. As you read, select appropriate headings from a–h for paragraphs 1–8.

4.4.2 Comprehension

Complete the following technical specifications using the text of 4.4.1 and Figure 4e (see below).

1 Memory capacity: . . .
2 Abbreviated address capacity: . . .
3 Speed: . . .
4 Printing type: . . .
5 Spacing: . . .
6 Paper: . . .
7 Ribbon: . . .
8 Mains input: . . .
9 Width: . . .
10 Depth: . . .
11 Height: . . .
12 Weight: . . .

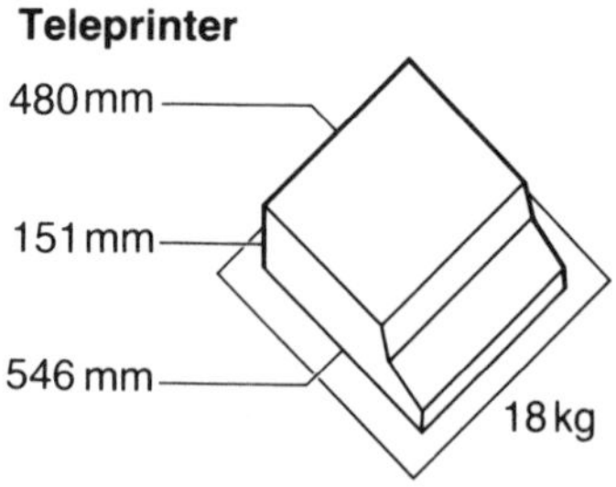

Fig 4e

4.4.3 Activity

You are thinking of changing over to a Puma telex machine. Your job is to convince your office staff of the advantages of this new machine. Pick out the advantages related to operator use and list them in order of importance (from the secretary's point of view).

Puma Telex Terminal

a	**Fast and quiet printing**	e	**Memory protection**
b	**Large memory store**	f	**Advanced keyboard**
c	**Keyboard calling**	g	**Internal directory**
d	**Automatic operation**	h	**Editing and justifying**

---

1. Puma's memory is used to store messages for later transmission. It can also store incoming messages. Each stored message is automatically allocated an index number. The capacity of the memory is 2,500 words, assuming a word consists of five characters plus a space.

2. In the event of temporary disconnection from the mains supply (240v), power to the memory is maintained by an in-built battery.

3. Puma can be instructed to make calls and transmit messages from its memory fully automatically while the machine is unattended, making great saving on the operator's time. Calls may be made automatically to most countries in the world. If a number is at first engaged, Puma makes further attempts by itself at approximately two-minute intervals.

4. Puma can store a choice of approximately 25 frequently used telex numbers, depending on their length. The numbers are given a two-character code by the user. These codes may be used instead of full numbers in any of Puma's functions involving calling or storing, saving the operator time and trouble.

5. Puma does not have a calling dial. The number required is typed on the keyboard or alternatively selected from the pre-stored internal directory.

6. Messages and calling information in the memory are easily edited: the operator can insert, correct or delete parts of messages in store. Puma's memory can be searched to identify the sequence for editing, and print the required passage up to the point to be edited. It is then possible to edit the appropriate text and in conjunction with the 'justification' function the text can be rearranged ensuring that there are no split words at the end of a line.

7. Puma's keyboard is a solid-state system which eliminates mechanical damage and wear and makes it resistant to liquid spillages. It is laid out in the same way as a conventional typewriter, with special function keys separated to the right and left. Some of the letter keys are also used for selecting functions.

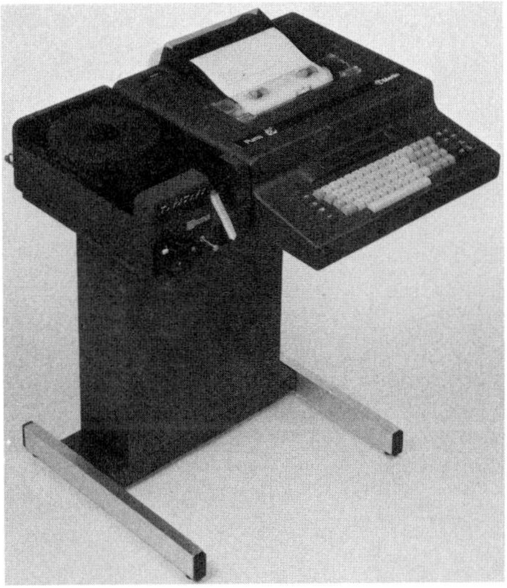

8. Without the clatter associated with earlier teleprinter machines, Puma prints using a highly readable 7 x 5 dot matrix technique to make up the characters. The machine operates at normal telex speed 'on line' ie 400 characters or 66 words per minute, but has the capability of speeds up to 1,800 characters per minute in 'local'. It can print up to 69 characters or spaces on each line. Puma uses standard teleprinter paper, or multi-ply paper giving up to three under-copies. Further copies can be made by reprinting the message from the memory in the local mode. It takes normal nylon typewriter ribbon with two colours - typically red and black.

4.5 Writing

You have received the following telex from Mr Dale of Dale Recruitment Agency. (Use glossary for telex abbreviations, if necessary.)

83. 10. 31 15.45
054321 BS LEEDS G.
743321 DALEREC Y.
TLX NO: 1145

ATTENTION: MR BURNS

REF OUR TEL CALL RE SUPPLY OF M3300 WORD PROCESSING PACKAGE, PLS SEND ASAP INFO RE PUMA TELEX MACHINE:
1. IS KEYBOARD SAME AS NORMAL TYPEWRITER?
2. CAN WE USE NORMAL TELEX PAPER?
3. MUST WE BUY A STAND FOR TELEX MACHINE?
4. MUST WE BUY PAPER TAPE ATTACHMENT?

THANKS IN ADVANCE
REGARDS
J. DALE

743321 DALEREC Y.
054321 BS LEEDS G.

Reply to the above telex, using the information below and in Reading 4.4.

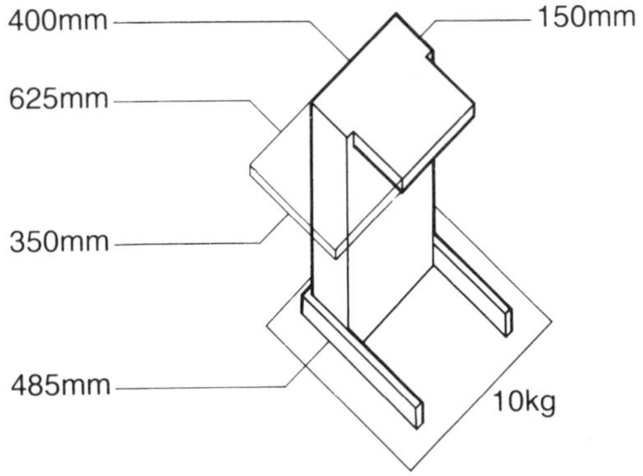

Plinth

Mounting and installing
Puma can be supplied with its own plinth as an optional extra, users may provide adequate alternative mounting. The user must provide a standard 13 amp three-pin socket mains power outlet.

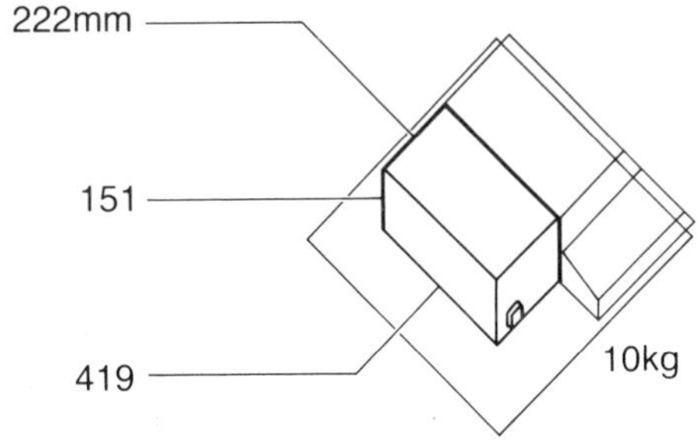

Paper tape attachment

Paper tape attachment
The attachment can be used to put messages into Puma's memory and to produce paper tape from messages already held in store. Operationally, the attachment allows Puma to be used in two distinct roles:

1. As a clean tape preparation unit using Puma's editing capabilities, and subsequently punching out a tape of the edited message. In this mode it can be used for tape preparation for feeding to earlier types of automatic machines.
2. For automatic calling: Messages are prepared 'off line', possibly on earlier types of machine or other devices. The automatic calling information is added on and any editing that may be required is carried out once the message has been put into the store.

In your reply, make sure you include the following:

Date and time	Attention
Telex address	Reference to enquiry
Your telex address	Answers to enquiry
Telex reference number	Sign off

4.6 Discussion

Choose one of the following for discussion:

a What problems do you foresee in creating an integrated service network?
b Look at Figure 4a—the BIGFON Experiment. Which services do you think will be the most popular, and why?
c What will the office of the future look like? Who will work in an office and what will they do?

4.7 Word list

Data communications

remote data processing p. 43 decentralized, in many different locations.
memory to memory p. 43 from one computer to another.
alphanumeric p. 44 a system of display using letters (e.g. a, b, c . . .) digits (e.g. 1, 2, 3 . . .) and other characters (e.g.: ?,).
graphic p. 44 a system of display using symbols (e.g. graphs, diagrams etc.).
store p. 199(T) to keep in a computer memory.
access p. 199(T) entry into.
data banks p. 199(T) stores of information—may be public (i.e. available to all), or private (for certain companies).
feed in p. 200(T) to enter (data) into.
asynchronous p. 52 (of a network) a system in which transmission is only possible in one direction at a time. (Opposite of **synchronous**.)
ISDN p. 44 Integrated Services Digital Network.

Hardware

solid-state p. 53 in electronics, depending on electrical and magnetic signals in solids (not gasses, compare with relays) e.g. transistors, integrated circuits.
modem p. 199(T)
screen p. 199(T) a VDU.
keyboard p. 199(T)
terminal p. 200(T) usually a VDU and keyboard.

Text services

telegraph p. 43
telex p. 43
teletex p. 43
telefacsimile p. 43

Voice

telephony p. 43
PSTN p. 44 Public Switched Telephone Network.

Broad-band transmission

videotex p. 44
viewdata p. 44
teletext p. 44

Word processing functions

to edit p. 53 to check, shorten, lengthen text.
to insert p. 53 to add extra text.
to delete p. 53 to take away unnecessary or incorrect text.
to justify, justification p. 53 to print a document with even alignment to left and right hand margins.

Printing

a character p. 53 one letter (a, b, c . . .), digit (1, 2, 3, 4 . . .) or punctuation mark (., ?, ; . .).
a space p. 53 the gap between two words.
dot matrix p. 53 a pattern of pin-points used to form characters.
to lay out p. 53 to organize text into a certain format.
multi-ply p. 53 (of paper) having 2 or 3 sheets for copying purposes.

intermediate paperwork p. 199(T) unnecessary production of text on paper between formation of message and transmission of message.

Transmission

incoming message p. 199(T) message received.

outgoing p. 199(T) message sent.

on-line p. 53 machine connected for transmission.

off-line p. 53 machine not connected for transmission.

local mode p. 53 machine not connected for transmission.

Miscellaneous

to promote p. 43 to make more popular, in demand.

to adapt p. 43 to change, modify.

to launch p. 43 to introduce onto the market.

spectrum p. 44 a range (as in colours of the rainbow).

stand p. 200(T) a site at an exhibition where a company displays its products/services.

stand p. 54 a support (e.g.: hat-stand).

plinth p. 55 see *stand* above.

to allocate p. 53 to give a certain address or number to something.

to maintain p. 53 to keep.

directory p. 53 an alphabetical list of names and numbers.

spillage p. 53 liquid that has run out of the container.

clatter p. 53 a regular noise made by printing.

socket p. 55 an entry point into mains electricity supply.

Telex abbreviations

ref p. 54 with reference to . . .

tel p. 54 telephone.

re p. 54 regarding, on the subject of . . .

pls p. 54 please.

asap p. 54 as soon as possible (often 'soonest').

info p. 54 information.

Unit 5 Radio communications 1

In this unit we begin to examine the different forms of radio communications.

5.1 Reading 1

5.1.1

Read the following description of certain types of radio communications. As you read, fill in Figures 5a, 5b, 5c and 5d.

Communicating by radio is a method of sending or receiving sounds, pictures and data through the air by means of electrical waves.

We use the airwaves for many purposes: broadcasting most of our local and national radio and TV stations, in our mobile radio and telephone services, and to communicate on a global scale through distant satellites, which act as a kind of reflector in the sky, redirecting the information we send up to them.

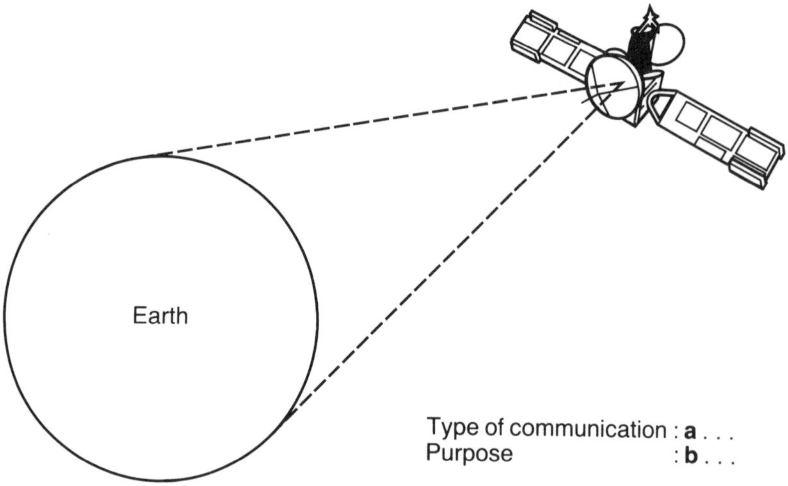

Type of communication : **a** . . .
Purpose : **b** . . .

Fig 5a

Another important use of this means of communicating is in shipping. A ship that is in difficulty can call the nearest coast station, giving details of its situation and, if necessary, ask for help. We call this 'ship-to-shore' radio. Radio can ensure greater safety in navigation (for example, to warn of bad weather or of hazards in the shipping lanes) and it enables large amounts of information to be sent over land or water without the support of several hundred kilometres of wires and cables. Radio networks can, therefore, be cheaper to install but often have fewer circuits than cable links. Radar systems also enable air-traffic controllers to follow and guide the flight paths of planes from take-off to landing.

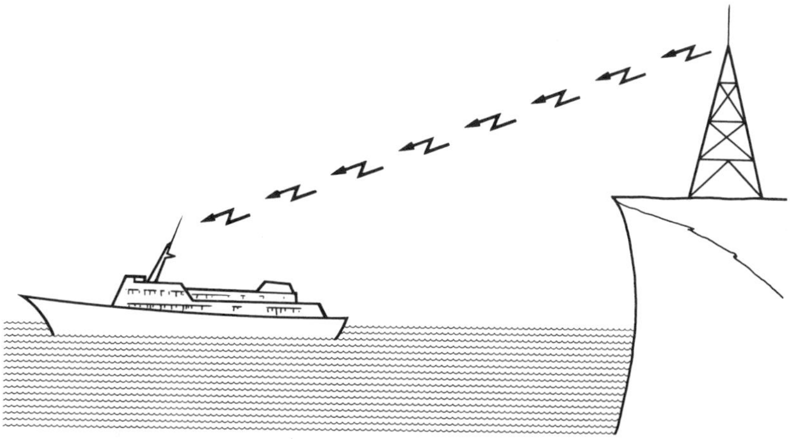

Type of communication : **c** . . .
Purpose : **d** . . .

Fig 5b

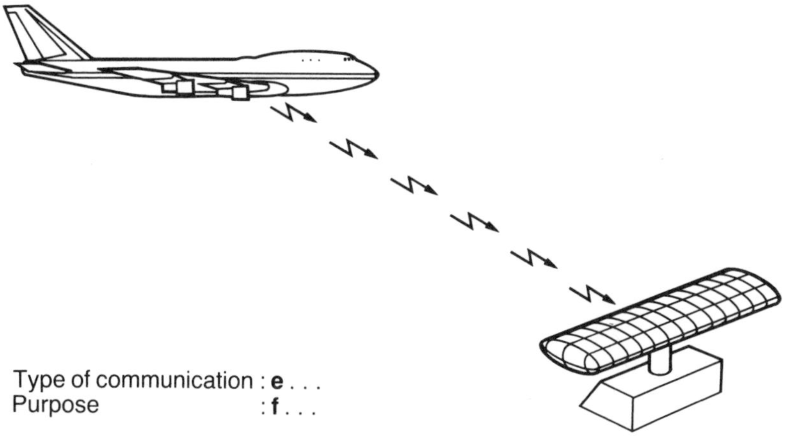

Type of communication : **e** . . .
Purpose : **f** . . .

Fig 5c

Radio-paging systems enable us to be contacted even though we do not have a telephone within easy reach. It is a way of letting us know that something important has just happened and that we must act quickly. The system works through a pager or 'bleeper', a small receiver about the size of a packet of cigarettes, which you can keep in your pocket. When people want to contact you, they simply pick up the nearest telephone, dial your personal paging number free of charge, and wherever you are in the coverage area, your pager will bleep. (You must, however, be above, not below, ground level, for the signal will not get through if you are underground.) The bleeping informs you that someone is calling you. You can identify up to four callers on some types of equipment. The most modern type of radio-pager displays the number of the telephone the caller is ringing from. The main advantage of radio-paging is that you can be contacted wherever you are, even though you may be a long way from a telephone set.

Many companies which have personnel on business trips have found that radio-paging improves their competitive position and allows them to be more responsive to a lot of their customers' needs. It also increases company efficiency by cutting out many unnecessary and expensive journeys that are sometimes made by salesmen. This saves time and fuel costs. Doctors can be contacted immediately and return to their surgery or hospital, thus possibly saving the life of a very sick patient.

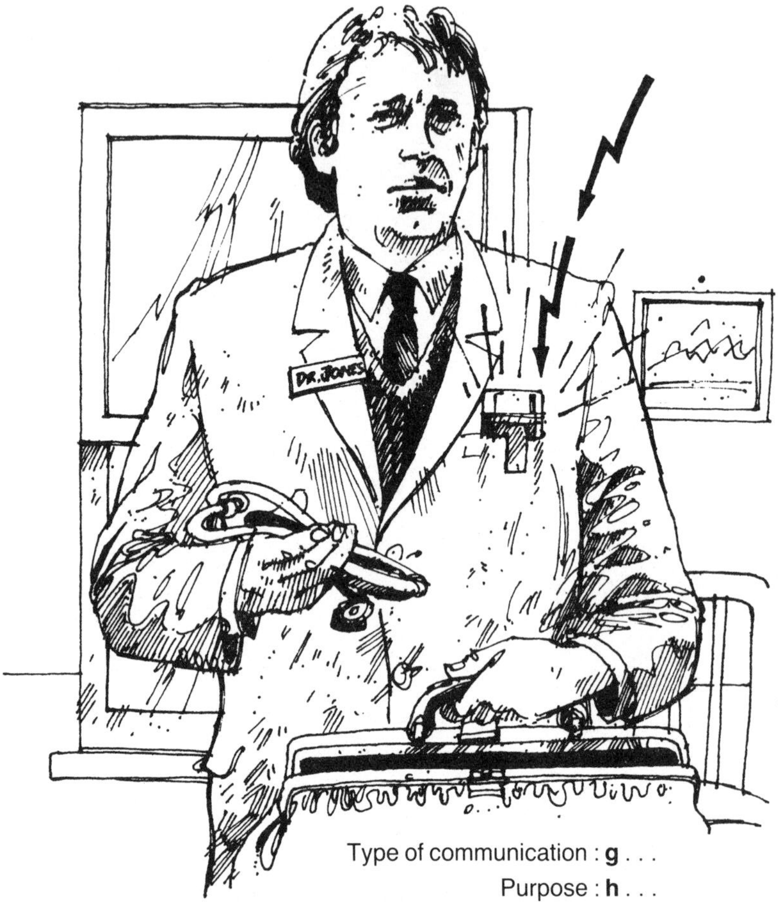

Type of communication : **g** . . .
Purpose : **h** . . .

Fig 5d

5.1.2 Comprehension

Answer the following questions:

a How does the text define radio communications?
b What examples does the text give of radio communications?
i) ship-to-shore radio ii) . . . etc.
c Why can radio networks be cheaper to install?
d What equipment does the radio-paging user need?
e Where does the user keep this equipment?
f Where must you not go if you wish to be contacted by radio-paging?
g How can companies benefit from radio-paging? (Give three ways.)
h Why do many doctors carry a bleeper?

5.2 Listening

5.2.1

Listen to the following radio telephone conversation between Peter Needham (PN), a salesman from Bradfield Electronics Ltd., Nutley, and John Brown (JB), area manager for Bradfield, who is in the factory at Nutley. Peter Needham is in his car heading for Greenwood, where he has to deliver some electronic equipment.
As you listen, complete Figure 5e by labelling the landmarks.

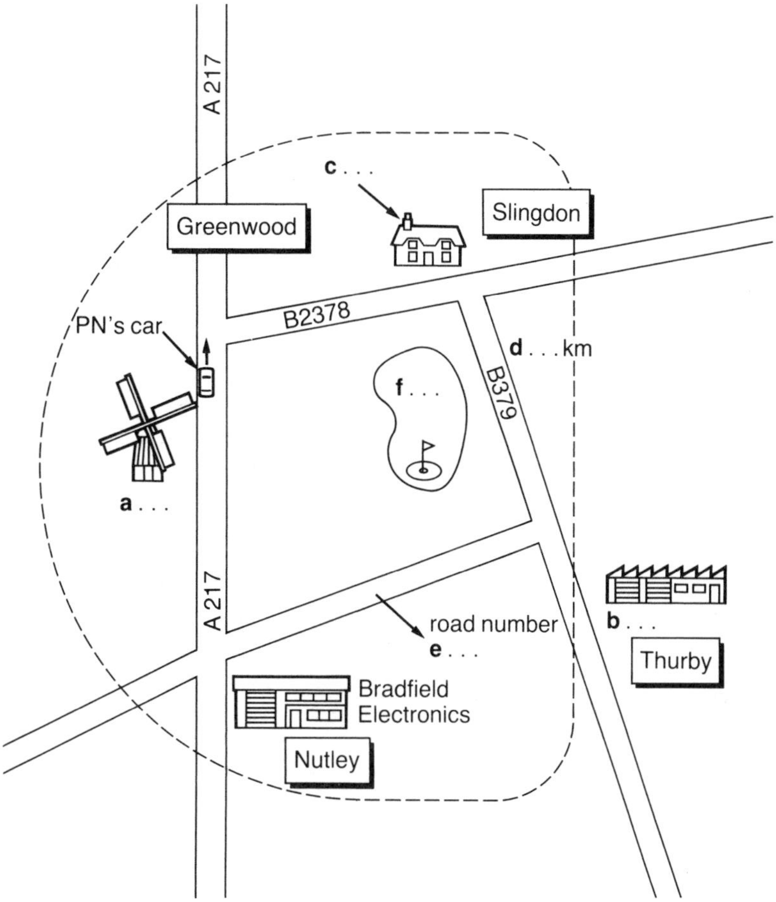

Fig 5e

5.2.2 Comprehension

Answer the following questions:

a Where is PN during the conversation?
b Why did JB get a call from Swanford Tools at Thurby?
c What road must PN take to Slingdon and where must he turn right?
d What does Derek Salvage do at Swanford Tools?
e What must PN not do when he meets Derek Salvage? Why?
f What four arguments must PN bring out concerning the advantages of the RPH radiophone?
g PN says he will be back in Nutley by:
i) 3.30 ii) 4.30 iii) 4.15.

5.3 Language practice

5.3.1 Quantity and Amount

When we talk about quantity and amount, it is important to know if what we are talking about is countable or uncountable. Look at the table below:

Countable	Uncountable
calls companies people telephone sets	news equipment information knowledge

Use the words below to express quantity and amount:

Approx.	Countable	Uncountable
100%	every/all	all
85%	most	most
↑	many/a lot of	much/a lot of
	some	some
	several	—
↓	a few	a little
5%	few	little
0%	no/none	no/none

If you need to count something which is uncountable, you must add a countable noun. **Four pieces of equipment**. **One type of information**.

Use the tables to help you fill in the blanks in the sentences below:

Year	1960	1980	2000	2050	2100
Calls going via satellite	0%	10%	70%	90%	100%
Calls going via sub-ocean cable	100%	90%	30%	10%	0%

a In:

<table>
<tr><td>1960</td><td>i . . .</td><td rowspan="5">calls</td><td rowspan="3">were</td><td rowspan="5">transmitted
by
satellite</td></tr>
<tr><td>1980</td><td>ii . . .</td></tr>
<tr><td>2000</td><td>iii . . .</td></tr>
<tr><td>2050</td><td>iv . . .</td><td rowspan="2">will be</td></tr>
<tr><td>2100</td><td>v . . .</td></tr>
</table>

b In:

<table>
<tr><td>1960</td><td>i . . .</td><td rowspan="5">information</td><td rowspan="2">was</td><td rowspan="5">transmitted
by
satellite</td></tr>
<tr><td>1980</td><td>ii . . .</td></tr>
<tr><td>2000</td><td>iii . . .</td><td rowspan="3">will be</td></tr>
<tr><td>2050</td><td>iv . . .</td></tr>
<tr><td>2100</td><td>v . . .</td></tr>
</table>

c Now choose the correct answers:

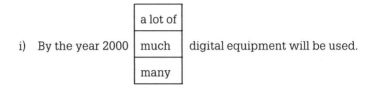

i)	By the year 2000	a lot of much many	digital equipment will be used.

ii)	Little Few	information was given about that	much piece of	equipment.	

iii)	The switchboard received	a little a few	calls about the future of satellites.

iv)	A few A little Some	good weather can normally be expected in England during August.

v)	Many Much	people think that	a few a little	knowledge is a good thing.

vi)	Many A piece of	news came in concerning	a lot of much many	engineers.

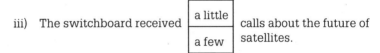

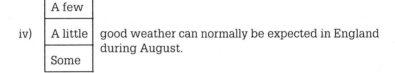

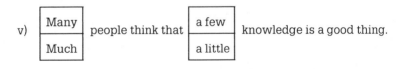

5.3.2 Prepositions of location

The following diagrams will help to make clear which preposition you should use:

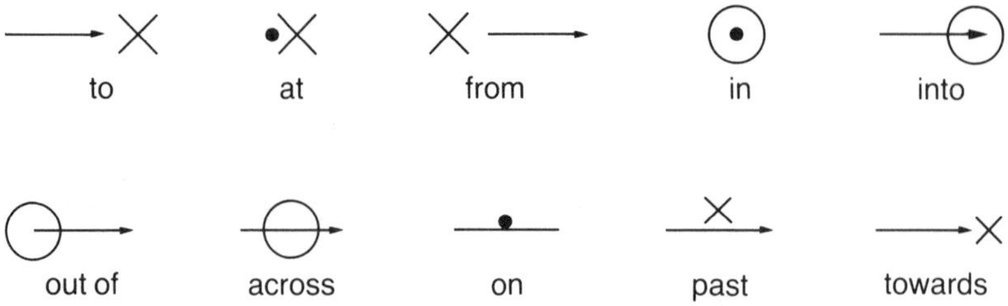

Fig 5f

Look at the map and then fill in the blanks in the exercise that follows:

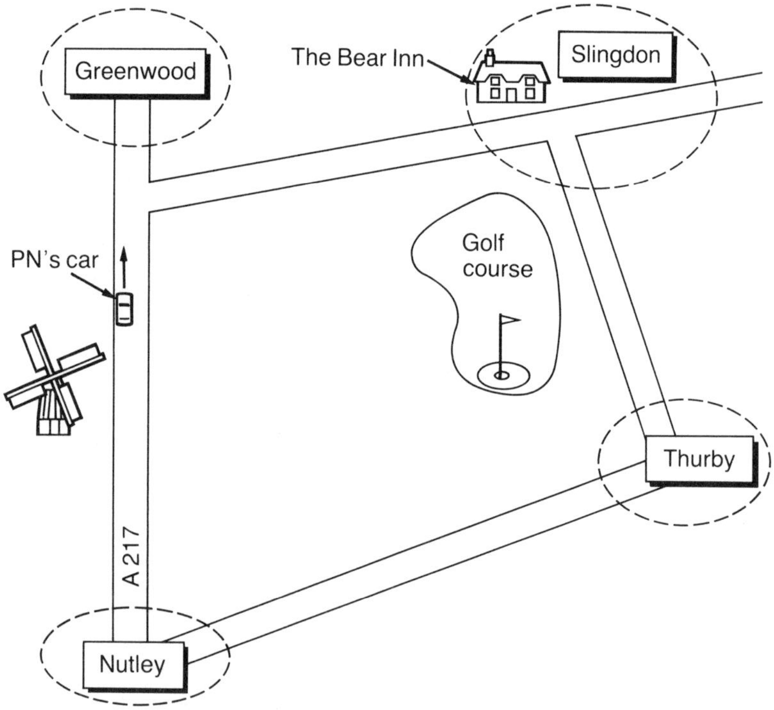

Fig 5g

a He's . . . the A217.
b He's coming . . . Nutley.
c He's going . . . Greenwood.
d He'll go . . . to Thurby.
e He's just gone . . . the windmill.
f When he's . . . Slingdon, he'll turn right . . . Thurby.
g Just after he's gone . . . Slingdon, he'll see the Bear Inn.
h When he comes . . . Slingdon, he'll see the golf course . . . his right.

5.3.3 Questions

Notice the difference between direct questions and polite questions in the examples below:

Direct Is she coming tomorrow?
When is she coming?

Polite Could you tell me when she's coming, please?
Would you mind telling me what the number is?

Now read the following dialogue and put in suitable questions. The information after each blank will help you decide what the question should be. In the dialogue, Chris Bradley (CB) is talking on the phone to Tom Davies (TD) about Bradfield Electronics' radio-paging system.

CB: Good morning. Bradfield Electronics. Research Division.
TD: **1** . . .
CB: Chris Bradley speaking.
TD: Hello Chris. It's Tom Davies from Swanford Tools here.
CB: **2** . . .
TD: I'm very well thanks. I'm phoning about your latest radio-paging system. I'd like a bit more information.
CB: **3** . . .
TD: There's quite a lot I'd like to know, actually.
CB: OK, off you go!
TD: **4** . . .
CB: No, very little. Just a small device called "a pager" or "bleeper".
TD: **5** . . .
CB: In his pocket, because it's very small.
TD: **6** . . .
CB: Oh, about the size of a packet of cigarettes.
TD: **7** . . .
CB: He's simply telephoned in the normal way and the pager bleeps.
TD: **8** . . .
CB: Nothing. It's free of charge.
TD: **9** . . .
CB: No, it doesn't. The user must remain at or above ground level.
TD: **10** . . .
CB: Not at all. The quarterly rental's only about £30.
TD: **11** . . .
CB: No problem at all. We've got a large amount in stock.
TD: **12** . . .
CB: No, fine. We could organize a demonstration next week. Would next Thursday at 2p.m. be alright for you?
TD: **13** . . .
CB: i) Good.
ii) (**14**) . . . ?
TD: No, there'll be several other people with me, mainly from the Sales Department.
CB: **15** . . .
TD: Of course. It's 53260. Extension 208.
CB: Good. I look forward to seeing you next Thursday at 2p.m.
TD: **16** . . .
CB: Yes. Come straight up. My office is on the second floor.
TD: Fine. Goodbye Chris.
CB: Bye Tom.

5.4 **Reading 2**

5.4.1

Read the description of the Nordic Mobile Telephone System (NMT) on page 67. As you read, complete Figure 5h.

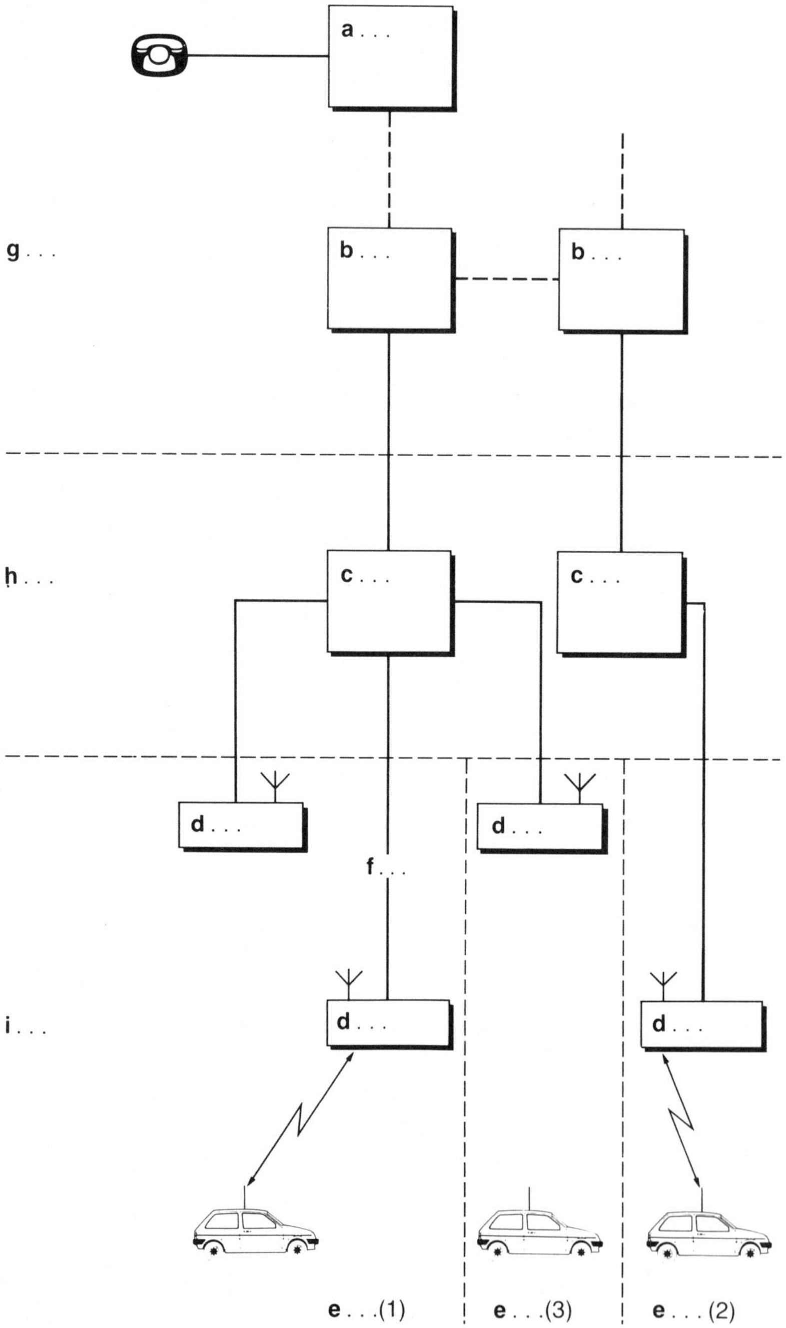

Fig 5h

Description of System

The NMT system is made up of the following component parts:

MTX (Mobile Telephone Exchange) is the brain of the system and is technically the most complicated part. The MTXs form the interface between the NMT system and the fixed telephone network. Whereas signalling and other system components of NMT are the same in all Nordic countries, their telephone networks differ in some respects. One of the functions of the exchanges is therefore to compensate for these differences.

The Base Stations are intermediary links without switching function between the wire and radio transmission. There will be about 1,000 base stations when the system is developed to full capacity.

The Mobile Stations i.e. the subscriber equipment, will be available in various forms, e.g. vehicle-borne, portable or of coin-box type. A mobile station is owned or leased by the subscriber and must be type-approved by the Administrations.

The adjoining figure shows the structure of the NMT system. Each country is divided into a number of traffic areas. In a traffic area there are a number of base stations spaced between about 8 and 80 km apart. Each traffic area belongs to a single exchange. This means that all base stations in the area are connected to this exchange and that all traffic in the area is channelled through it. The exchange communicates with the telephone network via the trunk exchanges. Every mobile subscriber is registered in a so-called home MTX, usually the MTX controlling the traffic area in which the subscriber normally resides.

Setting up of calls

A call from an ordinary telephone subscriber is connected on the basis of the first digits of the mobile subscriber's number to his home MTX. The latter stores data of his present location and transmits a call signal via all base stations in that traffic area. The mobile system answers automatically with a call acknowledgement and the MTX then assigns the mobile station a traffic channel. The call is set up.

If the mobile subscriber is in a traffic area not belonging to his home MTX, the home MTX hands over the call to the MTX controlling the visited traffic area, and the latter MTX takes over the subsequent setting up of the call.

5.4.2 Comprehension

Answer the following questions:

a Where does the NMT system compensate for the differences in the four countries' telephone networks?
b What does the distance 8–80 km refer to?
c How many exchanges does each traffic area have?
d What happens after the mobile station transmits a call acknowledgement?
e When does the home MTX hand over calls to another MTX?

5.4.3 Activity

The table below is from the July/August (1983) issue of *Personal Communications*. Look carefully at the list of headings below and choose one for the columns of information in the table which do not have a heading (a–g).

World Report

Commercial Cellular Systems In Operation in the World Today
(Latest figures available as of July 1, 1983)

a. . .	b. . .	Maximum subscriber capacity	c. . .	d. . .	e. . .	Maximum channel capacity	Equipment f. . .	Equipment RF Base	Equipment Mobiles	g. . .
AUSTRALIA Melbourne Sydney	 500 500	 4 000 4 000	 3 000 3 000	 Sep 81 Dec 81	 3 5	 120 120	All NEC equipment			Australian Telecommunications Commission
CANADA Edmonton metropolitan area	450	1 500–1 600	300	Feb 83	6	29	Nearest Class 5 tel office	G.E. Westech	Systooms-AGT Nova	Alberta Gov't Telephones
HONG KONG	800	13 000	1 000	June 83	14		All NEC equipment			
JAPAN Tokyo	800	100 000	12 532	Dec 79	13	1 000	NEC	NEC	NEC Matsushita	Nippon Telegraph and Telephone PC
Tokyo Megalopolis				Mar 81	24					
Osaka		100 000	5 654	Nov 80	11	1 000				
Osaka Megalopolis				Sep 81	16					
Nagoya		100 000	1 019	Jan 82	11	1 000				
Fukuoka		20 000	303	Dec 82	12	1 000				
Sappono		20 000	197	Dec 82	10	1 000				
Hiroshima		20 000	82	Mar 83		1 000				
Sendal		20 000	66	Mar 83		1 000				
MEXICO Mexico City	400	8 000	1 400	Aug 81	1	80	All NEC equipment			Telefonos de Mexico
SAUDI ARABIA Riyadh Jeddah Damman	450	200 000	2 000	Sep 81	20	Depends on System Growth	Ericsson (3 switches)	Ericsson Philips	Ericsson Philips	Kingdom of Saudi Arabia PTT
SCANDINAVIA Sweden Norway Denmark Finland	450	200 000	 16 500 16 100 10 500 5 000	 Oct 81 Nov 81 Jan 82 Mar 82	 155 120 30 30	About 10 000	LM Ericsson 6 switches	Ericsson Magnetics Mitsubishi Mobira	Ericsson NEC AP (Philips) Motorola Mitsubishi Matsushta Mobira (Finnish) Slomo (GE subsidiary) Siemens (German) Simonsen (Norwegian)	The 4 PTTs in Denmark Finland Norway Sweden
Totals			48 100		335					
SINGAPORE	400	6 000	2 000	Nov 82	4	180	All NEC equipment			Telecommunications Authority of Singapore
SPAIN Madrid	450	Will be extended to entire country	500	mid-82	20	Depends on System Growth	All Ericsson equipment			Spanish PTT
USA Chicago	800	2 000	2 000	Jan 79	10	136	Western Electric		EF Johnson OK1 Motorola	AMPS of Minors Bell
Washington Baltimore	800	up to 2 500	250	Dec 81	7	48	All Motorola equipment (mobiles and portables)			Amn Radio-Telephone

Fig 5i

Number of cells
Date service started
Operated by
Frequency (MHz)
Country and Service area
Switch
Number of subscribers

5.5 Writing

Now read the letter sent by Tom Davies's secretary to Chris Bradley (see 5.3.3) confirming the subject matter of their telephone conversation.

Swanford Tools Ltd.,
Slingdon Road,
Thurby. TH2 SY3
19th April, 19. . .

Tel: 0432 - 53260
Ext: 208
Ref: TD/368
Mr. C. Bradley,
Bradfield Electronics,
Nutley, NU6 SR7

Dear Mr. Bradley,

Following your telephone conversation yesterday with Mr. Tom Davies, I should like to confirm that Mr. Davies will visit you at Bradfield Electronics on Thursday 26th April at 2 p.m.

Mr. Davies hopes that you will be able to provide a demonstration of the radio–paging system which is of great interest to Swanford Tools Ltd.

I can also confirm that three other members of our Sales department will be present with Mr. Davies.

Yours sincerely,

J. Whitfield

Ms J. Whitfield,
(Secretary)
p.p. Mr. T. Davies

On Monday, April 30th, Ms Whitfield received the following telex from Mr Tom Davies, who was on a business trip to Spain.

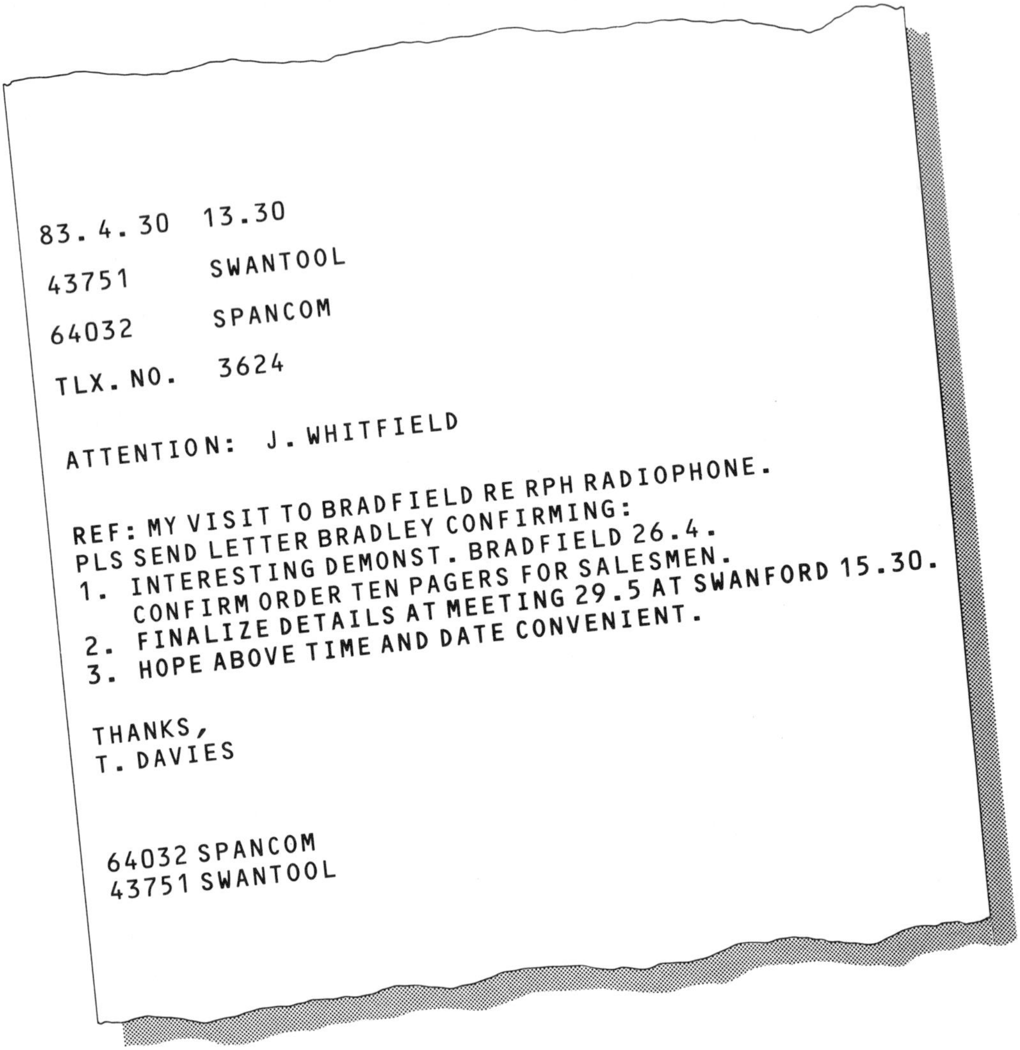

83.4.30 13.30

43751 SWANTOOL

64032 SPANCOM

TLX. NO. 3624

ATTENTION: J. WHITFIELD

REF: MY VISIT TO BRADFIELD RE RPH RADIOPHONE.
PLS SEND LETTER BRADLEY CONFIRMING:
1. INTERESTING DEMONST. BRADFIELD 26.4.
   CONFIRM ORDER TEN PAGERS FOR SALESMEN.
2. FINALIZE DETAILS AT MEETING 29.5 AT SWANFORD 15.30.
3. HOPE ABOVE TIME AND DATE CONVENIENT.

THANKS,
T. DAVIES

64032 SPANCOM
43751 SWANTOOL

Using this telex, write Ms Whitfield's letter to Chris Bradley, including all the information in the telex, and basing your letter on the example provided.

5.6 **Discussion**

Choose one of the following themes for discussion:

a What kind of people/organizations will find radio-paging a great advantage? Why?
b Discuss your country's plans for a mobile telephone service.
c What are the advantages and disadvantages of having a mobile telephone?

5.7 **Word list**

Radio communications

airwaves p. 58
ship-to-shore radio p. 58
radar system p. 58
radio-paging system p. 59
a pager (a bleeper) p. 59
a receiver p. 59
a radiophone system p. 200(T)

Mobile telephone services

interface p. 67 a connection.
coverage area p. 59
vehicle-borne p. 67 carried in a vehicle.
mobile telephone exchange p. 67
base station p. 67
mobile station p. 67
traffic channel p. 67
traffic area p. 67

Miscellaneous

type-approved p. 67 accepted for use by a Telecom Admin.
to assign p. 67 to give responsibility to.
to compensate for p. 67 to pay back the value of something which is lost.
to belong to p. 67
to reside p. 67 to live.
to hand over p. 67 to give to someone.
a demonstration p. 65
a surgery p. 60
a device p. 65

Revision Unit A Meeting the customer

In this unit you will analyse information about a large company's telecommunications activities and needs, and the Telecommunications Administration with whom it will have contact. At the same time, you will practise the language introduced in Units 1–5.
(Later Revision Units will continue this study)

Objectives: To study and analyse:
A the structure and operation of a large multi-national company
B the economic and geographical background to a developing country
C the state of development of the Telecommunications Administration of the same country.

1 Reniat

Reniat is an automobile company which is planning to set up a subsidiary in the South Pacific.
Study the information on Reniat and complete exercises **1a**, **1b** and **1c**.

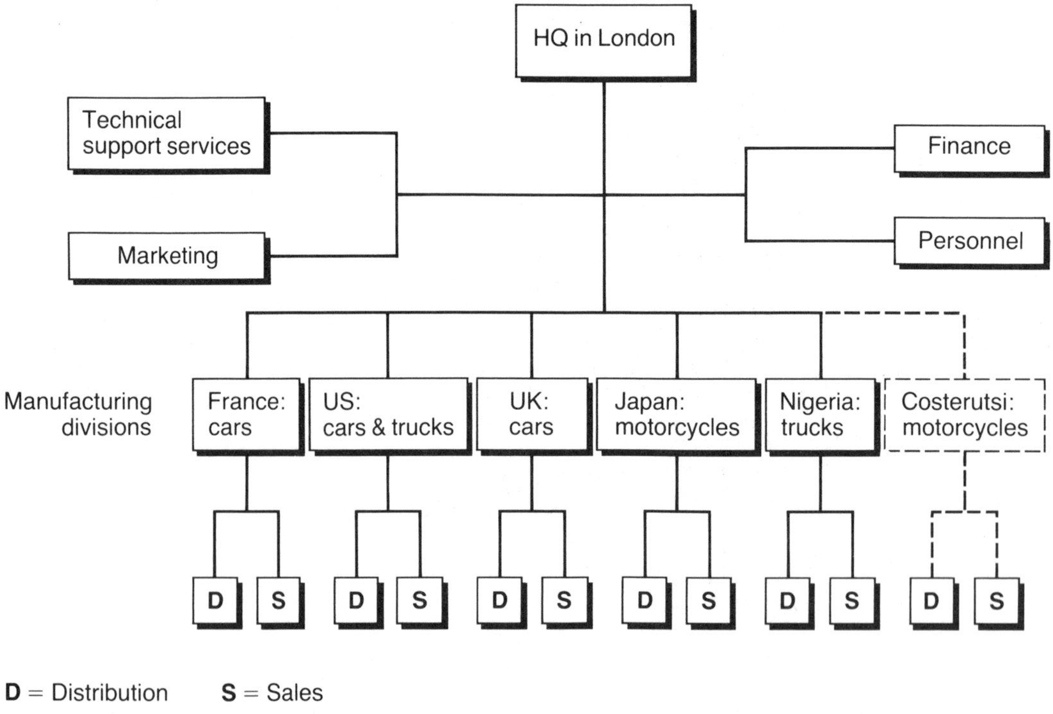

Figure Revision A 1

1 a

a Reniat . . . into 5 manufacturing divisions.
b There are . . . divisions which produce cars exclusively; . . . are in Europe, . . . in France, . . . in the UK.
c . . . plant produces cars in the USA, but it . . . produces trucks.
d The HQ organization . . . 4 sections, namely Technical, Marketing, Finance and Personnel.
e . . . manufacturing division . . . 2 main departments: Distribution and . . . .

1 b

The planned subsidiary in Costerutsi.
Use this extract from a report, written by the future Managing Director of the Costerutsi Division, to complete the data sheet below:

Extract from report

> Unlike other major divisions, the Costerutsi division will not be a manufacturing division. It will only assemble, distribute and sell products, using components imported from Japan. Models to be marketed will be the 75 cc, 125 cc and 250 cc motorcycles.
>
> Assembly will take place in the capital, Leyport, and distribution to the 7 main dealers will be via the warehouse, just to the East of Leyport.
>
> There will be 2 dealers in Leyport, and one in each of the larger towns: Ellton, Woodburn, Fort Gray, Sonley and Bloosburg.
>
> The management team will consist initially of 3 from the UK and 2 local distribution managers; there will be a total of 30 supervisory staff for the 570 operators and 15 maintenance mechanics. The payroll will be administered by the Costerutsi National Bank, all other support services being supplied initially by HQ in London.

COSTERUTSI DIVISION : DATA SHEET

Products:	**a**. . .	**b**. . .	**c**. . .
Activities:	**d**. . .	**e**. . .	**f**. . .
Source of Components:	**g**. . .		
Factory Location:	**h**. . .		
Warehouse Location:	**i**. . .		
Sales Outlets:	**j**. . .	**k**. . .	**l**. . .
	m. . .	**n**. . .	**o**. . .
Employees:	Management (total) **p**. . . Supervisors **q**. . . Operators and mechanics **r**. . .		
Support Services:	**s**. . .	**t**. . .	

1 c

Complete the description of the following flow chart by

i) putting the verb in brackets into the correct form, and
ii) inserting an appropriate preposition.

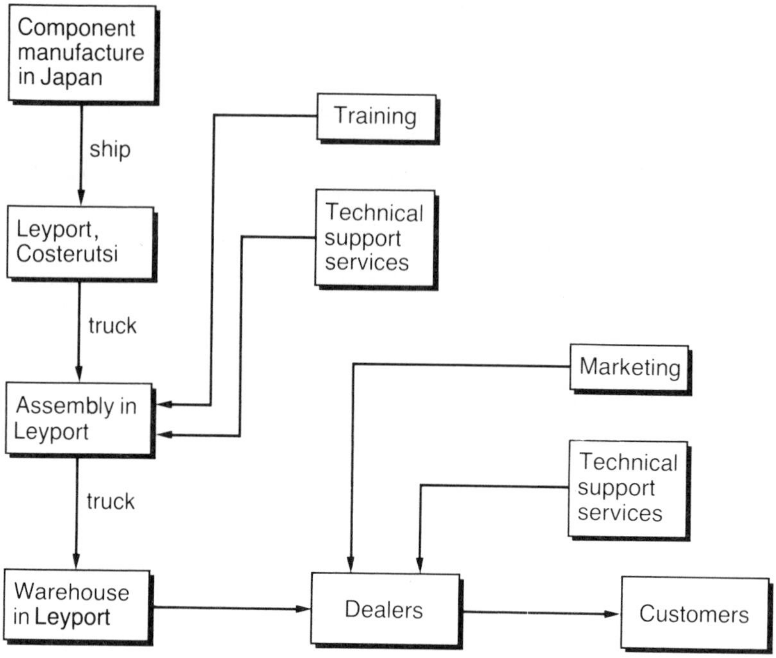

Fig Revision A 2

The components . . . (manufacture) in Japan and . . . (ship) to Leyport docks. From here, they . . . (transport) direct to our assembly plant . . . Leyport. Three models . . . (assemble) . . . the plant: the 75 cc, 125 cc, and 250 cc motorcycles. When they . . . (assemble), they . . . (take) . . . truck . . . the warehouse . . . the suburbs of Leyport. . . . here they . . . (distribute) . . . dealers throughout the country.

The technical support services department . . . London is available to assist the assembly plant and to help dealers . . . service problems. The training section, which . . . (come) under Personnel, . . . also (be) available to train assembly workers. The marketing department . . . (liaise) . . . the dealers . . . promotion campaigns . . . the public.

2 Costerutsi: A brief description

Use the information in Figures Revision A 3, 4 and 5 to complete the text.

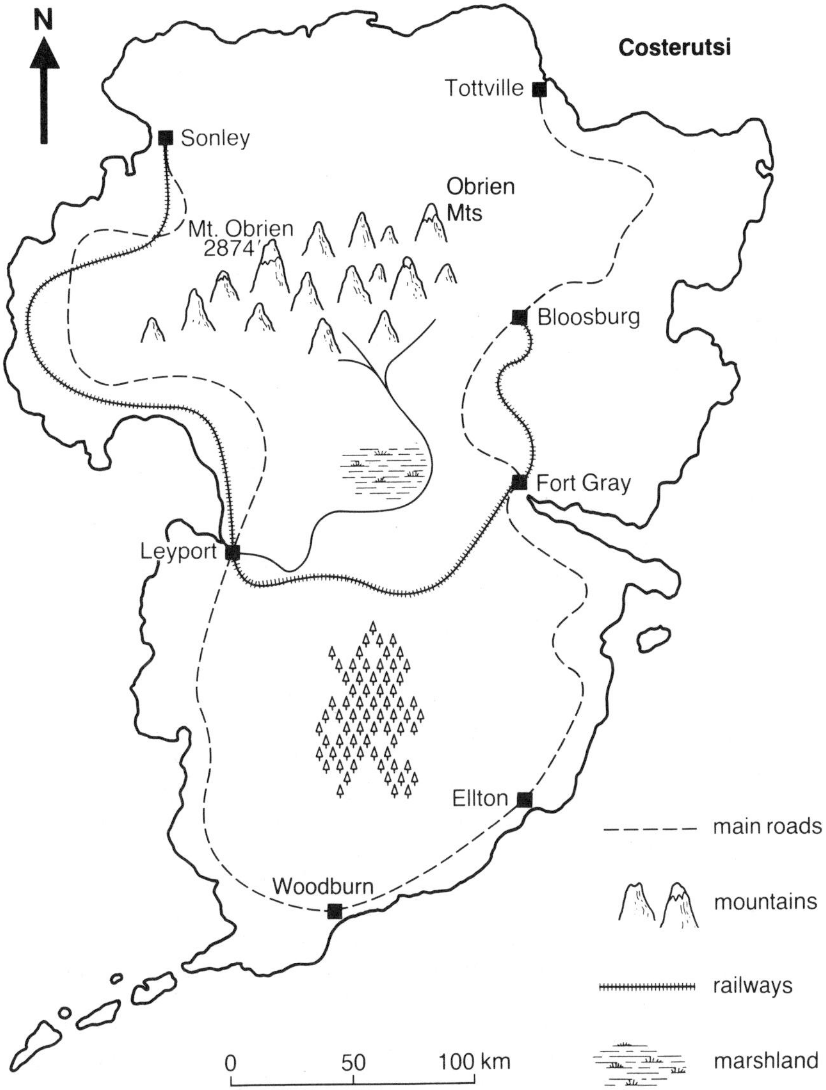

Fig Revision A 3

Situation

Costerutsi is an independent country in the South Pacific with a total population of more . . . three and a half million inhabitants.
It is approximately 400 km . . . and 200 km . . . . Its . . . point is Mount Obrien, which stands 2874 metres . . . sea level.
The capital city, Leyport, is situated . . . the west coast and . . . of the other towns are also situated on or . . . the coast.

Communications

There are relatively good road links . . . the main towns, but only . . . towns enjoy railway communication. . . . communication links follow the coast, the main exception being the railway line which carries uranium . . . Bloosburg . . . Fort Gray.

Costerutsi : Population

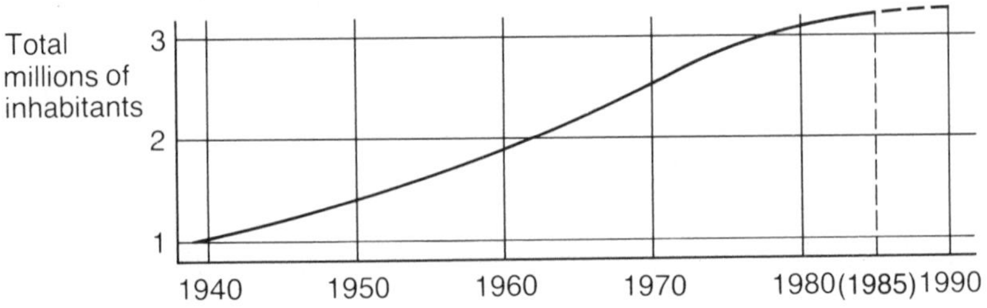

Fig Revision A 4

Individual towns

	Inhabitants	
	1950	1980
Leyport	150 000	360 000
Fort Gray	110 000	180 000
Ellton	90 000	175 000
Bloosburg	40 000	190 000
Others	550 000	1 245 000
TOTAL	940 000	2 150 000

Fig Revision A 5

Population

Over the last few years the population of Costerutsi . . . (rose/has risen) dramatically.
This is because of the discovery of uranium, which . . . (took/has taken place) in 1959 in the Obrien mountains. In 1960 the population . . . (was/has been) just . . . (over/under) 2 million, but, since then, it . . . (increases/has increased) to . . . (over/under) 3 million. The capital, Leyport, is by far the . . . (biggest/bigger) city. At the last census, in 1980, it was . . . (almost/more than) twice . . . big . . . the next town, Bloosburg.
The increase in the population of the other large towns . . . (was/has been) . . . (more/less) dramatic, as they offer . . . (fewer/more) attractions to the new urban population.

Products

In 1959 uranium . . . (discover) near Bloosburg and shortly afterwards a large mining operation . . . (set up) with the help of foreign capital and technology. The traditional exports of maize and rice were soon . . . (replace) by uranium, which now . . . (form) 80% of Costerutsi's exports.
The uranium . . . (extract) from the hills near Bloosburg and . . . (take) by rail via Fort Gray to Leyport. From there it is . . . (export) to Australasia and the USA.

3 The Costerutsi Telecommunications Administration

3 a

Listen to the Director General of the Costerutsi Telecommunications Administration (C.T.A.) giving a presentation on the present state of telecommunications in his country.

When you have listened to it, make brief notes on the subjects given below, which you have been asked to report on to your colleagues:

C.T.A. Points to watch for:

Monopoly?—**a**

Responsibilities: **b**
Services: **c**

No. of telephones per capita: **d**
Types of switching equipment: **e**
No. of free local calls (%): **f**
Relative cost of trunk calls: **g**
Average business rental cost: **h**
Trunk transmission techniques: **i**
Any traffic increase: **j**
Data services: **k**
Data speeds: **l**
Facsimile: **m**
Mobile radio-phone stations: **n**
Mobile radio-phone subscribers: **o**
Mobile radio-phone vehicles: **p**

International links:— satellite: **q**
undersea cable—present: **r**
future: **s**

3 b

Examine these statements of fact and opinion, and select those which you think are justified by the C.T.A. Director General's talk. Discuss your choice with a colleague.

- The C.T.A. will never be privatized.
- There is a need to replace a lot of switching equipment.
- The telephone is under-used in Costerutsi.
- C.T.A. policy on rental is unfair to businesses.
- Extra revenue would be raised by abolishing toll-free areas.
- Transmission techniques are out of date.
- Telex traffic shows a healthy increase.
- International telephone traffic increases are due to IDD facilities.
- The change to Datex will not increase data traffic.
- Leased data circuits are likely to prove popular.
- Mobile radio telephone services are not sufficient for a population of 2 million.

Unit 6 **Networks 2**

In this unit we look at local area networks (LANs).

6.1 Reading

6.1.1

As you read the following text, complete Figure 6d.

Local Area Networks (LANs) may be defined as transmission and switching systems that provide high-speed communication between devices located on a single site. This could be an office complex, an industrial estate, a college campus or any closely linked group of buildings in which a variety of workstations need to communicate with each other. A typical LAN may cover a distance ranging from a few metres to around ten kilometres. As much of our daily work in the office involves using different kinds of communication media, LANs have been seen to be particularly useful in the fields of office automation (OA) and distributed data processing (DDP). Several studies have shown that there are four fundamental levels of communication in office systems:

1. Communication within a group, which could be a particular department in a company. The distance of transmission ranges from a few metres to about one hundred metres.
2. Communication with other internal groups or departments in the same company. The transmission distance ranges from a few hundred metres to perhaps two or three kilometres.
3. Communication with branch offices of the same company. The distance here ranges from a few dozen kilometres to hundreds of kilometres.
4. Communication with the outside world. The transmission distance ranges from a few kilometres to thousands of kilometres.

Typically we find that about 50% of all office communication circulates within one geographic site and that 70% of all communication circulates within the same company. Only 30% ever goes beyond the company into the outside world, to customers and suppliers, for example.

Many large companies, or groups working on the same site, are being faced with the choice of continuing with their own PABXs, which may be electromechanical or electronic, or of installing a LAN. Installing a LAN is certainly very expensive but it offers a great variety of advantages over a PABX. Suppliers of LANs have been offering systems based on two major classes of architecture, the ring and bus topologies.

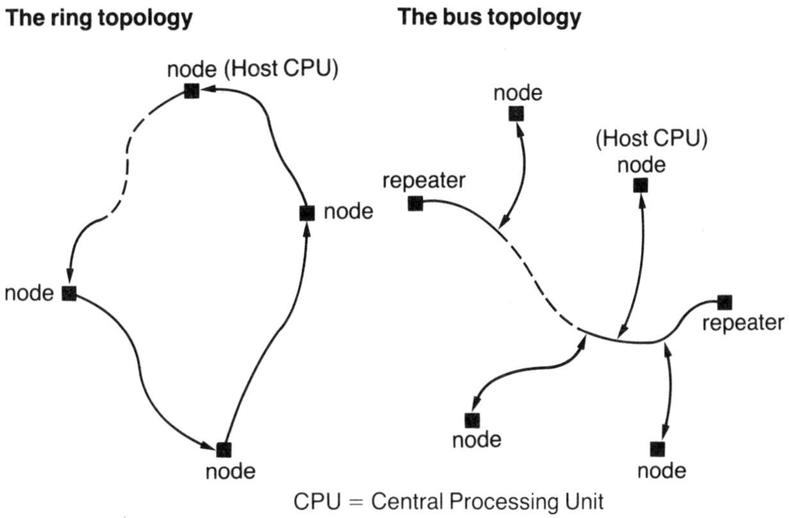

Fig 6a

A third solution that is also sometimes suggested is based on the classic star network, in which a central processor controls all other nodes in a master/slave manner.

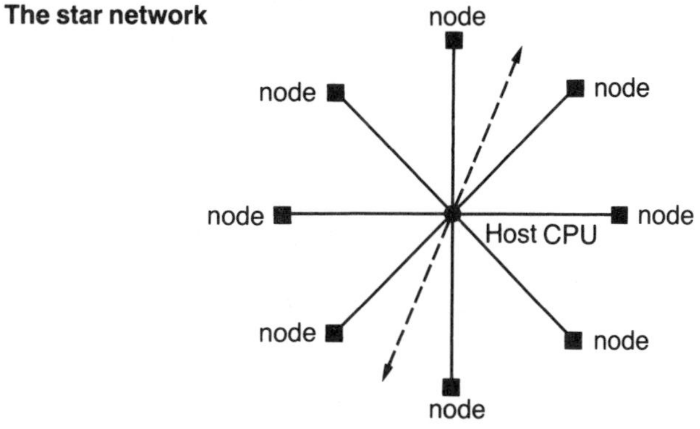

Fig 6b

The central processing unit (CPU) in ring and bus topologies can be located anywhere in the network, making for truly decentralized processing, whereas it controls every operation in a star network. In contrast to LAN suppliers, the effort of PABX suppliers has been placed, for the main part, on replacing electromechanical systems with modern, electronic PABXs where the customer's requirements have been almost exclusively for voice-only systems. The late entry of PABX suppliers into the OA market has been seen by many as the chasing of a new expanding market with 'second best' technology.

So which is the better for the office: a PABX or a LAN system? A lot obviously depends on the size and specific needs of each company, but LAN topology and architecture seem to be more suitable for levels one and two because of the very high data rates, high occupancy and transaction levels that are involved. PABXs, on the other hand, seem to be more suitable for levels three and four, where communication over longer distances is required.

Other arguments in favour of the PABX are that most people are already familiar with it and know how to use all its facilities. A PABX can normally be easily upgraded through software modifications to provide new facilities for the office of the future. It also offers full access to all national telecommunication services and an electronic PABX gives the user features such as call detail recording. The PABX has single wire connectivity and cabling probably already runs from the PABX to every workstation in the company. A final argument is that most users have limited budgets and prefer to continue with a technology that has been tried and tested, especially as they consider that voice traffic, rather than data, will remain the dominant form of communication.

The principal argument in favour of LANs is their ability to handle large amounts of data at high speed. Also their networks, either ring or bus, require less cabling than the star networks of PABXs, and LANs offer distributed control rather than the very centralized systems provided by PABXs. This gives LANs more power and flexibility. It is also easier to share specialized resources with a LAN and different terminals can be connected more economically than on a PABX. Finally, the LAN frees the PABX for other functions.

Against the LAN, we can argue that it is costly to install; it is limited in communications distance; there is a lack of privacy and a relatively small bandwidth; and it can only accommodate a limited number of terminals. For some operations a LAN may also be less reliable than a PABX. An enormous market for office automation is opening up, as we can see in Figure 6c.

Growth of terminals in USA			
Devices	**1979**	**1984**	**Approximate % growth in 5 years**
Computer terminals	3 300 000	7 600 000	130%
Desktop computers	400 000	3 600 000	800%
Computers	500 000	1 200 000	140%
Telex teleprinters	480 000	740 000	50%
Communicating word processors	25 000	500 000	1900%
PABXs	235 000	400 000	70%
Facsimile units	180 000	380 000	110%

Fig 6c

Since LANs appear to be particularly well-suited to the electronic office, they will certainly continue to develop in different forms using transmission media (coaxial cable and/or optical fibres) which meet the specific requirements and technical possibilities of individual companies in terms of architecture and investment.

	Levels and volume of communication in an office system				
Level	Type of communication	Distance covered	Volume of traffic	Suitability of system	
				PABX	LAN
1					
2					
3					
4					

Fig 6d

6.1.2 Comprehension

Answer the following questions:

a How does the text define a LAN?
b Give four examples of places where LANs could be installed.
c What are the two major classes of LAN architecture?
d What market have PABX suppliers been aiming at, according to the text?
e Give five possible advantages of a PABX over a LAN.
f Give six possible advantages of a LAN over a PABX.
g What do the following acronyms mean: CPU, OA, DDP?

6.2 Listening 1

6.2.1

Listen to the following extract from an in-house training seminar on LANs. As you listen, fill in the key for Figure 6e.

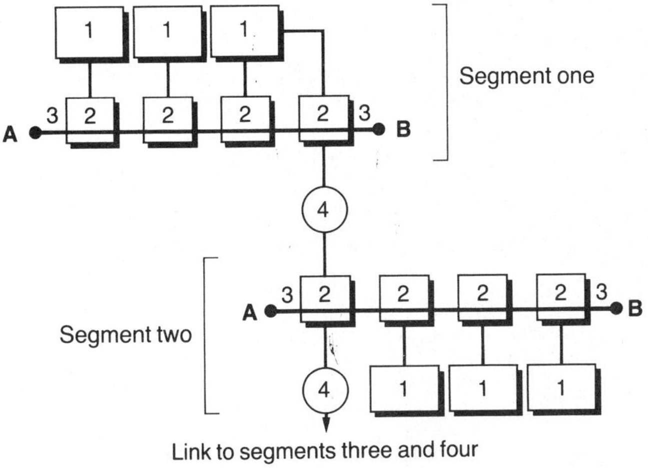

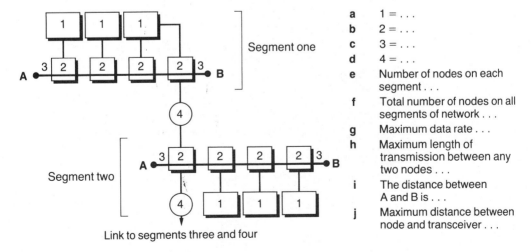

a 1 = . . .
b 2 = . . .
c 3 = . . .
d 4 = . . .
e Number of nodes on each segment . . .
f Total number of nodes on all segments of network . . .
g Maximum data rate . . .
h Maximum length of transmission between any two nodes . . .
i The distance between A and B is . . .
j Maximum distance between node and transceiver . . .

Fig 6e The Ethernet LAN (Xerox Corporation)

6.2.2 Comprehension

Answer the following questions:

a Give three technical reasons for the interest in LANs in an office environment.
b Give two marketing reasons for this interest.
c Name eight types of information system that can be linked to a LAN.
d What does the instructor mean by the expression 'a multimedia concept'?
e Why will fibre optic LANs be especially useful?
f Give six advantages of an optical fibre LAN.

6.3 Language practice

6.3.1 The present continuous tense

Look at the following examples of the present continuous:

Managers **are** now **beginning** to realize that . . .
Modern office systems **are evolving** towards . . .
I'm going to the USA tomorrow.

The present continuous is used:
a for an action which is taking place at the present time, but which will soon be over (first and second examples above).
b for a fixed arrangement which will take place in the future (third example above).

The main uses of the simple present tense are expressing:
a a habit (e.g. She always **gets up** at 6.30 a.m.)
b a state (e.g. I **like** computers.)

Now put the verbs in brackets into the correct present tense (continuous or simple).

a You can't see Mr Jones now. He (work) in the computer centre.
b He usually (arrive) at 8.30 a.m., but he phoned a few minutes ago to say that today he (arrive) at 10.
c He's already made his plans. He (fly) to New York next week.
d (Like) you computer programming? Yes, I (love) anything to do with computers.
e Where (live) she? For the moment, she (live) in London.
f Operators (work) a 3-shift system.
g Nowadays, many executives (lose) their fear of the keyboard.
h With the arrival of bureautics, a new market in local area networks (open up).
i Modern office systems (move towards) a multimedia concept.
j What (stand for) OA? It (stand for) office automation.

6.3.2 The use of modals

Look at the following examples:

a The CPU **can** be located anywhere in the network.
b LANs **ought to** be designed on a fibre optic system.
c LANs **cannot** be tapped.
d Fibre optics **should** offer higher bit rates.
e The equipment **must** be able to handle information in different forms.

Decide what ideas the words in bold type express. Use the table below.

Idea expressed	Modal verb
Possibility	can/could/may/might
Probability	should/ought to
Permission	may/can
Obligation	must/have to
Advice/recommendation	should/ought to
Ability	can/could/be able to

Now complete the sentences below with appropriate modal verbs.

f The report . . . be finished by 6 o'clock. (Obligation)
g Your telephone . . . be installed by Friday. (Probability)
h This equipment . . . be exported to certain countries. (Permission)
i You . . . wear protective clothing at all times. (Advice)
j We . . . not deliver until we receive the parts. (Ability)

Continue completing the sentences below. Also indicate the idea expressed.

k A LAN . . . be installed in most modern offices. (. . .)
l He doesn't look very well. He . . . stay in bed. (. . .)
m Optical fibre . . . come down in price as production expands. (. . .)
n You . . . only export this electronic equipment if you get a special licence. (. . .)
o According to the timetable, the plane . . . land in 20 minutes. (. . .)

6.3.3 Expressing opinions

Look at the table below. It contains phrases that will help you to express your opinion about something.

Neutral	Positive	Negative
According to him/her	You're quite right	Not at all
I think it's the best system available	I really do think it's the best system available	I don't at all approve of spending money on a system like that
In his/her/their opinion . . .	I'm more or less certain that . . .	It's not true that . . . I'm not at all sure that . . .
I suppose so	I really think so	I don't think so

In short answers, **so** replaces part of the original question:

Question: Has the meeting already begun?

Answer: I think { the meeting has already begun.
{ **so**.

Now listen to Listening 1 again. Pick out phrases similar to the ones above, and put them in the same categories as the phrases in the table.

6.4 **Listening 2**

6.4.1

Listen to the discussion between John Baker, marketing manager at Bromfield Equipment, and Stuart Henderson, a telecommunications systems engineer. They are talking about the optical fibre local distribution network at Biarritz in southwest France. As you listen, complete Figures 6f and 6g.

Key
Switching
a ▭ . . .
b ● . . .
c ☒ . . .
d ○ drop terminal
e ☎ . . .
Transmission
f —— intercentre optical fibre link
g – – – . . .
h ······· . . .

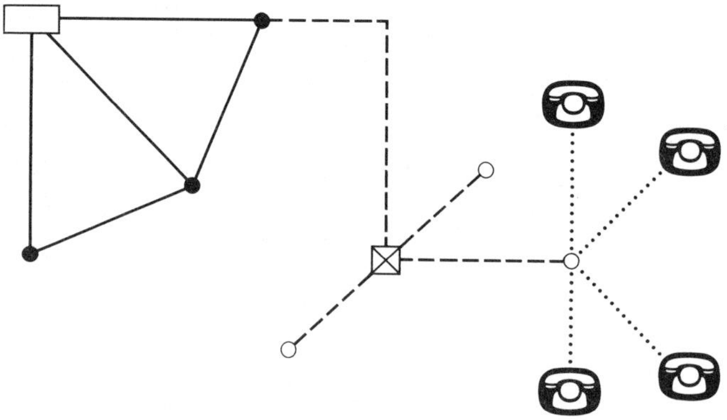

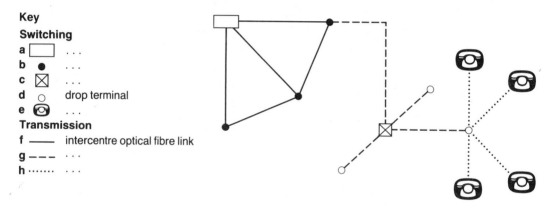

Fig 6f The organization of the Biarritz network

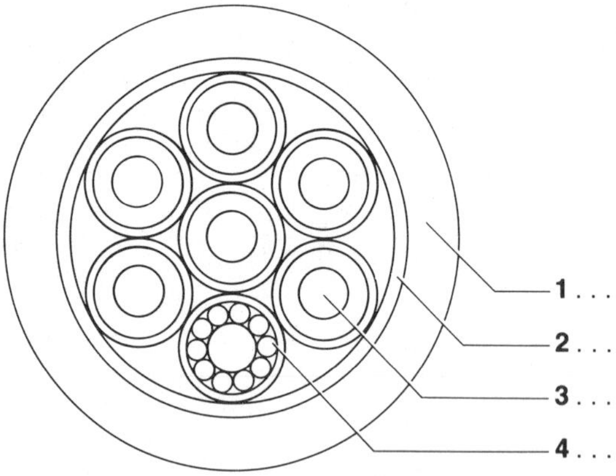

Fig 6g Cross section of an optical fibre

6.4.2 Comprehension

Answer the following questions:

a Why is John Baker particularly interested in the Biarritz project?
b Why were fibre optics chosen as the transmission medium?
c What is the main objective of the Biarritz project?
d What are the two categories of service provided and what facilities are offered in each one?
e How does John Baker summarise the Biarritz project?
f What does John Baker decide at the end of the discussion?

6.4.3 Activity

Below are some of the objectives of the Biarritz project as defined by the French Telecommunications Administration.

1. Acquiring the necessary competence to design high bandwidth optical fibre networks.
2. Winning a large part of the fast-developing optical fibre market.
3. Designing and producing well-adapted, reliable components.
4. Defining the applications of the videophone in order to produce commercially viable systems.
5. Creating new jobs in industry.
6. Obtaining the necessary technical know-how to enable installation of the equipment in a natural environment rather than in a laboratory.
7. Observing how use of the videophone changes people's behaviour (for example, letter writing or visiting friends) in order to produce high-quality non-expensive systems.
8. Creating new industrial companies.
9. Solving maintenance problems and rapidly detecting defective equipment.
10. Producing interactive services (such as reading documents by videophone and using it with a videocassette recorder) that may be marketed.
11. Designing a local videocommunications network (videophone + videoconference).

Now try to classify these objectives under the headings 'Technical Objectives', 'Commercial Objectives' and 'Industrial Objectives'.

6.5 Writing

After telephoning his old friend, Jean Dubois, John Baker has decided to visit Biarritz to see the network layout for himself. Write the letter sent by John Baker. You must include all the following information:

1. Polite enquiry about Mr Dubois' health and work.
2. John Baker suggests visiting Biarritz for two days in the week 12–16 May.
3. Visit, if possible, to a primary and secondary centre.
4. Themes for discussion: number of subscribers, types of equipment, frequencies on different parts of the network.

5 Possibility of Mr Dubois participating in a three-day seminar in London later in the year. The theme is 'Local Optical Fibre Networks'.
6 The seminar will be attended by a small group of British engineers.
7 Bromfield Equipment will pay for all Mr Dubois' expenses.
8 Hope it will be possible.
9 John Baker looks forward to seeing Jean Dubois again.
10 The letter, sent from Bromfield Equipment's London office at 24, Conway Street, EC4, is dated 14 February and is addressed to the Primary Switching Centre at 18, rue du Vieux Moulin, Biarritz, France. The letter reference is 374/JB/85.

6.6 Discussion

Choose one of the following for discussion:

a How may LANs transform the office in the near future?
b Would a LAN or a PABX be most suitable for *your* company/institution?
c What changes may there be in the everyday life of a family linked to a network like the one in Biarritz?

6.7 Word list

Local area networks

office automation p. 78
distributed data processing p. 78
ring/bus/star topology p. 78
bit rates p. 201(T)
high occupancy and transaction levels p. 80
single wire connectivity p. 80
bureautics p. 82
packet switching p. 201(T) a method of transmitting data in packets.
network architecture p. 201(T)
node p. 79 a point at which switching control functions take place.
workstation p. 78
transceiver p. 201(T) a transmitter/receiver.
bus p. 80

Local distribution networks

subscriber loop p. 202(T)
TV channel p. 202(T)
stereophonic hi-fi channel p. 202(T)
FM radio station p. 202(T)
videophone p. 202(T)
local videocommunications network p. 85

Miscellaneous

to upgrade p. 80 to extend/improve a system with new technology.
power station p. 201(T)
TV studio p. 201(T)
branch office p. 78 a local office that reports to headquarters.
subscriber's premises p. 202(T)
directory enquiries p. 202(T)
to design p. 201(T)

Unit 7 Transmission 2

In this unit we will see how modern transmission techniques are helping to provide the customer with new services.

7.1 Reading

7.1.1

Below are some typical customer complaints. Read the article about common channel signalling and see how this technique will provide services to help these customers:

A 'I waste hours trying to get through. No one ever seems to answer the phone.'

B 'I run my business on my own. I've no secretary. I'm out a lot and my customers get fed up listening to my telephone answering machine.'

C 'We must spend a fortune on international calls. You get through to a big company's switchboard and then you are left listening to the phone ringing in someone's office. After a minute or so, you put the phone down and call the switchboard again!'

D 'The phone's always engaged. I keep trying but never seem to catch you when you're not already on the phone.'

E 'I would like to use the phone more for bookings but it costs so much. If you call long distance in the day, it'll cost you a fortune!'

Common Channel Signalling and the subscriber

During recent years, the dramatic progress made in the field of telecommunications has paved the way for the introduction of new and improved services. It will be of vital importance for TA's to be able to satisfy customer demands regarding such services. Whatever new services come, and regardless of their implementation, one thing is certain: they will require signalling resources which cannot possibly be provided by the conventional signalling systems in use today.

With conventional signalling, a large number of pieces and many types of signalling equipment are required. With Common Channel Signalling (CCS), the signalling equipment is limited to relatively few signalling links. These links are used for the transfer of signalling messages between SPC exchanges. One link can be used for signalling many simultaneous transactions and hence is called a 'common channel'. The signalling information is digitally coded and transmitted in the form of discrete messages; each message being a discrete block of binary coded data. See Figure 7a.

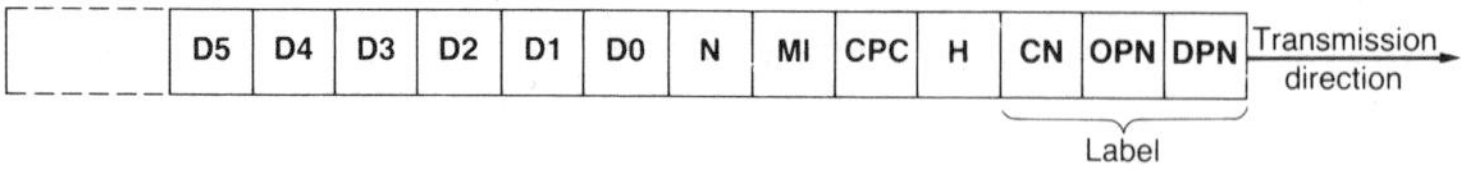

DPN Destination Point Number
OPN Originating Point Number
CN Circuit Number
H Header (indicates message type: in this example that the message is an Address Message)
CPC Calling Party Category (e.g. ordinary subscriber or operator)
MI Message Indicator (indicates for example whether the address information includes country code or not, and whether a satellite link is part of the connection)
N Number of address signals
D0-D5 Address signals (i.e. the called telephone number).

The last, dotted, field illustrates that the signalling message may be extended in the case when additional information is required; for example information associated with new supplementary services.

Fig 7a

Each message is logically associated with the transaction concerned (e.g. the set up of a call on a certain circuit) by means of a label (address).

To summarize, CCS makes it possible to transfer signalling information directly from one digital exchange to another without setting up a speech-path.

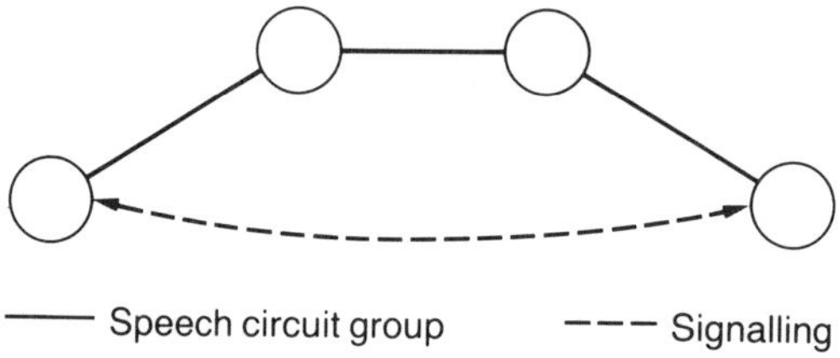

Illustration of the 'direct signalling' feature.

Fig 7b

As mentioned above, this 'direct signalling' is an important feature for the efficient realization of certain new subscriber services. Later, this feature may also be employed for ordinary calls to investigate the status (busy, disconnected etc.) of a called subscriber line, by setting up a speech path through the network.

One important new service which will require CCS is call diversion. This involves automatically diverting a call destined for a particular number (the B-number) to another number (the C-number). Today the use of this facility is limited by transmission restrictions; a call may not be routed via more than a certain number of transmission links in tandem. With CCS, by returning the C-number to the calling exchange, the call may be rerouted to a path that meets transmission requirements. This also gives a better utilization of network resources, as the number of occupied circuits for a diverted call is reduced.

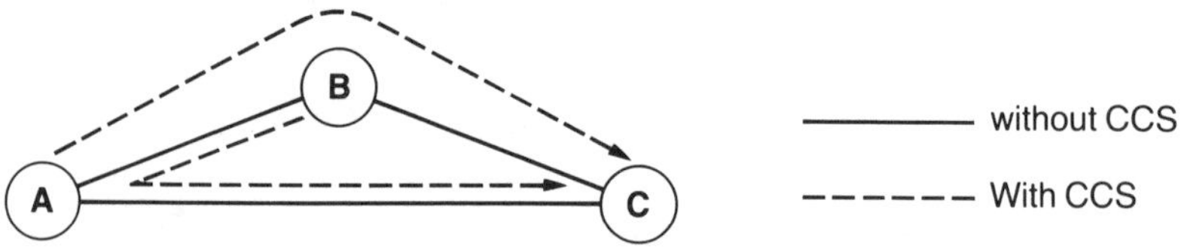

Illustration of how the subscriber service "diversion of call to another number" is realized today and how it may be realized when common channel signalling becomes available.

Fig 7c

For a fully developed diversion service, facilities for also charging the B-subscriber should be available. The A-subscriber would then only be charged for the cost of a call from A to B, whereas the B-subscriber would pay the additional cost to C. In cases where a call is rerouted at exchange A, the charging during the call will be performed at A. CCS will be used to transfer charging information from A to B after the call is completed.

CCS may be used also in connection with the activities of diversion. Exchange B asks exchange C whether or not diversion to the C-number in the enquiry message is allowed and the C exchange makes a positive or negative response. Moreover, the functions above may be applied to other diversion services such as 'diversion to operator'; 'diversion on no reply'; 'diversion on busy'; 'call transfer' etc.

Completion of 'call to busy subscriber' is another service planned in a digital network. When available, this will mean a new call will automatically be established at the moment a B-subscriber becomes idle. A rational implementation of this service requires that the call status of both the A- and B- subscribers can be monitored continuously. Changes in call status would then be signalled to the remote exchange, together with the identities (numbers) of both the A- and B- subscribers.

The exploitation of CCS will be a gradual process, which proceeds in step with the evolution of the telecom network as a whole. The potential of CCS can be illustrated by examples from the USA, where it is already an established technique. Here CCS is used in conjunction with centralized data bases to provide various subscriber services. When a call is established, information is exchanged between a particular switching centre and a data base which gives instructions as to the way a call should be handled.

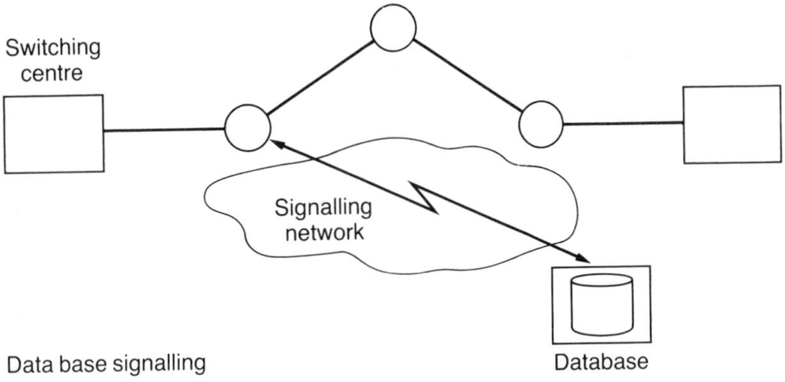

Fig 7d

For example, this technique will be employed for improving the already widespread INWATS services. It will be possible to call certain subscribers (companies, authorities etc.) without being charged for more than a local call, regardless of the destination of the call. These subscribers may be assigned a unique number (800. . .), which is automatically routed to one of the companies' offices. By using CCS, companies may centralize customer enquiry services, booking services etc. without discouraging customers from calling.

7.1.2 Comprehension

Answer the following questions:

a Look back at the customer complaints. Match the following services with their problems (**A–E**).
   i) Call to busy subscriber
   ii) Diversion to subscriber
   iii) INWATS
   iv) Diversion on no reply
   v) Call diversion

b What type of message is indicated in Fig 7a?
   i) Clear back (indicates called subscriber has terminated call)
   ii) Address-Message (indicates the telephone number of the called subscriber)
   iii) Release Guard (indicates the circuit is available for a new call)

c Which advantage does CCS offer TA's from a traffic handling point of view?
   i) makes more services available
   ii) reduces number of occupied circuits

d Who will pay *more* for the following diverted call?
   i) Subscriber A
   ii) Subscriber B

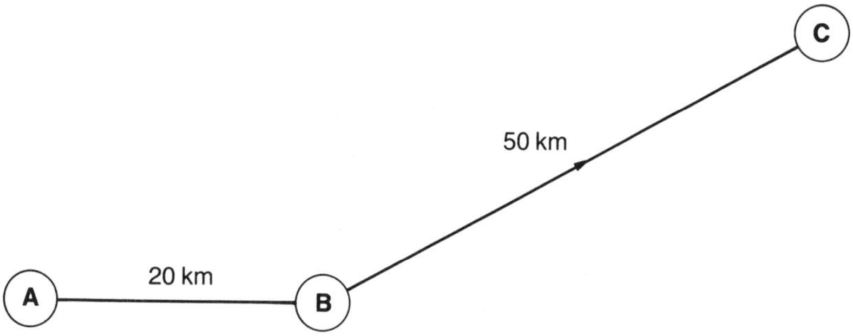

e Why is continuous monitoring of the A- and B-subscriber necessary for effective implementation of the 'call-to-busy-subscriber' facility?

f Who pays *more* for the following INWATS call?
   i) Subscriber A
   ii) Subscriber B

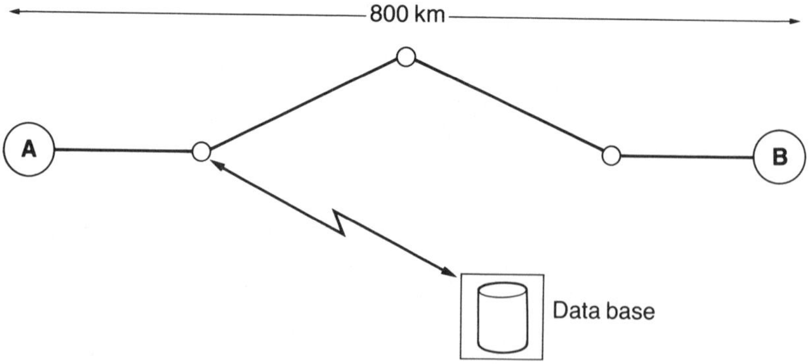

7.2 Listening 1

7.2.1

The following meeting takes place at a B.T. Sales office in London on 14–10–83.
Mr Roberts, Administrative Manager for VIDEOTEC Ltd. is talking to Mr Callan from B.T. Sales about call diversion facilities.

As you listen, label Figure 7e.

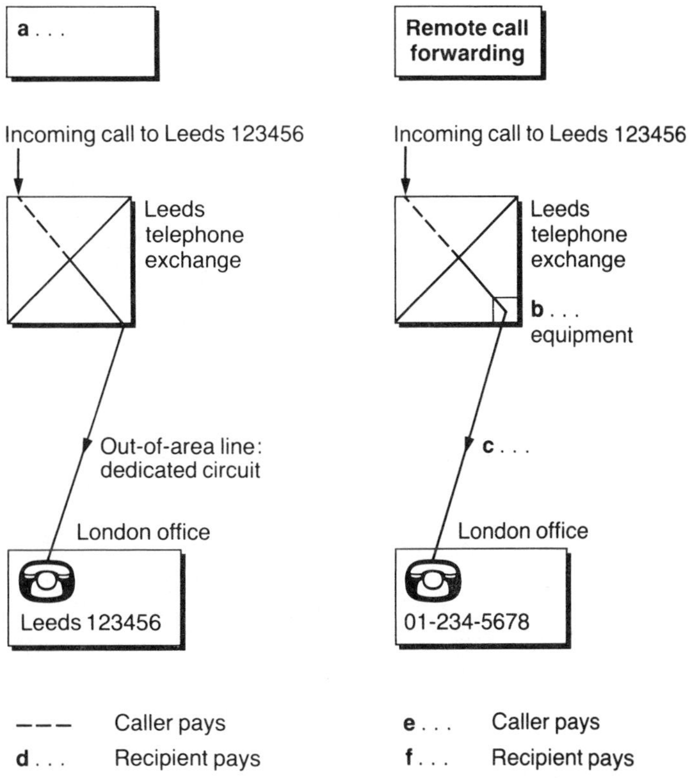

Fig 7e

7.2.2 Comprehension

Now listen again, and complete the following table which compares the two systems:

	Rental costs	Call costs	Call connection time	Transmission quality
Out-of-area	a . . .	Customer: local call Subscriber: trunk call		**
Remote call forwarding	b . . .	c . . . d . . .	e . . .	f . . .

7.3 Language practice

7.3.1 The future and conditional

In the reading section you saw the following statements:

1 No Condition
One thing is certain: they will require signalling resources which cannot possibly be provided by existing equipment.

2 Condition 1
In cases where a call is rerouted at exchange A, the charge during the call will be performed at A.

3 Condition 2
Facilities for charging the B-subscriber should be available. The A-subscriber would then be charged for the cost of a call from A to B.

2 and 3 can be expressed in another way:

Condition 1
If the call is rerouted at exchange A, the charge will be performed. (This is possible. It happens sometimes.)

Condition 2
If the facilities were available, the A-subscriber would be charged. (This is not yet possible. The facilities are not available.)

Use the table below to make sentences. Base your decision to choose either Condition 1 or 2 on the information given in Reading 1 and Listening 1.

Condition	Result
a Remote call forwarding/cost/ £400 a year	We/not subscribe/to the service
b Caller/pay for/the diverted call	This service/not used
c Customer/phone/Leeds number	The call/divert/to London
d CCS/available/nationwide	New services/available/ nationwide
e Subscriber/receive/fewer than 20 calls/day	Out-of-area line/not economic
f You/subscribe/to RCF	We/install/divert-a-call equipment in local exchange
g Customer/has to wait/ for connection	He/hear/pre-recorded announcement
h I/understand/CCS	I/explain/to you

7.3.2 Past continuous tense

In the last unit, we saw how the present continuous can be used to talk about events happening temporarily in the present.

e.g. We **are only getting** about 20 calls a day.

The past continuous, in the same way, is used to talk about temporary events in the past.

e.g. At that time, we **were getting** a lot of enquiries.
I **was just saying** . . .
I **was looking** at it, just before you arrived.

We use the past continuous:
i) to indicate that an event took place at a certain time in the past.

e.g. At 3p.m. yesterday, I **was standing** outside your office.

ii) when an event in the past was interrupted:
e.g. I **was looking** at the report, when you came in.

Use the table below to make sentences using the past continuous:

Time/Type of interruption	Action
a This time last year	I/work/Saudi Arabia
b The lightning struck	the exchange/operate/fine
c 14.45 yesterday	I/write/a report
d Just	He/make/a phone call
e He telephoned	We/discuss/the project
f The power was cut	Engineers/install/the equipment
g 10 in the evening	Technicians/still/replace/the circuit
h It started snowing	They/lay/the cable
i Friday morning	I/wait for/my plane
j Car broke down	He/drive/to work

7.3.3 Responses (expressing approval/ confirmation/ under-standing)

In the Listening section you heard responses to the following statements or questions:

a 'No problem, you let us know what you want and we'll arrange it.'
b 'I wondered if you could fill him in on the details?'
c 'So you had an out-of-area line?'
d 'The equipment automatically dials a second call.'

Which response would be appropriate to each?

i) Of course.
ii) That's right.
iii) Good.
iv) I see.

Listen to Listening 1 again, and write down under the following headings the responses you hear:

e Expressing approval, e.g. 'Good!' (3 responses)
f Expressing willingness, e.g. 'Of course' (2 responses)
g Expressing agreement with a fact, e.g. 'That's right' (1 response)
h Expressing understanding, e.g. 'I see' (1 response)

7.4 Listening 2

7.4.1

Listen to the following extract from a meeting, held in London on 10–11–83, between Mr Cornwall (London branch) and Mr Mackintosh (Glasgow branch) of MITEC Ltd. They are discussing the possibility of using teleconference facilities for an inter-branch meeting.

As you listen, complete the table:

Alternative A: 3 people fly to London from Glasgow for a 3-hour meeting. 3 participants are based in London already.

Alternative B: 3 Glasgow participants remain in Glasgow and a TV meeting is arranged.

A **Conventional meeting**		**B** **TV meeting**
Charge for studio	**a** . . .	**e** . . .
Travel costs for Glasgow participants	**b** . . .	**f** . . .
Man-hours for Glasgow participants	**c** . . .	**g** . . .
Man-hours for London participants	**d** . . .	**h** . . .
Cost saving (excl. time allowance)		**i** . . .
Cost saving on time (at £15 per hour) Time-saving		**j** . . . **k** . . .

7.4.2 Comprehension

Listen again and answer the following questions:

a What advantage does a teleconference have over a telephone conference?

b What is the maximum number of active participants allowed in the studio?

c How many cameras are there in the studio?

d Does Mr Mackintosh think £15 per hour is i) too high } a value? ii) too low }

e Are they planning to use teleconferences for all meetings in the future?

f Which meeting will probably be the first teleconference?

7.4.3 Activity

Below are listed some features and benefits of Confravision. Match up feature and benefit. Note some features have the same benefit.

Features

1 Studios in major cities

2 Dedicated coaxial cable and microwave links between studios

3 Sound-proof studios

4 Room for 5 conferees

5 Push button control of cameras i.e. no need for outside operators

6 An external studio telephone

7 Display camera

8 Audio-tape recorder

9 Overflow monitor

Benefits

a Contact with outside world

b Room for larger groups to listen and watch

c No long-distance travel

d Meeting capacity of 10 participants

e High-quality sound products

f Confidential discussion

g High-definition transmission of documentation

h No need for secretary to take minutes

Now discuss which features you would highlight in a brochure designed to sell this service to the business community.

7.5 Writing

Minutes

The minutes are a written record of a meeting. They should record the following:

1 Date and place of meeting
2 The participants
3 The main items of business and decisions reached.

They should be short and accurate. Below are some sample minutes of the discussion you hear in Listening 1.

Subject Meeting to discuss provision of RCF facility for Videotec Ltd., held at B.T. Sales, London on 14–10–83.

Present Mr Roberts (Videotec)
Mr Callan (B.T. Sales)
Mr Philips (Exec. Engineer—RCF)

1 Mr Roberts explained that Videotec rented an out-of-area line between London and Leeds. This service was no longer economical due to a reduction in use.
2 Mr Philips presented the RCF service. It was noted that Videotec required a special announcement.
3 Mr Callan quoted a price of £100 rental for divert-a-call equipment.
4 Installation of the above equipment at the Leeds exchange was agreed with effect from 1st December.

Now write up the minutes of the meeting in Listening 2. You can look at the tapescript at the back of the book, if necessary.

Use the frame below:

Subject:
Date:
Place:
Participants:

1 Teleconferencing facilities
2 Teleconferencing cost
3 Teleconferencing time-saving
4 Teleconferencing decision

7.6 Discussion

a What are the most common complaints of telephone subscribers in your country? Carry out a survey amongst your classroom or work colleagues. Discuss whether new services will overcome these complaints.
b What are the advantages to a company of using leased lines rather than the PSTN?
c Do you think teleconferencing has a future? Will the videophone replace this service?

7.7 Word list

Common Channel Signalling (CCS)

signalling link p. 87
discrete message p. 87
a label/address p. 88
a speech path p. 88
direct signalling p. 88

Subscriber status

idle/free p. 89
disconnected/off the hook p. 88

New services

call diversion p. 88
diversion to operator p. 89
diversion on no reply p. 89
diversion on busy p. 89
call forwarding p. 202(T)
call transfer p. 89
call to busy subscriber p. 89
INWATS p. 89

Traffic handling

to route a call p. 88
to re-route a call p. 88
to set up a speech path p. 88
call destined for . . . p. 88
transmission links p. 88
in tandem p. 88
occupied circuits p. 88
dedicated/leased line p. 202(T)
transmission loss p. 203(T)
to compensate for transmission loss p. 203(T)

Unit 8 Switching 2

In this unit we look at the development of electronic switching systems and some of their applications in the field of telematics.

8.1 Reading

8.1.1

Read the following text and then complete the key for Figure 8g.

The purpose of every switching system is to establish a temporary circuit or link between the caller and the subscriber being called. This circuit must be terminated when one of the subscribers decides to replace his/her handset. In handling a telephone call an exchange performs three essential functions:

- it establishes a path enabling a signal to be transmitted between two subscribers.
- it dialogues with other parts of the network.
- it processes all other information from the network and decides whether calls can be established or not.

Two main types of switching technology have evolved: space division switching and time division switching.
The principles of these two types of switching are illustrated in the following figures in which we follow the speech paths of two subscribers through a small exchange.

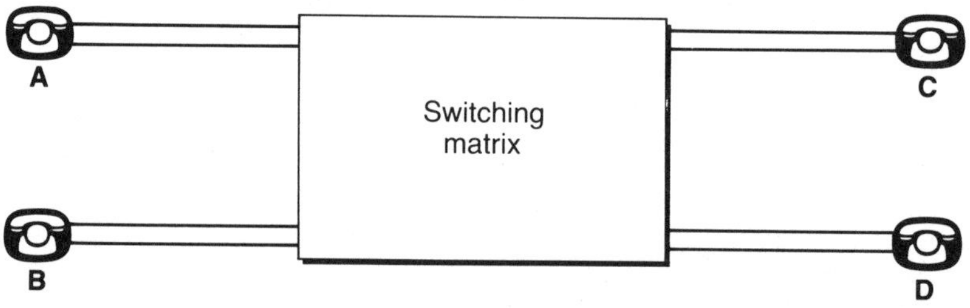

Fig 8a

The switching matrix consists of a number of cross points made up of a series of horizontal and vertical wires at the intersection of which a relay is installed. The relay has two positions, on or off.

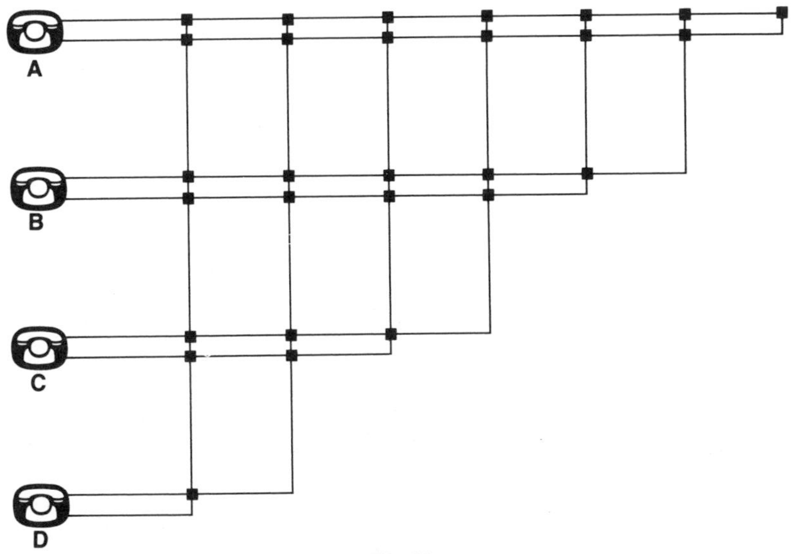

Fig 8b

If two subscribers are to converse, a two-wire channel must be established capable of transmitting a signal in the 300–3400 Hz band in both directions. Figure 8c below shows the speech paths taken by two conversations, subscriber A to subscriber C and subscriber B to subscriber D. The relays used to direct the calls (i.e. relays in the on position) are indicated with a star.

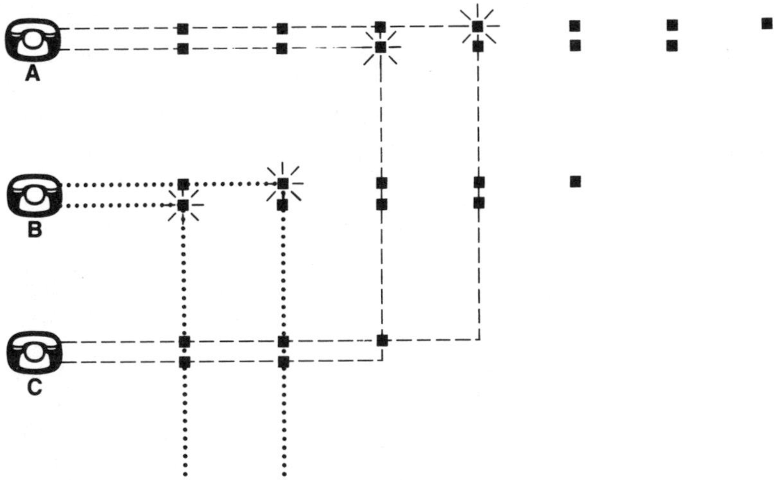

Fig 8c

The physical path of each conversation can be clearly distinguished. As soon as one of the subscribers hangs up, the physical link is broken and the call terminated. The technique used in this exchange is known as space division switching.

Time division switching has begun to replace space division techniques in nearly all the most modern systems. If we imagine two conversations between four subscribers as in the previous example, we can see that they no longer share the physical space in the switching matrix but that time slots are allocated to each party. During their conversations, none of the subscribers will, of course, be aware that their speech is being broken up into small batches of time.

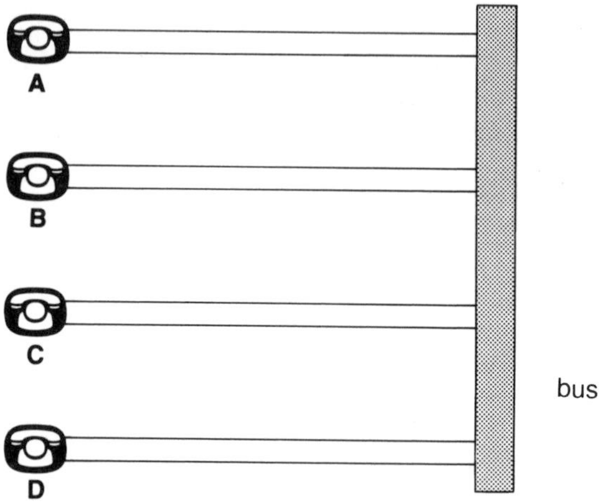

Fig 8d

When subscriber A speaks to subscriber B, the analogue signals in the 300–3400 Hz range are transmitted to the exchange, sampled (using Pulse Amplitude Modulation) and are then transported on the bus before being reconverted into analogue form and sent on to subscriber B. The sampling rate is determined by using Shannon's Theory which states that the sampling frequency must be double the maximum frequency of the signal. In practice, sampling is done at 8 kHz. The time slot between two samples is thus 125 microseconds (1 second ÷ 8 000 = 0.000125 seconds). In other words, the signal is sampled once every 125 microseconds. In the conversation between subscribers A and B, 16 000 samples are transported every second, 8 000 in each direction. When two conversations take place at the same time, 32 000 samples have to be transported per second. An observer with an oscilloscope connected to the bus would see the samples corresponding to these two conversations in the form opposite.

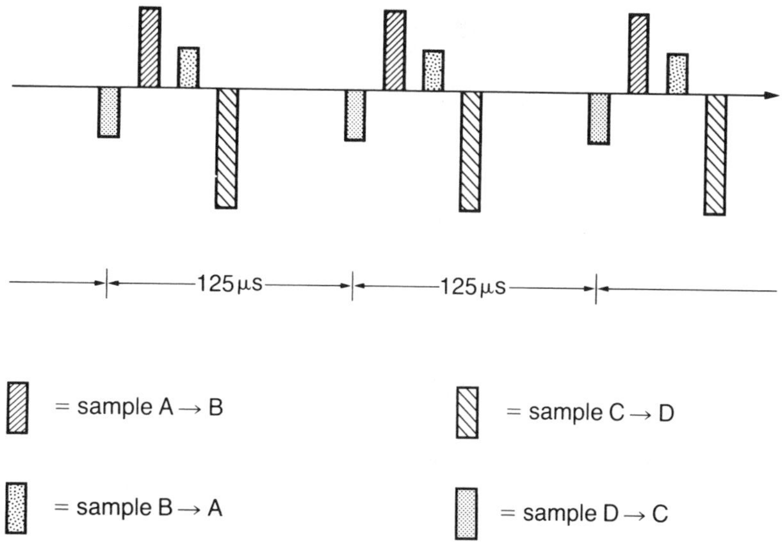

Fig 8e

This technique, known as time division switching, appears to be very attractive but has one great drawback: the PAM samples can only be transmitted over relatively short distances, and the capacity of the bus is limited. When an exchange handles more than 30 simultaneous calls, the PAM sample itself must be encoded so that it can be transmitted within the exchange without distortion. This is known as digital time division switching for each sample is encoded into eight bits (one byte).

In a digital time division switching exchange, all internal links are performed using four-wire PCM which allocates a time slot to each subscriber who is talking at a rate of 64 000 bits per second (bps), since 8 000 samples × 8 bps = 64 000 bps.

If subscriber A talks to subscriber B, he is allocated a time slot (DC A) on the PCM 1 line, while subscriber B has a time slot (DC B) on the PCM 2 line. Every 125 microseconds, a double transfer of bytes takes place. This operation can be seen in the diagram below in which we see the incoming PCM links on the left and the outgoing links on the right.

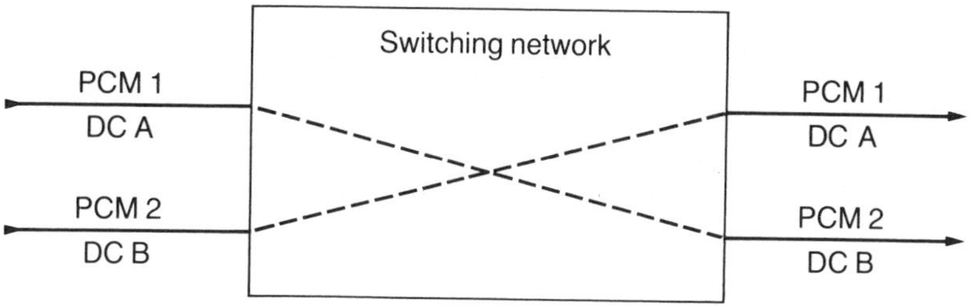

DC = Digital Channel

Fig 8f

By associating digital transmission and switching techniques, an integrated digital network is created. This will lead, in time and with the fusion of different digital networks, to an Integrated Services Digital Network (ISDN).

a  = . . . in - Hz frequency band.

b 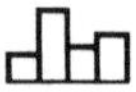 = . . .

c  = . . .

d Time slot between two samples = . . .

e Number of samples per second = . . .

Fig 8g

8.1.2 Comprehension

Answer the following questions:

a What is the objective of every switching system?
b Match the exchange function with the definition:

Definition	Function
1 Establishing a signalling path between subscribers through an exchange.	**a** Control
2 Dialoguing with other parts of the network.	**b** Subscriber connection
3 Processing network information and deciding whether to establish a call or not.	**c** Signalling

c What are the cross points composed of?
d What are the main differences between space and time division systems?
e What is Shannon's Theory?
f What are the two main characteristics of a digital time division switching exchange?
g What will enable the creation of an ISDN?

8.2 Listening 1

8.2.1

Listen to the discussion between two engineers, John Blackman and Peter Norman. They are talking about the French E 10 switching system. As you listen complete the keys for Figures 8h and 8i.

Key
1. . .
2. . .
3. . .
4. . .
5. . .
6. . .

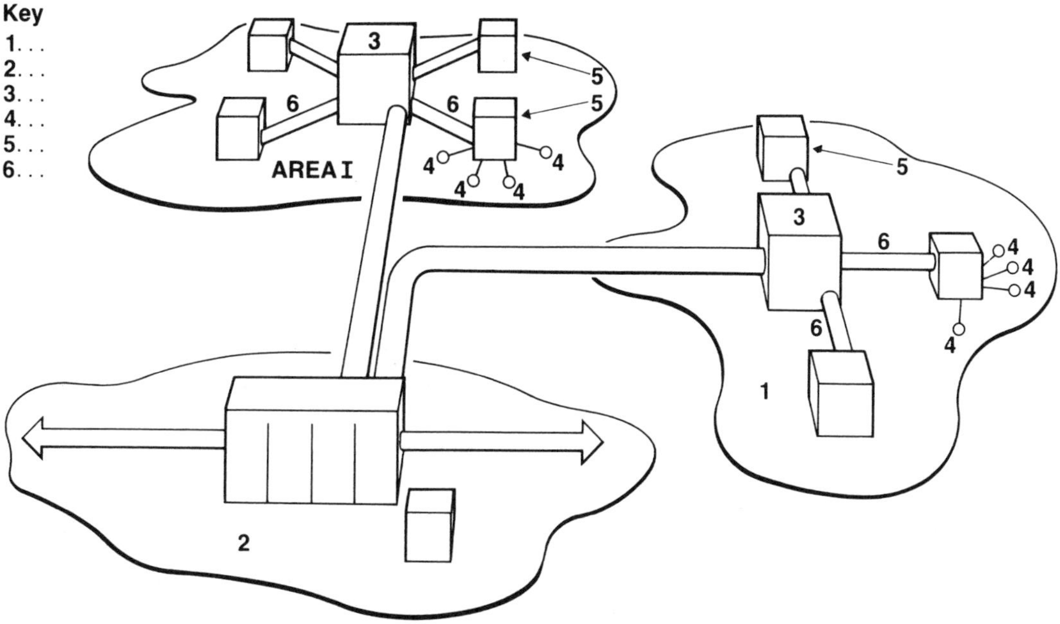

Fig 8h E 10 network structure

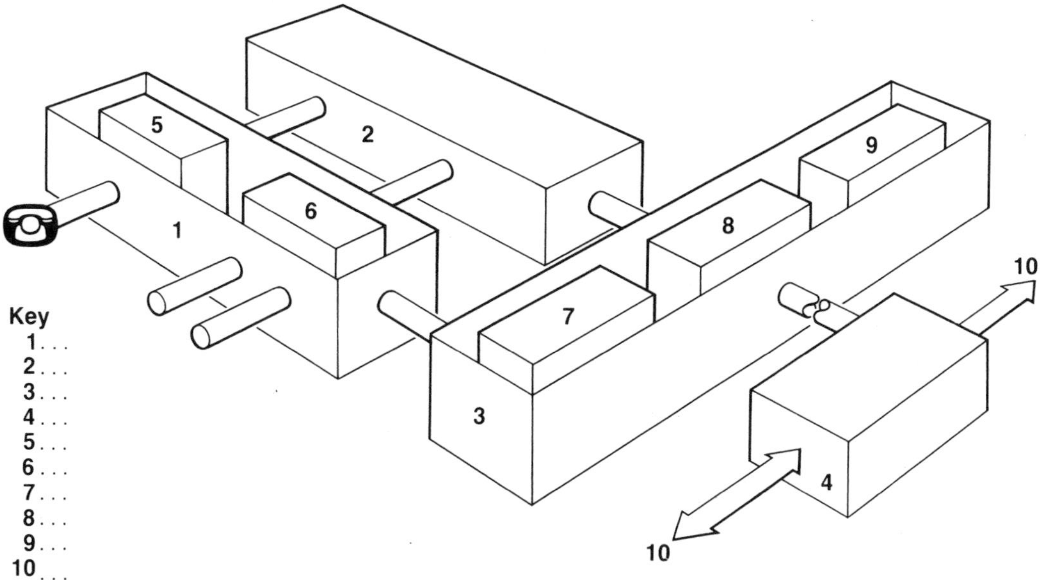

Key
1. . .
2. . .
3. . .
4. . .
5. . .
6. . .
7. . .
8. . .
9. . .
10. . .

Fig 8i E 10 exchange structure

8.2.2 Comprehension

Answer the following questions:

a What main idea has determined the design of the E 10 system?
b What is the maximum distance a concentrator can be from the exchange: 10, 25 or 50 kilometres?
c Why is this distance certainly an advantage?
d How many simultaneous conversations can a 4-line PCM link transport: 30, 90 or 120?
e What is the ratio between the maximum number of voice channels available and the number of subscribers?
f How many subscribers does the OMC handle?
g What equipment can be found in the OMC?
h Has the OMC reduced operation and maintenance costs by: 50%, 40% or 30%?
i What other service can be provided by the E 10, if the subscriber asks for it?

8.3 Language practice

8.3.1 Combining sentences

Look at the following sentences. Notice how the different parts of the sentence are linked using : (a colon) or 'which' or 'who'.

1 Two main types of switching technology have evolved. **2** The two main types are space division switching and time division switching.
→ Two main types of switching technology have evolved: space division switching and time division switching.

1 The principles of these two types of switching are illustrated in the following figures. **2** In the following figures we follow the speech paths of two subscribers through a small exchange.
→ The principles of these two types of switching are illustrated in the following figures **in which** we follow the speech paths of two subscribers through a small exchange.

1 This was confirmed by Shannon. **2** Shannon developed a theory. **3** Shannon's theory states a formula for finding the correct sampling frequency.
→ This was confirmed by Shannon **who** developed a theory **which** states a formula for finding the correct sampling frequency.

Now join the following sentences in a similar way.

a 1 The switching matrix consists of a number of connection points.
2 The connection points are made up of a horizontal and a vertical wire joined by a relay.
b 1 Two types of switching equipment predominate in Sweden.
2 These two types are crossbar equipment and digital systems.
c 1 This technique appears to be very attractive.
2 A lot of money has been invested in this technique.
3 This technique has one great drawback.
d 1 The first rotary switch was invented by Almon Strowger.
2 This switch is still in use today.
3 Strowger was an undertaker in Kansas City.

e 1 The analogue signals are transmitted to the exchange.
2 The analogue signals are in the 300–3400 Hz range.
3 The signals are sampled using PAM.

8.3.2 Frequency

Expressions of frequency are used to answer the questions: 'How often?' or 'How many times?'.

For example: PCM is **hardly ever** used on subscriber loops.
Occasionally there are no staff present at all.
All the connections are checked **once a year**.

The table below illustrates expressions of indefinite frequency:

100% ↑	always
	almost always, nearly always
	usually, normally, generally
	often, frequently
	sometimes
	occasionally, now and then, now and again
	seldom, rarely
	hardly ever, scarcely ever
↓ 0%	never

Definite frequency expressions:

1 once a week, twice an hour, three times a year
2 every day, every afternoon, every six years
3 hourly, daily, weekly, monthly, yearly/annually

Now use this extract from a factory inspector's diary, which shows a typical month, to answer the questions on the next page. Try to give two answers to each question, one expressing definite frequency and one indefinite frequency.

MARCH									
S	3		10		17		24	
M	4	Factory inspection	11	Annual Board meeting	18	Factory inspection	25	Monthly production review
T	5		12	10,000 km car service	19	Factory inspection	26	Six monthly dental appointment
W	6	Do quarterly financial rpt	13		20		27	Factory inspection
T	7	Factory inspection	14	Factory inspection	21	Factory inspection	28	Factory inspection
F	8	Sales meeting	15	Sales meeting	22	Sales meeting	29	Sales meeting
S	9	Tennis match	16	Tennis match	23		30	Tennis match

a How often does he inspect factories?
b How often does he play tennis?
c How often does he review production figures?
d How often does he attend sales meetings?
e How often does he attend board meetings?
f How often does he have to prepare financial reports?
g How often does he go to the dentist?
h How often does he get his car serviced?
i How often does he play football?

8.3.3 Question tags

Tag questions added to the end of a statement ask for confirmation of the statement, said with a falling tone (A), or make the complete sentence a question, said with a rising tone (B). For example:

A The E 10 was one of the earliest TDM systems, **wasn't it**?
B I don't suppose the subscriber's line uses PCM, **does it**?

There are three things to think about when forming these tag questions:

1 The subject and the tense must be the same in statement and tag, e.g. **It must** be an advantage to have greater capacity, **mustn't it**?
2 Positive statements are followed by negative tags and negative statements by positive tags.
3 Auxiliary verbs (do, have, be, must, can, should etc.) are always repeated in the tag. If there is no auxiliary verb in the statement, you must choose an appropriate auxiliary (do, does or did) for the tag, e.g. Those exchanges **seem** to be rather expensive, **don't** they?

Now end the following sentences with the correct form of tag.

a He's coming at 8 o'clock, . . .?
b He said his name was Johnson, . . .?
c A new electronic exchange has just been installed, . . .?
d They didn't call us yesterday, . . .?
e You'll write before the end of the month, . . .?
f It was raining when you left London, . . .?
g It can't be replaced before next month, . . .?
h The delivery's late, . . .?
i You couldn't lend me five pounds, . . .?
j The PAM unit samples the signal, . . .?

8.4 Listening 2

8.4.1

Listen to the conversation between a telephone subscriber (TS) and a telecommunications authority employee (TAE). The conversation takes place in a 'teleshop' (telephone shop). As you listen, complete the keys for Figures 8j and 8k.

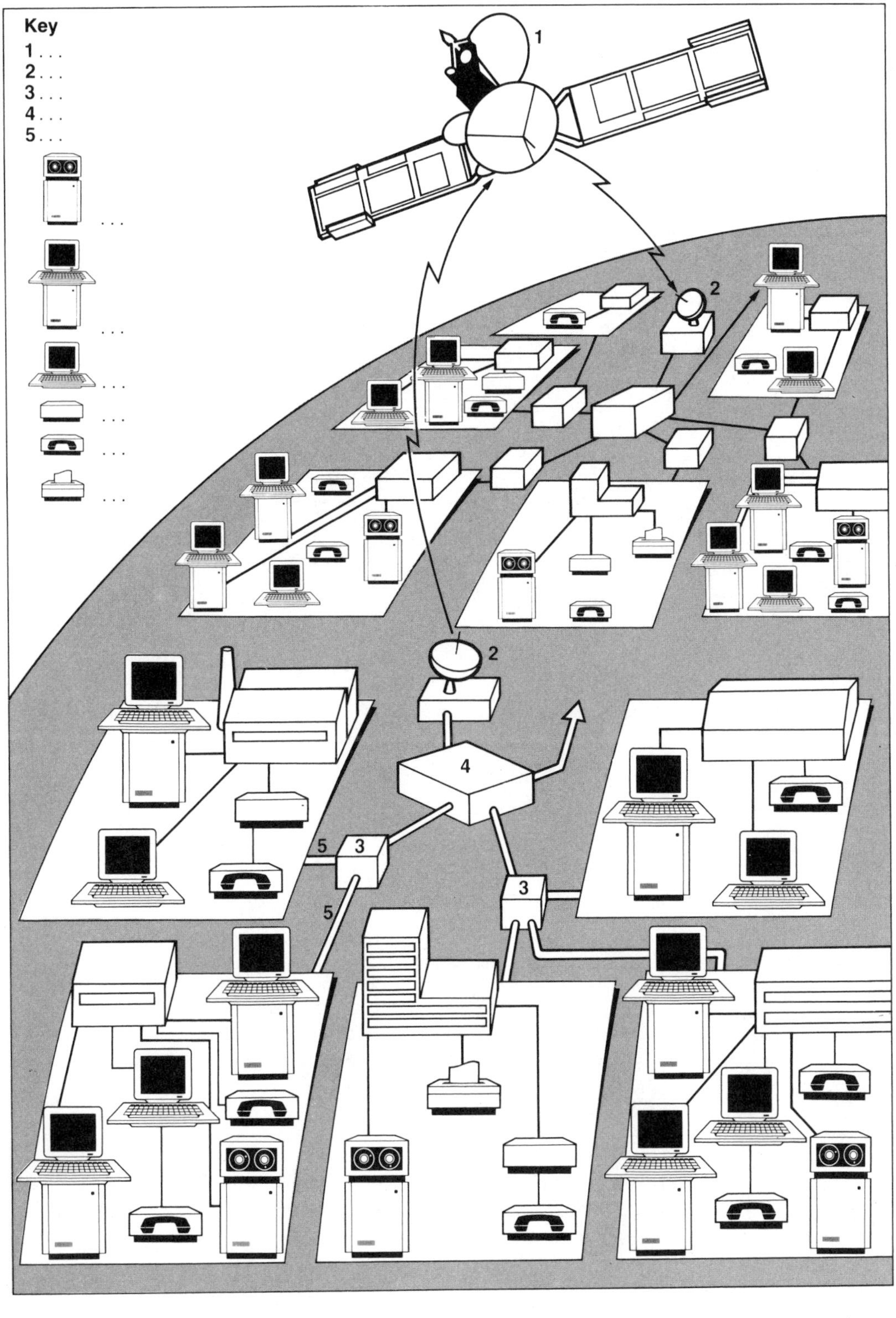

Fig 8j Telecom 1 network principles

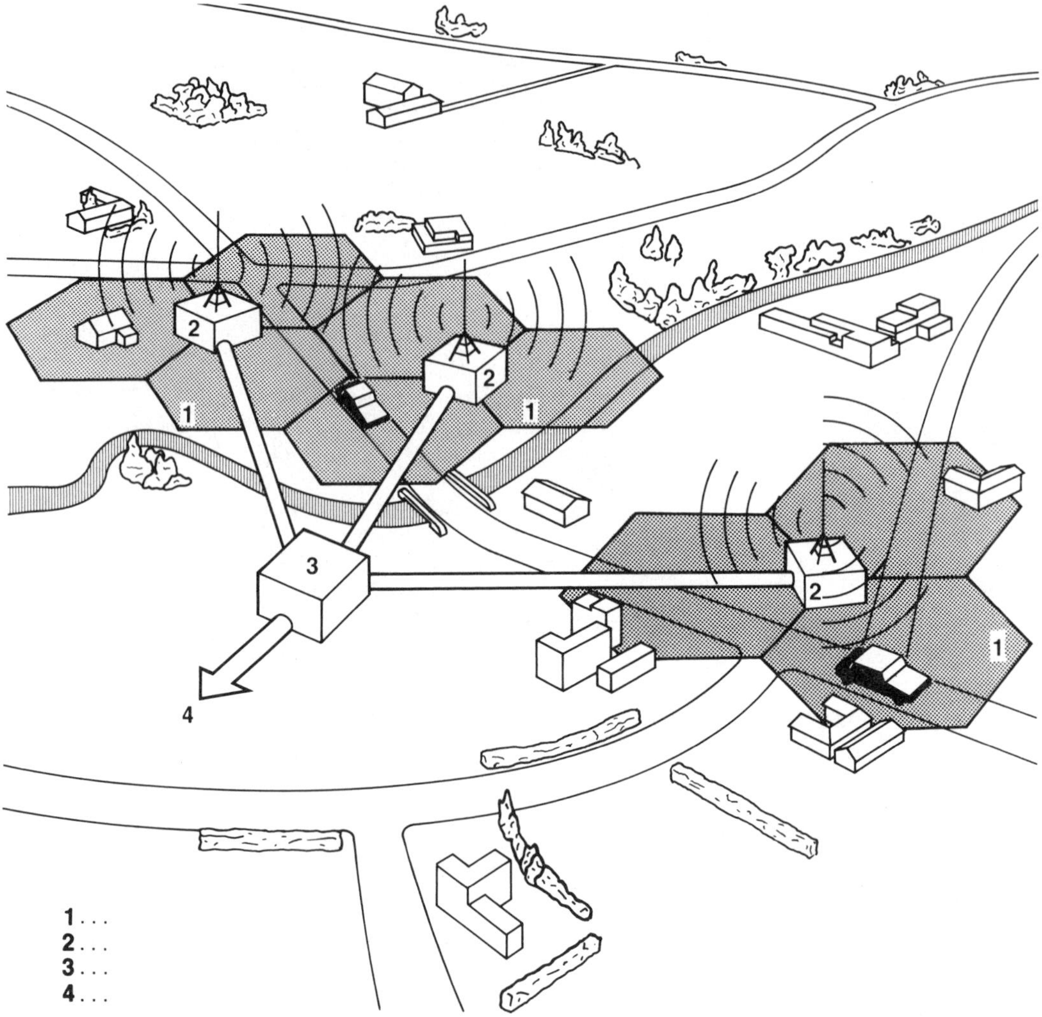

Fig 8k Principles of a cellular radiotelephone network

8.4.2
Comprehension

Answer the following questions:

a Why has the subscriber called in at his local teleshop?
b How does the TAE define the term telematics?
c Identify the three main telematics groups and give an example of a service in each of them.
d What is a multiservice network?

8.4.3
Activity

Read the following text about multiservice networks for business users and fill in the blanks using the solutions below. Use each solution once only.

Until the distribution network is fully digitalised, **a** . . . will cope with most applications intended for use by the **b** . . . .

Business users, often with their own powerful **c** . . . resources, require more sophisticated services. For this reason, in several parts of the world it has been decided to set up **d** . . . , initially to cater for industrial requirements and business users, subsequently to become more generally available for other applications. The basic intention is to provide **e** . . . between different locations of the same organization or company, to provide **f** . . . for hooking up computer systems, high-speed facsimile, electronic fund transfer (EFT) and more generally all **g** . . . making use of high-capacity data processing resources.

The first multiservice networks to be installed use **h** . . . as the transmission medium since existing **i** . . . are generally unsuitable for the functions required. The simplest approach consists of equipping each major location or group of locations with **j** . . . providing ground-to-satellite communication using the time division multiple access (TDMA) technique.

Attractive in theory, this approach is **k** . . . in terms of transmission equipment, management and maintenance. To make it more **l** . . ., a structure can be adopted in which a single earth station serves an entire region. Industrial locations are connected to the station via high-speed data switches which also provide facilities for **m** . . . other regions and other multiservice networks. Whichever approach is adopted, installations are required to provide compatibility between transmission rates, signalling systems and interfaces between **n** . . . of very different kinds and the transmission system. The French E 10 multiservice system has been **o** . . . for precisely this purpose.

Solutions	**Place in text**
economical	**l**
integrated service digital networks	**d**
designed	. . .
videotex	. . .
business transactions	. . .
costly	. . .
terminals	. . .
geostationary satellites	. . .
facilities	. . .
general public	. . .
cable networks	. . .
earth stations	. . .
high-speed digital links	. . .
data processing	. . .
interconnecting	. . .

8.5 Writing

Systems description. You will remember from Listening 2 that the applications of telematics can be divided into three main groups:

	Group 1	Group 2	Group 3
Target groups	general public (ord. subscribers)	large companies (business users)	specialized users (mobile users)
Application	videotex	multiservice n/w	specialized services
Example	electronic dir.	Telecom 1	cellular radio tel. n/w
Components	home terminal data terminal	geost. satellite earth station industrial locations high-speed data switches	mobile users transceivers PSTN switching centre
Function	search for telephone numbers	access to high-speed data switches	ability to telephone from car

Now complete the systems description below using the information in the table. Use the first completed paragraph as a model.

1 The first group is aimed at the general public. The term normally used to describe this application is videotex, an example of which is the electronic directory. This consists of a home terminal linked to a data bank enabling the ordinary subscriber to search for telephone numbers.

2 The second group . . . . This consists of . . . which, in turn, is linked to . . . through . . . . This service . . . .

3 . . .

8.6 Discussion

a Why are digital time division switching systems generally considered to be the most suitable for networks of the future?

b What are some of the applications of telematics?

c How do you think the association of telecommunications and data processing will change your everyday life in the future?

8.7 Word list

Switching systems

space division switching p. 98
time division switching p. 98
switching matrix p. 99
oscilloscope p. 100 a device for displaying voltage waveforms.
byte p. 101 the smallest addressed unit of data storage, normally eight bits long.
man/machine dialogue p. 204(T) interaction between the network and human operators.
multiplexing p. 204(T) the process of combining signals so that they share a common transmission facility.
multiregisters p. 204(T)
translators p. 204(T)
metering units p. 204(T)

Telematics

electronic directory p. 204(T)
multiservice network p. 204(T)
geostationary satellite p. 205(T) a satellite which circles the earth every 24 hours (see Unit 10).
earth station p. 205(T)
high-speed data switch p. 205(T)
transceiver p. 205(T) a transmitter/receiver.

General

drawback p. 101 a disadvantage.
field (of activity) p. 204(T) an area (of activity).
roughly p. 204(T) approximately.
the norm p. 204(T) the usual standard.
sparsely populated p. 204(T) with few inhabitants per unit area.
concisely p. 204(T) giving much information in few words.
consumer p. 204(T) a user or customer.
premises p. 204(T) building, or space in a building, used for activities (often commercial).

Unit 9 Computer communications 2

In Unit 4, we introduced some of the services which have resulted from the 'marriage' between telecommunications and data processing. In this unit we will be looking at one of these services—videotex—in more detail.

9.1 Reading 1

9.1.1

Read the following article about the evolution of Prestel, the British videotex service. When you have read it, complete Figure 9c.

'The strategy pursued by Prestel in the business field has been simple and successful—that of initially marketing specific information services to key business areas with defined and special needs. The case of the travel industry, where 80 per cent of travel agents now use Prestel, is a good and telling example of how Prestel can become indispensable in a business context.

Fig 9a

However, the hurdle of gaining mass public acceptance of Prestel was still to be overcome. The British public would not buy Prestel simply for information but would do so for a joint package of information and interactive services. The first move towards a full range of interactive services aimed directly at the ordinary person was the 'Homelink' system.

Banking, and the problems of transferring and disposing of money, is a chore that is universal. At a time of increased automation in a traditionally conservative industry and as the traditional roles of both building societies and banks become blurred, Prestel launched the most ambitious home banking scheme in the world—Homelink. Together with the entrepreneurial Nottingham Building Society and the Bank of Scotland, Homelink offers its customers a wide range of financial services which previously had to be carried out in person at a branch. Through Homelink pages, bank and building society accounts can be securely seen on the screen, money transferred electronically and simple tasks like paying a telephone bill easily performed.

Prestel's other major initiative to promote home usage this year revolves around another piece of technology—the microcomputer. More than half a million micros are now in use in the UK and all require programs before they can function. The broadcasting of computer programs over viewdata and teletext systems—known as telesoftware—is not a new idea, but Prestel's Micronet 800 Series, launched in February 1983, is the largest telesoftware facility in the world.

Fig 9b

Together with East Midlands Allied Press, a publisher of computer magazines, Prestel provides a library of some 2,000 programs on a wide range of subjects—from the obligatory games to complex educational and business programs.

Most microcomputers can be connected to Micronet 800 using a simple modem and associated software. Having selected the program required, the pages are simply called up on Prestel and the screenfuls of software then activate the microcomputer. As well as supplying more lighthearted programs, Micronet 800 provides plenty of scope for educational purposes. Schools can link in with other schools and educational users around the country to swap ideas, techniques and even programs they have written themselves. Business users are equally well catered for with special closed areas of Micronet that can be used for private business communication.

In short, Prestel's move towards the residential market marks another evolutionary stage in the service. What was originally perceived as a 'world of information at your fingertips' has become a series of very specialized information services allied to a growing series of interactive facilities.

Until earlier this year (i.e. 1983), Prestel meant the supply of fast, updated information for travel agency users but with the introduction of 'Skytrack', Prestel's airline reservation service, there is a move towards interaction. Linking up the Prestel customer through a series of computer systems to US-based airline computers may seem technically advanced—and it is. But for the end-customer the interactive benefits of Prestel are that simplicity and user-friendliness are the two keystones of commercial success.

Prestel will continue to evolve, and the interaction of interfaces with other networks—notably the telex network—are no longer test bench dreams. The interconnection of first private computers with Prestel and, later this year, (i.e. 1983), with overseas viewdata systems, will form part of what is the next evolutionary stage.

Original perception:

'A world of information at your fingertips'

Stage 1
Specialized business sectors

Example:
a . . .

Co-operators

Stage 2
Residential sector

Service:
b . . .

Nottingham Building Society & Bank of Scotland

Stage 3
Residential & business sector

Service:
c . . .

East Midlands Allied Press

Stage 4
Business sector

Business sector	Service: **d** . . .	U.S. Airline Companies

Stage 5

Business sector	Service: **e** . . .	

Stage 6

Residential & business sector	Service: **f** . . .	Foreign Telecommunication Administrations

Fig 9c Evolution of Prestel Service

9.1.2 Comprehension

Answer the following questions:

a How was the 'hurdle of gaining mass public acceptance of Prestel' to be overcome?
  i) by providing more information on Prestel
  ii) by providing only interactive services
  iii) by providing both interactive and information services.

b What do you think 'chore' means in the sentence 'banking is a chore that is universal'?
  i) a task
  ii) a pleasant task
  iii) an unpleasant/inconvenient task.

c Which of the following are examples of the statement: 'Banking is a traditionally conservative industry'?
  i) banks have been slow to introduce automation
  ii) banks support the Conservative party in Britain
  iii) banks insist that their male employees wear ties
  iv) banks encourage investment in new technologies.

d What are Prestel's two major initiatives in order to promote usage in the residential sector?
  i) . . . ii) . . .

e Which of the following are examples of 'light-hearted' programs?
  i) space invaders
  ii) computer chess
  iii) simple home accounting
  iv) teach yourself German
  v) computer tennis.

f The evolution of Prestel has been . . .
  i) from a general information concept to . . .
  ii) from information services to . . .

g Who is the end-customer for their new 'Skytrack' service?

h What does 'interfaces with the telex network are no longer a test bench dream' mean?
  i) this development will certainly happen
  ii) this development is likely to happen
  iii) this development has happened.

9.2 Listening 1

9.2.1

Listen to the summary of a presentation on international developments in videotex. As you listen complete Figure 9d.

	Country	Name of system	Techniques	Data base controller	Special services
a	. . .	. . .	 . . .	. . .	Homelink Micronet 800
b	. . .	. . .		. . .	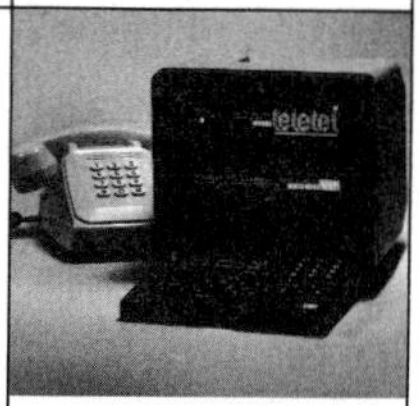 . . .
c	. . .	. . .	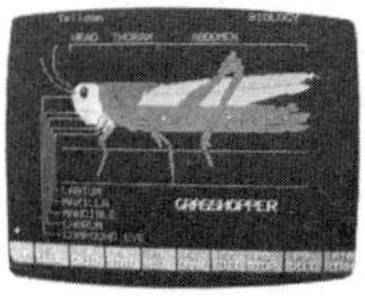 . . .	. . .	Not announced

Fig 9d

9.2.2 Comprehension

Listen again, and answer these questions:

a During the presentation the speaker tries to engage the audience by using expressions like 'As you know . . .'.
Pick out three similar expressions.
i) . . . ii) . . . iii) . . .

b What is the main difference in appearance between alphamosaic and alphageometric display?

c What examples of information providers are mentioned?
i) . . . ii) . . . iii) . . .

d Three questions are asked at the end of the presentation. The first one is: 'What effect will videotex have on traditional media, especially newspapers and postal services?'
What are the other two?
i) . . . ? ii) . . . ?

9.3 Language practice

9.3.1 Contrast and difference

The presentation on videotex pointed out some actual differences between the national systems and contrasted them.

Differences

Telidon uses a **different** graphic display system **from/to** Prestel.
Prestel, **unlike** Telidon, uses alphamosaic graphic techniques.

Contrasts

Prestel's data banks are owned by British Telecom. **In contrast**, Télétel is open to independent companies.
or
Prestel's central data banks are owned by B.T., **as opposed** to Télétel, where independent companies can set up their own data bases.
Télétel provides electronic mail facilities. Prestel, **on the other hand**, has been slow in offering this service to the general public.

Now use the language above to complete the following sentences:

a Videotex has an interactive capability. . . ., teletext simply provides information.
b Teletex is . . . from telex in that it is faster and offers more services.
c Videophone, . . . confravision, can be used directly from subscribers' premises.
d Telidon offers more sophisticated graphics. Prestel, . . . has the advantage of several years' operating experience.
e Coaxial cable requires repeaters every two or three kilometres, . . . optical fibre, which can transmit signals without repeaters for 30 or more kilometres.
f B.T., . . . many other TA's, has discontinued its telegram service.
g Many developed countries are now introducing electronic telex switching networks. . . ., some less developed countries have no telex network at all.
h Investment priorities in the Third World are often very . . . priorities in the industrialized world.

9.3.2 Adjectives and adverbs

Look at the examples below:

Use of adjectives

Prestel has pursued a **simple** strategy.
Prestel launched an **ambitious** scheme.

Use of adverbs

Bank accounts can be **securely** seen on the screen.
Money can be transferred **electronically**.
Paying a telephone bill can be **easily** performed.

Use of 2 adjectives together

Prestel meant the supply of **fast**, **updated** information.
The case of the travel industry is a **good** and **telling** example.
Marketing to business areas with **defined** and **special** needs.

Use of adverb and adjective together

Banking is a **traditionally conservative** industry.
Skytrack is a **technically advanced** system.

Now use the table below to build up acceptable combinations:

Adjective or adverb	Adjective	Noun
a good	qualified	candidate
b slow	complex	technique
c poor	planned	scheme
d simple	successful	strategy
e stringent	tested	equipment
f efficient	secure	system
g continuous	monitored	status
h cheap	old-fashioned	product
i direct	transferred	information
j extreme	experienced	salesman

e.g. **a** A well-qualified candidate. Now complete **b** to **j**.

9.3.3 Giving presentations

When giving a talk, it is important to signal to your audience the different stages/parts of your presentation:

Introduction

The topic	'I'd like to talk today about . . .' 'I'd like to say a few words about . . .'
The scope	'I shall be dealing with . . .' 'I have divided my talk into 2/3 parts . . .'
Signalling the main parts	'To begin with . . .' 'Let me leave that point . . .' 'Let's turn to/move on to . . .' 'That brings me to . . .'
Referring forwards	'I'll be dealing with that later . . .' 'I'll come to that in a minute . . .'
Referring backwards	'As I mentioned earlier . . .' 'To come back to that point . . .'
Concluding	'Finally, we come to . . .' 'That's all I have to say. Are there any questions?'

Now listen again to the Presentation on Listening 1. Note down expressions used to do the following:

a Introduce the topic of the presentation . . .
b Describe the scope of the talk . . .
c Signal the 3 parts i) . . . ii) . . . iii) . . .
d Refer forwards . . .
e Refer backwards . . .
f Conclude the talk . . .

9.4 Listening and Reading 2

9.4.1

Listen to the potential customer's enquiries about HOMELINK.

Use the information below to answer his/her questions (**a–m**). You will probably need to switch the tape off after each question to write down the answer.

YOUR INTRODUCTION TO THE WORLD'S FIRST HOME BANKING AND SHOPPING SERVICE.

Homelink is the first service of its kind in the world. It links your home to the Nottingham Building Society, the Bank of Scotland and a range of shopping services via your ordinary television set. Not surprisingly, it has aroused enormous interest and comment. To help you understand the way it works and its many unique advantages this leaflet summarises the answers to many of the questions you are bound to ask. If you have any further queries the Nottingham Building Society will be happy to try and deal with them.

WHAT CAN HOMELINK DO FOR ME?

A. Using your ordinary home TV set, it enables you to carry out all these activities– 18 hours a day, 7 days a week:

1 See your Nottingham Building Society (N.B.S.) account statement "on screen" showing all transactions and interest up to the current day. See your Bank of Scotland (B. of S.) account statement "on screen" showing all debits and credits, etc.

2 Transfer funds between bank and building society and vice versa.

3 Instruct us to pay domestic household bills at the touch of a button.

4 Arrange to direct debit any bank account and credit the funds to your Nottingham Building Society account.

5 Correspond "on screen" with N.B.S. and Bank of Scotland; replies sent to you on screen too.

6 Apply for a mortgage "on screen."

7 See your N.B.S. mortgage account statement "on screen"–showing debits, credits and interest to the current day.

8 Obtain an automatic instantaneous additional loan quotation on your N.B.S. mortgage account–and receive the money within 48 hours.

9 Make "on screen" electronic reservations with Thomas Cook at the **guaranteed lowest prices** available on any holiday you care to select.

10 Enter remarkable competitions and auctions, offering big prizes and real bargains.

11 See houses for sale, London restaurant guides, gardening tips, opinion polls, place **free** classified advertisements etc.

12 Armchair shop–often at discounts that can save more than the total cost of using Homelink–see later.

13 Receive nearly all the Prestel services, which include news, weather, sport, stock market prices, bus, train and airline timetables etc.

14 If you wish, join Prestel specialised services like Micronet (which links many micro-computers for games, business and computing etc.).

HOW DOES HOMELINK WORK?

Thanks to advanced microchip technology and secret development work which has taken several years, it is now possible to link any ordinary black and white or colour T.V. set into the remarkable HOMELINK/Prestel range of services. Nottingham Building Society will provide a small console called a "Home Deck" that simply plugs into the aerial socket of your T.V. set. In many cases, British Telecom will install the equipment and provide a demonstration. For many thousands of customers, all this is provided free of charge (see later). Without any further amendments it converts your T.V. set into a type of cable T.V. network that enables you to send and receive electronic signals and pictures. When you press buttons on the console, the signals go through your T.V. set, down your telephone line, into a national network of computers and back to you the same way.

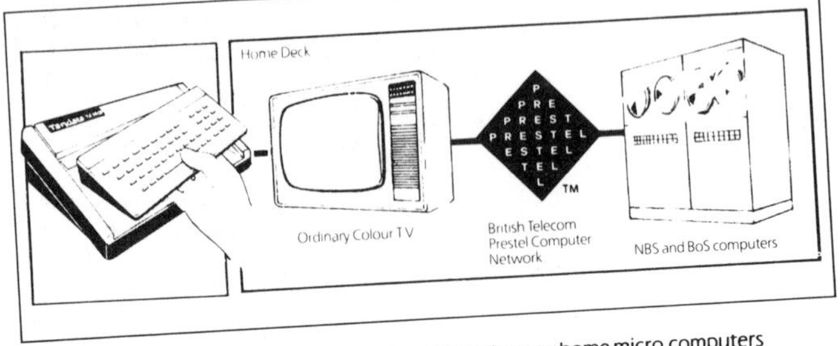

Using a special "Home Deck" you can, if you wish, link many home micro computers to HOMELINK.

Once you have the equipment, by simply pressing the keys, you are connected to the whole HOMELINK Prestel network and can carry out the remarkable functions referred to earlier. If you want to send letters etc., on the service, the keypad enables you to do so. No special skills are required and the "Home Deck" is as easy to operate as a calculator or video recorder. The technology used is the most advanced of its kind anywhere in the world and many millions of pounds have been spent on building the system.

SECURITY & CONFIDENTIALITY

HOMELINK uses 10 different security checks (some of which are too secret to be revealed) to protect your account from unauthorised access or use. Once you have familiarised yourself with the procedures, you can see your building society or bank account statement "on screen" within one minute. See the system in operation and you will recognise just how much time and thinking has been put into the security system. It is so good, that if you input the wrong security codes yourself, even you cannot get access!

WHAT DOES HOMELINK COST?

* To obtain HOMELINK you have to open an account with Nottingham Building Society, investing a minimum of £1,000 (or by opening a mortgage account). You will receive the **full Paid Up Share Interest rate** recommended by the Building Societies Association and paid by most leading societies.
* Full details are provided in the Society's leaflet "Guide to Homelink Costs & Savings".
* Because of the special status of N.B.S. customers, the Bank of Scotland current account can be opened without an initial payment and can immediately be overdrawn up to the pre-determined overdraft limit. If used wisely the Bank of Scotland 'No. 2' account can be **completely free.**
* You pay Prestel £5 per quarter for use of the Prestel computer network.
* You pay telephone call **local** charges each time you use HOMELINK (except 8% of population in remote areas). Off peak charges are 5p for 8 minutes. Peak charges are 5p for 1½ minutes. If you use HOMELINK during the day, you will also have to pay Prestel computer charges (currently 5p per minute). However, most HOMELINK use will be in the evenings and weekends when these charges are not incurred.

9.4.2
Activity

Classify the following displays under the headings below:

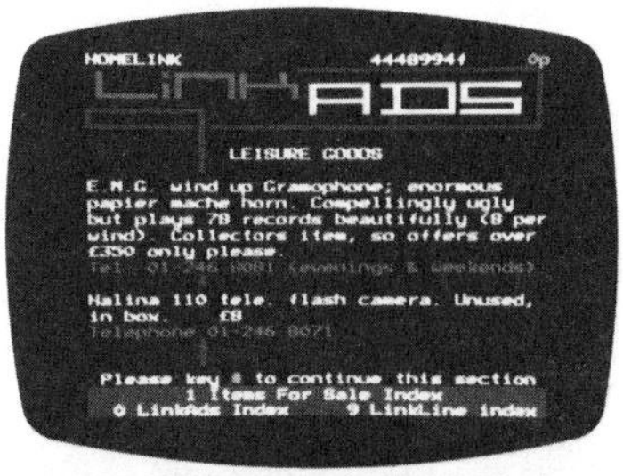

a

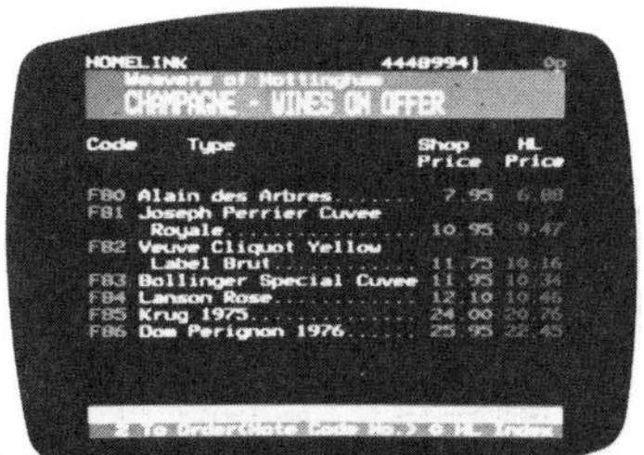

b

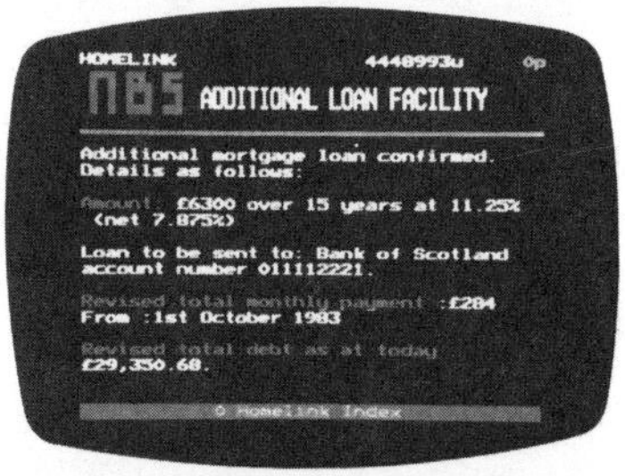

c

d

e

f

g

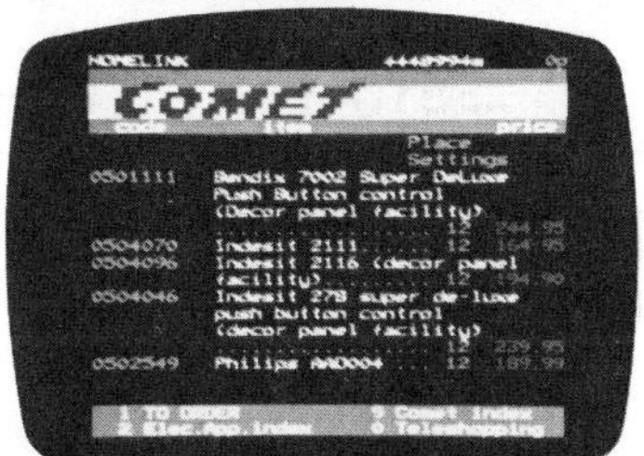

h

i

j

Headings

i) Money management
ii) Classified advertising
iii) Shopping/bargain discounts
iv) Prestel information services
v) Holiday bookings

9.5 Writing

Short reports and summaries

All reports are divided into 3 main parts:

1 **Introduction**—statement of the **purpose** and **scope** of the report.
2 **Findings/Main part**—all the necessary **facts**, **evidence** and **results**.
3 **Conclusions and recommendations**—based on the above findings.

Summaries of reports should also follow this pattern.

You work for a consultancy firm, HITECH LTD., involved in a lot of overseas work. Your boss is considering joining the HOMELINK scheme. Having found out about HOMELINK (see Reading 1 and Listening/Reading 2), you have been asked to submit a summary of your findings to your boss.

Your summary should include the following:

1 Introduction	Purpose	– to decide whether it is cost-effective to join HOMELINK
	Scope	– an analysis of the benefits and costs of HOMELINK
2 Findings	Benefits	– money management
		– travel reservations
		– Prestel information services
	Costs	– initial costs
		– running costs (see below)

PRESTEL COMPUTER TIME CHARGES

No charge during off peak periods (weekdays 6p.m.–8a.m. Saturdays 1p.m. until Mondays 8a.m.) which is when most Homelink customers use the service. (During peak periods a Prestel computer time charge of 5p per minute is payable).

TYPICAL ANNUAL COSTS OF USING HOMELINK

Assuming Homelink is used on 100 occasions, each of 4 minutes duration, the total cost payable to British Telecom would be as follows:

1 Private Customers (100 4 minute calls)	100 calls CHEAP RATE	100 calls PEAK RATE
Prestel quarterly charge (4 x £5)	£20	£20
Prestel computer charges for 100 calls	-	£20
Telephone Calls 100 @ local call rate	£4.94	£14.83
Total	£24.94	£54.83

In fact you may currently use a telephone for 8 minutes during the CHEAP RATE period for under 5p i.e. in the exampie above you may make 100 8 minute CHEAP RATE calls for £4.94.

2 Business User (100 4 minute peak calls)	
Prestel quarterly charge (4 x £15)	£60
Prestel computer charges for 100 calls	£20
Telephone Calls (100 on-peak @ local call rate)	£14.83
Total	£94.83

PAGE CHARGES
Some of Prestel's specialised services, e.g. Stock Market quotation etc., have "page" charges (one screen of information is a "page") ranging from 1p to 50p. Customers always have the option not to take such services before incurring a page charge. Approximately 200,000 of the Prestel pages are free of charge.

3 Conclusions Saving in secretarial time – banking
– travel reservations
– information seeking
Faster decision-making – cash-flow
– budgeting

Recommendations Join HOMELINK if Nottingham Building Society and Bank of Scotland can handle foreign currency transactions.

9.6 Discussion

Choose one of the following for discussion:

a What effect, do you think, videotex will have on traditional media, such as newspapers?
b Is there a danger of creating two types of people—the informed and the uninformed?
c What effect will services such as home banking and shopping have on local communities?

9.7 Word list

Telecomputing

alphamosaic graphics p. 205(T)
alphageometric graphics p. 205(T)
telesoftware p. 113
user-friendliness p. 114
information-providers (IPs) p. 205(T)
electronic telephone directory p. 205(T)
a console p. 120 a keyboard.
to plug in p. 120 to connect.
aerial socket p. 120 the hole for antenna.
adaptor p. 206(T) 'black box' used to convert ordinary devices into specialized devices.
test bench p. 114 where prototypes are tested.

Banking

to open an account p. 120
to deposit £X in an account p. 206(T)
to debit (direct debit) p. 119 take out money.
to credit p. 119 put in money.
funds p. 119 money.
building society p. 113 a type of bank which deals principally with finance for buying houses.
mortgage p. 119 a loan from a building society to buy a house.
overdraw/overdraft p. 120 to take out more money than you have in your account.
account statement p. 119 a balance of credits and debits.
to transfer p. 113 to move money from one bank to another.
a branch p. 113 a bank/building society office where you can pay in/take out money.

Security

to protect p. 120 to provide security.
unauthorized p. 120 not allowed/permitted.
access (to get access) p. 205(T) entry into the system.

a security code (password/ codeword) p. 120 a set of numbers or figures which enable access.

a safeguard p. 206(T) any means (e.g. *password*) which protects/ gives security.

Financial

cost/benefit analysis p. 122 an investigation of the relationship between the costs of a system/ product and its advantages.

cost-effectiveness p. 122 similar to above—a measure of the relationship between what you pay and what you get.

General

key (key business area) p. 112 main, important.

indispensable p. 112 absolutely needed, cannot do without.

hurdle p. 113 a barrier, which must be climbed or jumped in order to proceed.

chore p. 113 an unpleasant or inconvenient task.

to blur p. 113 to become unclear, undefined.

stringent p. 118 very strict.

lighthearted p. 114 entertaining, not serious.

to swap p. 114 to exchange.

to cater for p. 114 to provide service for.

appropriate p. 205(T) suitable, relevant.

Charges

In Britain there are 3 telephone charging times:

Peak	(08.00–13.00)
Standard	(13.00–18.00)
Off-peak	(18.00–08.00)

Unit 10 Radio communications 2

In this unit we look at the increasingly important role of communications satellites in the world of telecommunications.

10.1 Reading

10.1.1

When you have read the following text, complete the key to Figure 10c.

The launching of the first satellite by the Russians in 1957 began what has become known as the 'space race', the first stage of which culminated with the Americans landing on the moon twelve years later. A whole range of satellites now orbit the Earth and are used for a variety of purposes.

Low orbit satellites, the typical height of which varies from 150 to 450 kilometres, are of little use for telecommunications for they are only in line of sight of each earth station for about 15 minutes. Their rotation period around the Earth is about one and a half hours and their main use is for remote sensing, a field in which digital processing techniques are proving especially valuable. A low orbit satellite, equipped with a multispectral scanner system (MSS), can observe the Earth in great detail providing us with extremely accurate information about agriculture, forestry, water resources and pollution patterns. It also has a multitude of applications in such fields as weather forecasting, environmental monitoring, geology, oceanography and cartography. There are important defence implications too, since they can be used to 'spy' on the activities of a potential enemy.

Medium altitude satellites are used for telecommunications, especially in countries which cover a vast geographical area like the USSR. They 'fly' at a typical height of 9 000 to 18 000 kilometres, orbiting the Earth in a period of five to twelve hours. They are in line of sight of the earth station for between two and four hours.

The most important type of satellite for telecommunications is the **geosynchronous,** or **geostationary, satellite** positioned over the Equator at a height of 35 800 kilometres. Its rotation period is 24 hours, the same as the Earth's, and consequently, seen from the Earth, this type of satellite appears to remain motionless in the sky. It is within line of sight of an earth station for its entire life.

A communication satellite is, in essence, a microwave relay station which receives signals in a given frequency band and retransmits them at a different frequency to avoid problems of interference between the weak incoming signal and the powerful retransmitted signal. The equipment which receives a signal, amplifies it, changes its frequency and then retransmits it, is called a transponder. A satellite can handle large amounts of traffic which it can send over vast areas of the Earth. It therefore represents a relatively cheap way of transmitting information over long distances. For countries which do not already have sophisticated cable or microwave networks the use of a satellite can be extremely beneficial as it can be used in their place.

The first satellites were seen as a way of communicating with people who lived in isolated areas of the world. As a result, earth stations began to appear in the remotest parts of the globe. The cost of satellite communication began to fall steadily and, consequently, satellites have to compete with submarine cables as a way of linking continents cheaply. With the arrival of optical fibre undersea cables, however, a more balanced division of intercontinental circuits between the two is likely. Satellites were soon used to broadcast TV programmes 'live' from one side of the Earth to the other, and then to link up computer terminals in different parts of the world. The use of digital transmission and multiplexing techniques has led to an enormous increase in the capacity of satellites.

The international organization INTELSAT was created in 1964 to provide international communication services by satellite. In 1983 it operated and owned 16 spacecraft in geosynchronous orbit representing an investment of over three billion US dollars. In 1983 it handled two thirds of all international telephone and data communications and transmitted virtually all 'live' international television broadcasts. 109 nations are members of INTELSAT. Between 1979 and 1983 INTELSAT's traffic doubled, yet its communications charges decreased, despite a 73% rise in the worldwide cost of living index.

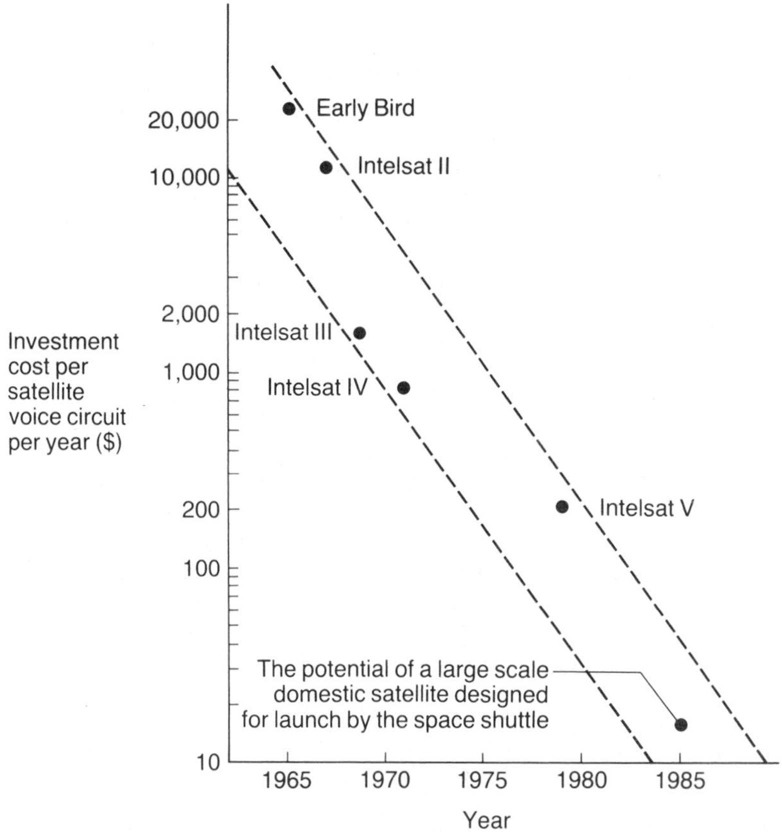

Fig 10a The falling investment cost of satellite voice circuits

A series of INTELSAT satellites has been launched, the next of which will be INTELSAT VI in 1986. The table below gives the main characteristics of the INTELSAT satellites.

Evolution of INTELSAT Spacecraft

SERIES	 I Early Bird	 II	 III	 IV	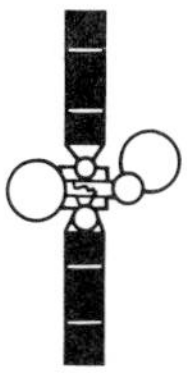 Va	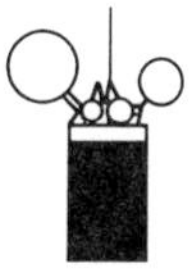 VI
First launch	1965	1967	1968	1971	1983	1986
No. of voice circuits	240	240	1200	6000	24 000	80 000
Bandwidth MHz	25	130	225	36	2570	3262
No. of transponders	2	1	2	12	27	50
Design lifetime (years)	1.5	3	5	7	7	7–10
No. of antennae	1	1	1	3	7	7
Weight in orbit (in kg)	38	87	146	703	950	2243

Fig 10b

Satellites are not simply replacements for point-to-point terrestrial lines. They have several unique properties, among which the most important are:

- a 270 millisecond propagation delay caused by the distance the signal has to travel (80 000 km–300 000 km/sec = 0.27 seconds)
- the possibility of very high bandwidths or bit rates if the user can avoid local loops by having an antenna on his premises, or a radio link to an earth station antenna.
- the special security problems that are posed when information is broadcast through a satellite.

Until recently all satellites were launched using rockets, which proved to be extremely costly as the rockets were lost in the sea a few minutes after being launched. The space shuttle, itself put into orbit by a rocket, parts of which are recovered and can be reused, heralds the era of routine access to space, for one individual shuttle will be able to perform not less than 100 separate missions. Its payload is also greater than that of any previous rocket's and its crew will be made up not only of professional astronauts but of scientists who will be able to conduct their research in the gravity-free environment of space.

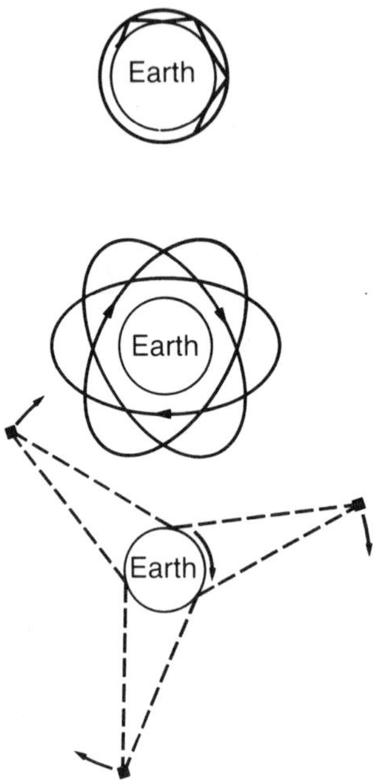

1 . . .
- **a** height . . .
- **b** rotation period . . .
- **c** time in line of sight of earth station . . .
- **d** use . . .

2 . . .
- **a** height . . .
- **b** rotation period . . .
- **c** time in line of sight of earth station . . .
- **d** use . . .

3 . . .
- **a** height . . .
- **b** rotation period . . .
- **c** time in line of sight of earth station . . .
- **d** use . . .
- **e** exact position . . .

Fig 10c

10.1.2 **Comprehension**

Answer the following questions:

- **a** Which event sparked off the 'space race'?
- **b** Which event ended the first stage of the 'space race'?
- **c** What does a transponder do?
- **d** Why are developing countries particularly interested in satellite communications?
- **e** What are the three main stages in the way satellites have been viewed?
- **f** Give the following information about INTELSAT: year of creation; number of spacecraft owned and operated in 1983; investment value of the above spacecraft; number of member nations; proportion of all international telephone and data traffic handled in 1983.
- **g** How has the investment cost per satellite voice channel changed over the last twenty years?
- **h** Give four apparent advantages of the space shuttle over conventional rockets.

10.2 Listening 1

10.2.1

Listen to the following interview between Roland Leijonflycht, Special Adviser to the Swedish Ministry of Communications, and Stanley Clayton, Science and Technology Correspondent of the *Financial Guardian* newspaper. Mr Clayton was writing an article entitled 'European Communications Satellites—a mid-1983 perspective'. As you listen, complete Figure 10d.

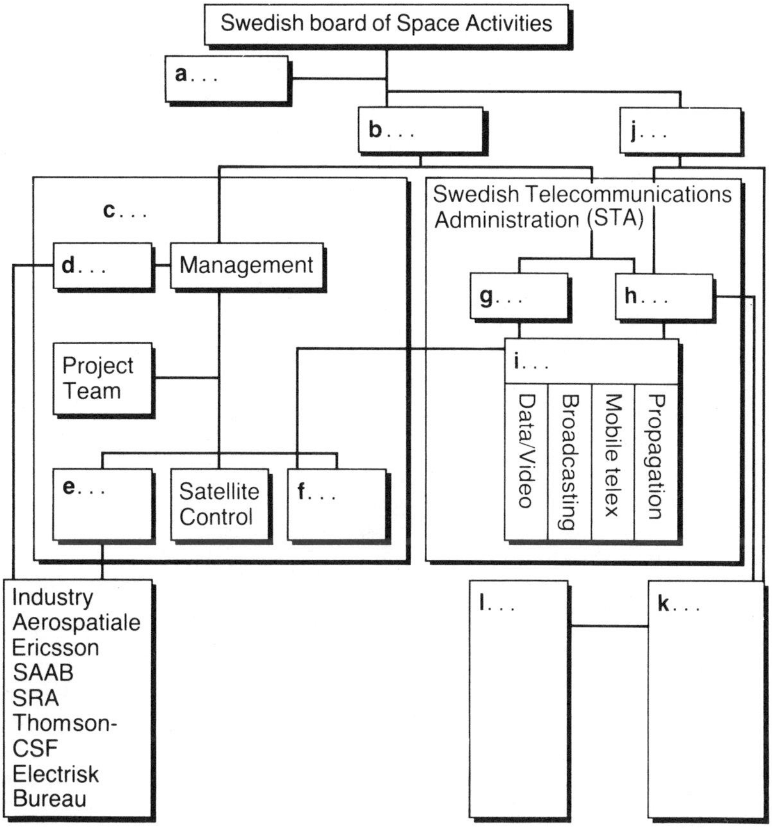

Fig 10d

10.2.2 Comprehension

Answer the following questions:

a Why does Mr Leijonflycht think that some of his answers may not be complete?
b Why does Mr Leijonflycht not want to comment on financial questions?
c Which organization has final responsibility for the project?
d What are the principal parties involved?
e How many of the parties do the private companies liaise with?
f Why is the SSC Earth Station group in direct contact with Swedish Telecom?
g Why doesn't Mr Leijonflycht give the journalist the full list of private companies involved?

10.3 Language practice

10.3.1 Reason and result

Low orbit satellites are of little use for telecommunications.
Reason = They are only in line of sight for about 15 minutes.

Low orbit satellites are of little use for telecommunications **for/since/as/because** they are only in line of sight for about 15 minutes.

The cost of satellite communication began to fall.
Result = Satellites began to compete with undersea cables.

The cost of satellite communication began to fall and, **therefore,/consequently,/as a result** satellites began to compete with undersea cables.

Now join the sentences below with either a reason marker or a result marker.

a Digital transmission and multiplexing techniques have developed considerably.	The capacity of satellites has increased enormously.
b There is a 270 millisecond propagation delay.	The signal has to travel thousands of kilometres.
c The rockets were lost at sea.	The launches were very expensive.
d The shuttle heralds a new era of space travel.	The shuttle can perform at least 100 separate missions.
e The Kennedy Space Center was fog-bound.	The launch was delayed by 24 hours.
f Mr Leijonflycht is not prepared to answer questions on financial matters.	He is not a financial expert.
g Geosynchronous satellites travel at the same speed as the earth.	Geosynchronous satellites are much used for telecommunications.
h The list of private companies involved in the project is long.	Mr Leijonflycht will not give the names of all the companies involved.

10.3.2 Plans and intentions

You will remember from **6.3.1** that we can use the present continuous to express **fixed plans**, e.g.:

We're flying via New York.

Now look at ways of expressing **future intentions**:

I intend to buy a copy of your newspaper.
I aim to be there before six o'clock.
We're going to reuse the shuttle about 100 times.

Notice, too, how we can express **routine arrangements**:

We'll be looking at the effects of propagation delay.
Will you be informing the Danes of your progress?

Roland Leijonflycht represents Sweden on one of the CCIR (International Consultative Committee on Radio) working groups. He is going to visit Geneva for one of the group's regular meetings.

Details of Visit	
1 Leave Stockholm	: 10.20 on Monday 17 September
2 Length of stay	: 3 days
3 Hotel	: Hotel Bristol, Geneva
4 Date of return	: 20 September at 19.15
Routine tasks	
5 Review previous meeting's minutes	
6 Present action taken since last meeting	
7 Assign tasks to various members of the group	
Special objectives	
8 Discuss frequency distribution in the 11.7 to 12.5 GHz band	
9 Have a meeting with the Nordic delegates	
10 Present latest details of Tele-X project.	

Now ask Mr Leijonflycht about his fixed plans (**1–4**), the routine tasks he'll be performing (**5–7**) and anything special he intends to do (**8–10**).

10.3.3 Dealing with difficult questions

Often we can't answer questions. Sometimes because we don't know the answer, sometimes because we don't want to give the answer. Here are some expressions that will help in such situations.

Not giving a complete answer	I'm afraid I can't give you a full answer.
Not giving an answer at all	I'm sorry. I'm not in a position to say.
Transferring responsibility	That's not my field.
	I think Mr X. is in a better position to answer.
Postponing an answer	I'd rather not say at the moment.
	It's too early to say.

Now listen to Listening 1 again. Try to pick out ways in which Mr Leijonflycht deals with difficult questions. Sort them into the four categories above.

10.4 Listening 2

10.4.1

Ebor Radio, a group of radio, TV and electronics shops in the north of England, are going to add a small home earth station to the range of products they sell. Listen to Douglas Wilson, a representative of the earth station's manufacturers, talking about it to a meeting of the shops' managers. As you listen, complete Figure 10e.

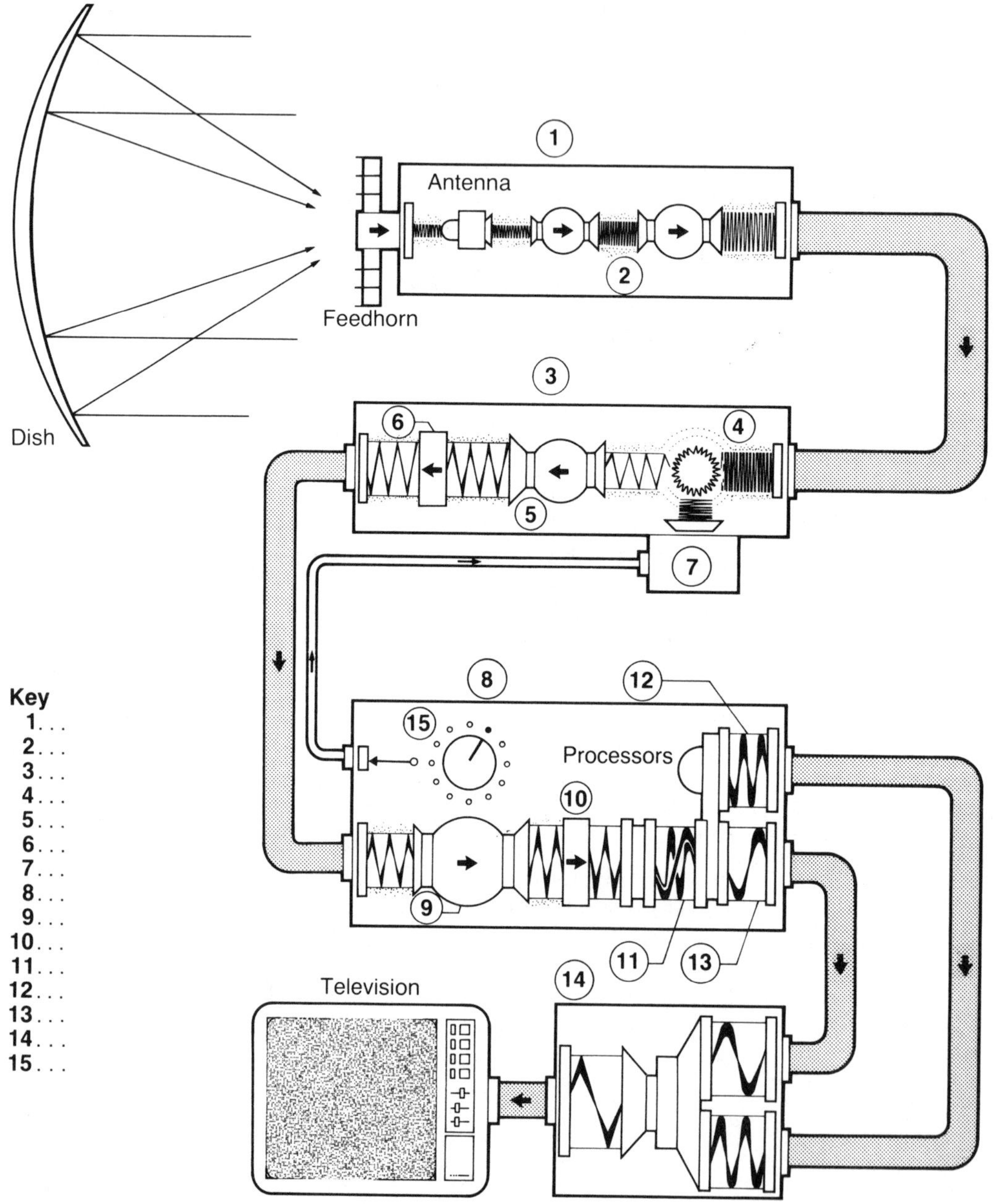

Key
1. . .
2. . .
3. . .
4. . .
5. . .
6. . .
7. . .
8. . .
9. . .
10. . .
11. . .
12. . .
13. . .
14. . .
15. . .

Fig 10e

10.4.2 Comprehension

Answer the following questions:

a What is the trade name of the equipment the speaker is talking about?
b How big is the dish antenna?
c Where is the feedhorn positioned?
d How strong is the incoming microwave signal?
e What do we really mean when we say the IF is 70 MHz?
f What is the original 4 GHz frequency also called?
g When do you need a CATV transformer connected to the TV?
h How many normal ways of tuning home earth stations are there?

10.4.3 Activity

Look carefully at the diagram below which shows the modular composition of the Tele-X satellite.

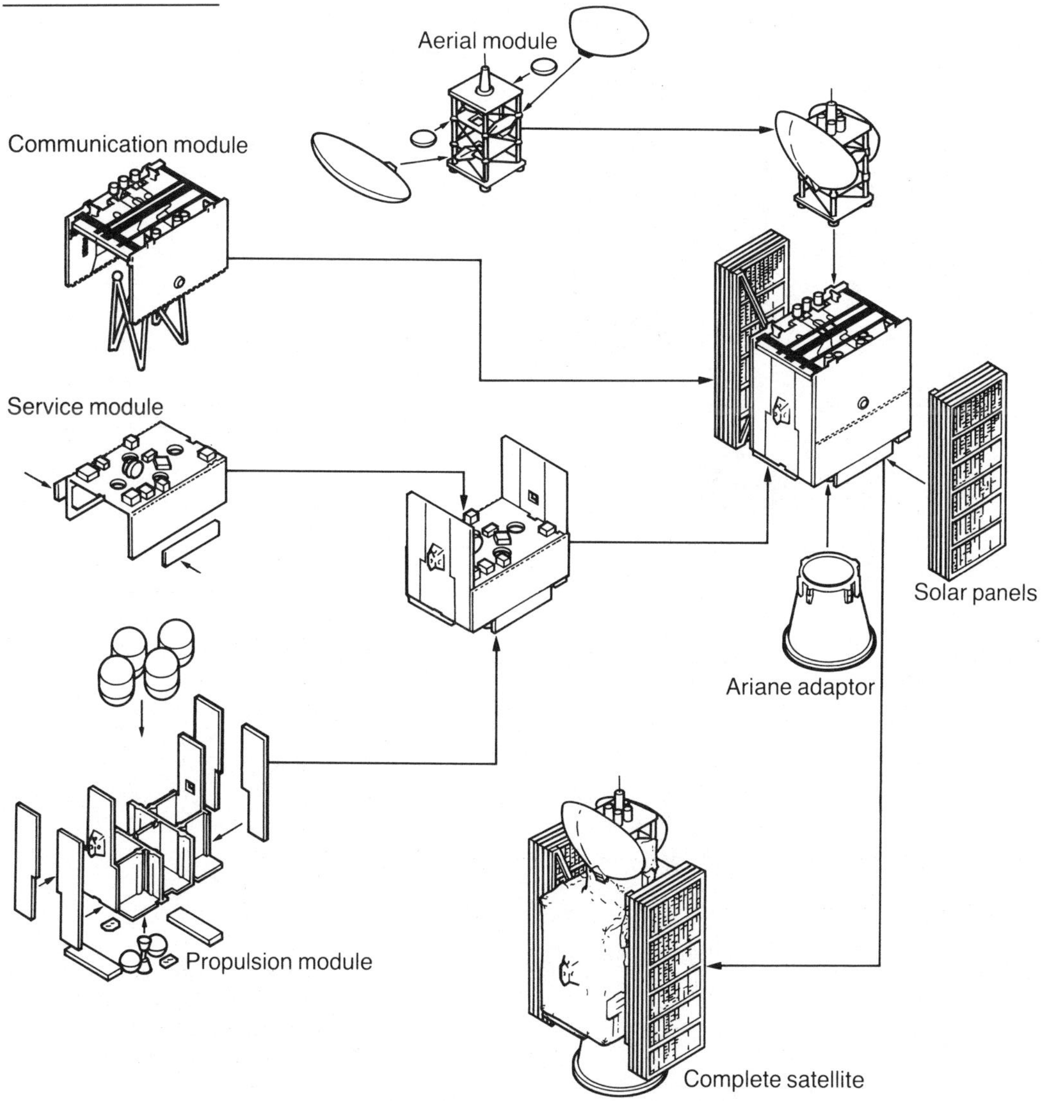

Fig 10f Tele-x module sections

Now look at the next diagram and attempt to identify the parts of the satellite. The list of parts is given below.

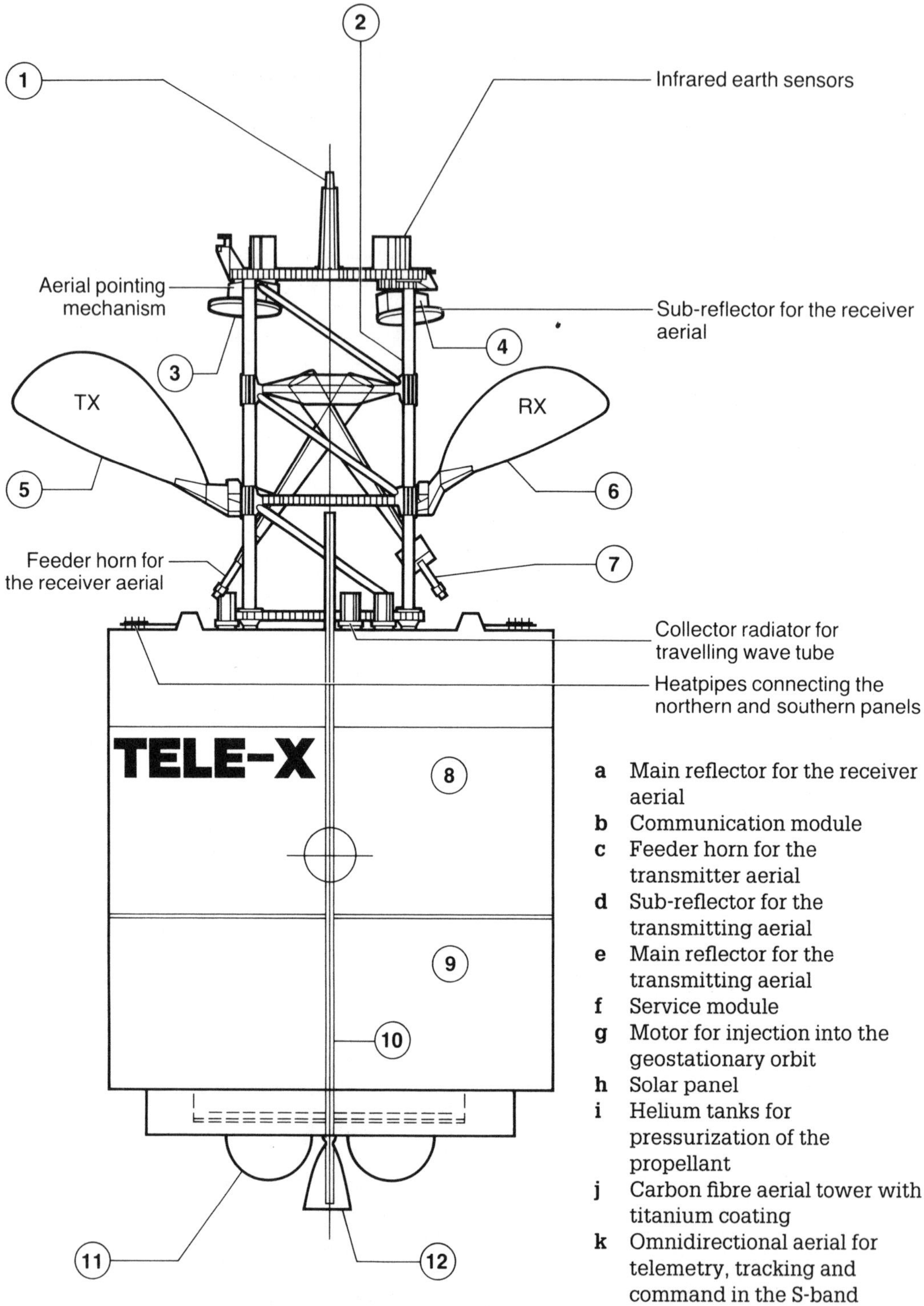

Fig 10g

- **a** Main reflector for the receiver aerial
- **b** Communication module
- **c** Feeder horn for the transmitter aerial
- **d** Sub-reflector for the transmitting aerial
- **e** Main reflector for the transmitting aerial
- **f** Service module
- **g** Motor for injection into the geostationary orbit
- **h** Solar panel
- **i** Helium tanks for pressurization of the propellant
- **j** Carbon fibre aerial tower with titanium coating
- **k** Omnidirectional aerial for telemetry, tracking and command in the S-band
- **l** Aerial pointing mechanism

10.5 Writing

Sometimes we have to make a report about what has been said at a meeting. When we do this we turn direct speech into indirect speech. For example, if you had been ill and missed the meeting about the Homearth Mark II (Listening 2), one of your colleagues might have reported Douglas Wilson's words like this:

Actual words After leaving the discriminator, the separated audio and video signals are sent to another unit called the RF modulator. This may be contained within the receiver or, in some cases, it comes as a separate unit.

Report He said that, after having left the discriminator, the separated audio and video signals were sent to another unit called the RF modulator. This might be contained within the receiver or, in some cases, it came as a separate unit.

Now listen to the first part of Listening 1 and write a report of what Mr Leijonflycht and Mr Clayton said to each other.

10.6 Discussion

Choose one of the following themes for discussion:

a The different uses of satellites.
b The influence of direct broadcasting satellites and readily available home earth stations.
c The importance of the space shuttle.

10.7 Word list

Space and satellite communications

to launch a satellite/the space shuttle p. 125
the rotation period p. 125
remote sensing p. 125
INTELSAT p. 126
a 270 millisecond propagation delay p. 127
an astronaut p. 128
the gravity-free environment of space p. 129
a spacecraft p. 126
a rocket p. 128

Project organization

joint project p. 206(T)
project team p. 129
group p. 206(T)
division p. 126
corporation p. 206(T)
to co-ordinate p. 206(T)
principal parties p. 206(T)
working party p. 206(T)
subordinate to p. 206(T)
to liaise with p. 206(T)
to maintain links with p. 206(T)
prime contractor p. 206(T) most important contractor.
overall responsibility p. 206(T)

Radio

microwave p. 125
broadcasting p. 129
transponder p. 125
(dish) antenna p. 127 also, aerial.
feedhorn p. 207(T)
signal loss p. 207(T)
amplifier p. 207(T)
filter p. 207(T)
to heterodyne p. 207(T)
discriminator p. 207(T)
carrier p. 207(T)
RF modulation p. 207(T) Radio Frequency.
to tune p. 207(T)
variable tuning p. 207(T)
channel selector knob p. 207(T)
up/down scan tuning p. 207(T)
CB radio p. 207(T) Citizens' Band radio.

Miscellaneous

payload p. 128
to monitor p. 125
terrestrial lines p. 127
weather forecasting p. 125
submarine cable p. 126 also, undersea, subocean.
to spy on p. 125
the cost of living index p. 126
a range (of products) p. 125

Revision Unit B Defining needs

In this unit you will continue to study the setting-up of the new Reniat subsidiary in Costerutsi, which you began in Revision Unit A.
You will have 3 tasks to perform, each one relating to the telecommunication requirements of Reniat.
In doing this you will practise the language introduced in Units 1–10.

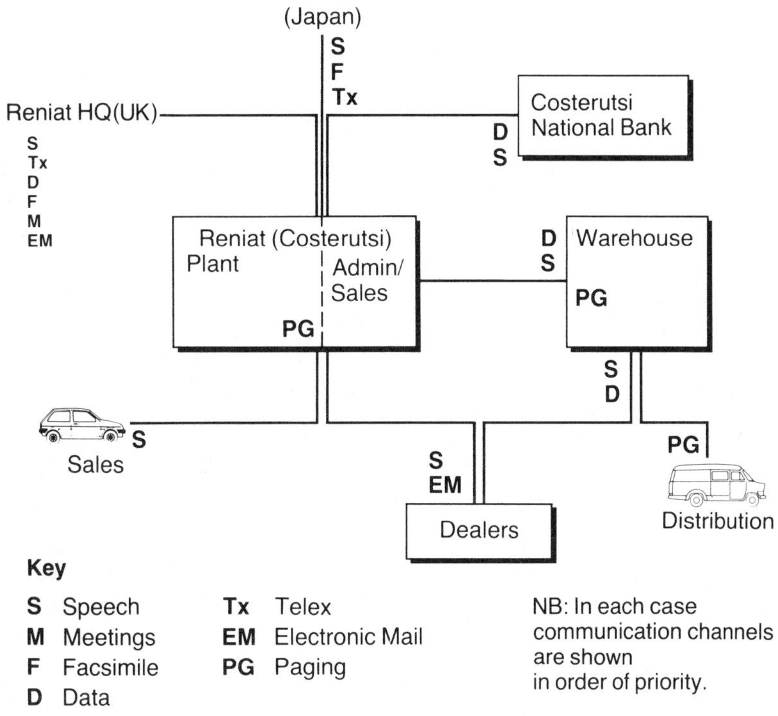

Fig Revision B1 Reniat (Costerutsi) communications needs

Task 1

Study Figure Rev B 1, which shows the communication diagram drawn up by the Communications Manager of Reniat, as a first step in assessing his company's communication needs.
The report is given on the next page, but is presented in an incorrect order.
Re-write it in the correct order. The headings and sub-headings used by the Manager are given in the correct order at the beginning.

Reniat (Costerutsi) Communication Needs

Introduction
Findings: Needs of individual parts of the Company
– Domestic
– International
Overall priorities of types of communication
Conclusion

A Facsimile transmission between the plant and the warehouse would enable us to keep up to date on documentation such as production schedules and warehouse allocation. Electronic mail would facilitate orders and invoicing, and enable instant discounting.

B Speech and data communication will be essential for our internal operations in Costerutsi. All departments will need speech communication. Data will be particularly important between the plant and the warehouse, between the warehouse and the dealers and between the plant and the Costerutsi National Bank.

C Inevitably, voice links are the most important need at all levels. Data and text communication are roughly equal in importance, and both growing rapidly. Less important at the moment, but also likely to increase, are facsimile transmission, mobile radio telephone and electronic mail. Radiopaging is, at the moment, perhaps the least important, but it must not be ignored.

D This report presents the estimated telecommunication needs of Reniat (Costerutsi).

E Finally, when planning the system, care must be taken to allow for future expansion and for the use of new services.

F Firstly for links with London the full range of telecommunications will be necessary. In addition to the usual telephone links, a teleconferencing facility will save valuable time and expense in travel and meetings. Similarly, electronic mail will save time and prove more reliable than conventional international postal services.

G It is of great importance that both domestic and international telephone services are efficient and readily available. Almost as important are high-speed data and text communications. The latter are almost exclusively international. Facsimile transmission to and from Japan must be available immediately, and eventually with HQ and Costerutsi. Other facilities, such as electronic mail, radiopaging and mobile radio telephone, are medium-term needs.

H Other important media are radiopaging and mobile telephone services. Radiopaging would be very useful within the plant, and from the warehouse to distribution vehicles. In order to speed up delivery, mobile telephone links would be an advantage for the sales force.

I The findings can be grouped into two main categories: the needs of individual departments and sections of the company and the priority to be given to the different means of communication throughout the company.

J Finally, two less pressing but still considerable requirements are facsimile transmission between plant and warehouse, and electronic mail between plant and dealers.

K Secondly, for links with Japan, telephone and text transmission will be essential. However, equally important will be the facsimile transmission of plans, diagrams and, in some cases, Japanese characters.

Task 2

As International Accounts Manager for the C.T.A., responsible for the Reniat account, you have just received the following letter from the Reniat Communications Manager.

Write a brief letter of reply, answering the main points and suggesting a meeting for more detailed discussion.
Your assistant has drawn up some notes for you to refer to, if necessary, and further information may be found by listening again to the Director General of C.T.A. on the tape for Revision Unit A.

The International Accounts Manager
C.T.A. (Costerutsi Telecommunication Administration)
Costerutsi

Reniat

Dear Sir

As Communications Manager for Reniat, I am writing to make some preliminary enquiries on the type and range of services available from your administration.

I should be glad to have the following information:

1. The types of telephone set and private exchange available in Costerutsi.	– 3 BASIC TYPES OF SET PABXs FROM 1+2 to 15+75
2. The availability of (high-speed) data links. At which point on the data network does your responsibility end?	– 9600 b/s LEASED CIRCUIT SOON AVAILABLE. – MODEM
3. Is Teletex available in Costerutsi? If so, may we use our own equipment?	– ONLY EXPERIMENTAL SO FAR – ? NOT DECIDED
4. What type of facsimile services are available?	– GP II & BUREAUFAX
5. What parts of the country are covered by MRT?	– MOST LARGE TOWNS
6. Is Radiopaging available?	– NOT YET
7. What is the cost of business telephone rental?	– UP TO \$C 700 pa
8. What kind of delays are experienced with international telephone links?	– SOME NOW – BETTER WITH NEW CABLE (→ 9 MONTHS?)
9. Does all or most telecommunications equipment have to be supplied by C.T.A.?	– YES, POSITION BEING REVIEWED

I look forward to having your reply at your earliest convenience.

Yours faithfully

Paul Bailey

Paul Bailey (Communications Manager)

Task 3

Either (class)

1 Divide the class into 2 groups, one group to represent C.T.A., the other Reniat. Each group should then:
2 Re-read this Revision unit and the information supplied so far.
3 Examine together the appropriate role-card below.
4 Practise the kinds of question and answer required to exchange the necessary information.
5 Meet the other group in a 'semi-formal' meeting, in order to get and give information and reach a conclusion.

Or (individual study)

1 Re-read the information so far given in this Revision unit.
2 Examine both role-cards below.
3 Write the minutes (a short report), showing what you imagine would be the results of a meeting between C.T.A. and Reniat. Use the following headings to help you:
   - Services and equipment available at present
   - Services available in the future
   - Costs
   - Training
   - Future arrangements for contact.

A

Reniat You are Paul Bailey, Communications Manager of Reniat. You are to meet Bill Wallace, International Accounts Manager of C.T.A. You wish to clarify these points:

1. When it will be possible to use privately-produced telecommunications equipment. (You have a good link with manufacturers.)
2. When teletex and radiopaging will become available.
3. Which towns are not yet covered by MRT.
4. What the details are of telephone rental costs.
5. What training facilities are offered with equipment.

B

C.T.A. You are Bill Wallace, International Accounts Manager for C.T.A. You are to meet Paul Bailey, Communications Manager of Reniat. Further to your letter (see Task 2) you have the following information:

1. A new PABX will shortly be available: 25 lines up to 150 extensions.
2. The Government has decided to liberalize the supply of phone sets, data terminals and facsimile transceivers within 3 years.
3. The Teletex experiments are experiencing difficulties with the software. No solution visible yet.
4. Radiopaging available within 6 months.
5. MRT unavailable only in country areas. —no problem?
6. Rental costs for business phones are high—but negotiable. Basic $C 700 p.a. may be reduced, depending on type of equipment, amount of traffic.
7. You'd like to meet Paul Bailey on a regular basis—say, once a month, or every 6 weeks, to discuss problems, training facilities, new services.
8. Training facilities come free with all equipment.

Unit 11 Telecoms in France

In this unit we look at the first of four case-studies of telecommunications in different countries.

11.1 Reading 1

As you read the following text, complete the key for Figures 11b and 11c.

France is a western European country with a population of just over 54 million and a surface area of some 550 000 square kilometres. Its population varies from more than 24 000 inhabitants per square kilometre in the capital, Paris, to 15 inhabitants per square kilometre in the Massif Central in central southern France.

Town	Town population	Town + Suburbs
Paris	2 300 000	8 550 000
Lyons	462 000	1 170 000
Marseilles	914 000	1 070 000
Lille	177 000	935 000
Bordeaux	226 000	612 000
Toulouse	383 000	509 000
Nantes	263 000	453 000
Nice	346 000	437 000
Grenoble	169 000	389 000
Rouen	118 000	388 000
Toulon	185 000	378 000

Fig 11a

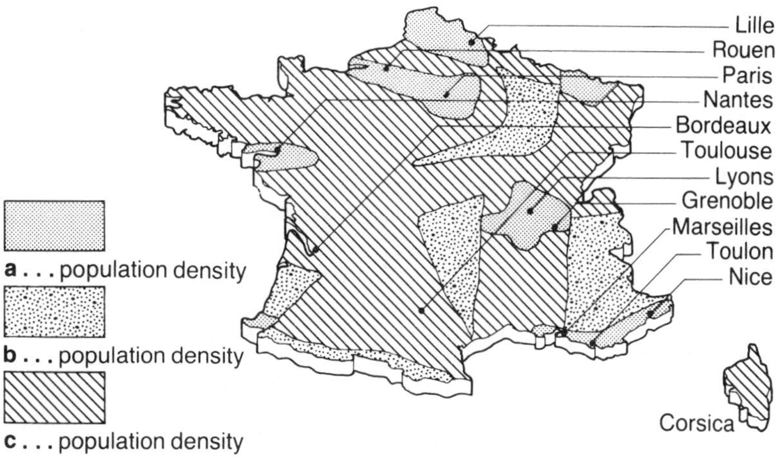

Fig 11b

About one Frenchman in every six lives in the Paris region, which, given the surface area of France, means that the country is very centralized in terms of transport. Should you wish to travel from Nantes to Nice, you will almost certainly have to pass through Paris.

While France is an important food-producing country (vegetables, fruit, cereals and meat) it is also one of the major industrial powers in Europe, and nowhere is this more true than in the field of telecommunications. In the ten-year period 1975–1985, the internal telecommunications network in France more than tripled in size, and French companies such as CIT-Alcatel and Thomson CSF have become world leaders in switching and telematics. Important pilot schemes are being carried out in France to assess the value and usefulness of certain networks; for example, the optical fibre network in Biarritz, the electronic directory experiment near Rennes and the new services project in Vélizy, a suburb to the south of Paris.

The Vélizy Project

In 1978, the French government made funds available for a project which has become known as Télétel 3V, Télétel being an interactive videotex system and 3V representing the first letter of the three neighbouring areas where the experiment was carried out; Vélizy, Versailles and Val de Bièvre. This zone, ten kilometres south-west of Paris, has a total population of some 140 000 made up of 45 000 households, 38 000 of which had their own telephone.

Interactive videotex makes use of the ordinary telephone line to transmit information. At the user's end, there is a terminal, consisting of a display unit (similar to a TV screen) and an alphanumeric keyboard. Whereas the early videotex systems had a relatively limited keypad, often comprising nothing more than the numbers 0 to 9 with a couple of function keys, the Télétel keyboard includes the complete alphabet, which means that far more sophisticated dialogues can take place between the user and the system.

The aims of the Vélizy experiment can be summarized under four main headings:

i) From the user's point of view, what are the most useful videotex services?
ii) How can the service providers best master and market the possibilities of this new way of communicating?
iii) Are the ideal products being used at hardware, software and network levels, by information providers and the Telecommunications Authority?
iv) What are the social consequences of videotex in a mass community context?

The first terminals were installed in subscribers' homes in April 1981 and by September of the same year, 2 500 subscribers were connected. It must be stressed that all the subscribers voluntarily agreed to participate and that a good cross-section of society was deliberately chosen . . . people who differed in age, academic background, profession and family situation. The aim was for each socio-economic group to be represented by a large enough sample of people to guarantee a meaningful result even though the tests were limited in terms of the geographical area covered and the number of subscribers involved. No such limitations, however, were imposed on the information providers. All sorts of organizations, public and private, local and national, were invited to provide computer-based services with a view to evaluating the potential of this new mass communication system.

The experiment began in June 1981 and ended, officially, on 31 December 1982. It was the first experimental system in the world to enable subscribers using the same type of terminal to access different data banks, and to perform operations ranging from the simple consultation of a file to high-level operations such as booking flights with an airline or ordering goods directly from chain stores.

It should be noted that Télétel billed all calls at a rate of about 10 US cents every five minutes, regardless of the distance covered. The users were not required to pay for the equipment or its installation in the 2500 households.

Location	**Telephone density (%)**	**Users' equipment**	**Size of sample**	**Cost to users**	**Facilities available to users**	**Duration of experiment**
a ...	**b** ...	**c** ...	**d** ...	**e** ...	**f** ...	**g** ...

Fig 11c Basic facts about Vélizy project

11.2 **Listening 1**

Listen to the following presentation of telecommunications in France, given to a group of visiting engineers. As you listen, complete Figures 11d and 11e.

Year	**Main characteristic(s)**
Mid-1960s	**a** ... **b** ...
1970	**c** ...
1976–80	**d** ...
1978	Funds are made available for: **e** ... **f** ... **g** ... **h** ... **i** ...

Fig 11d

Year	Number in millions	Density (%)
1954		
1965		—
1970		—
1974 (Dec)		—
1976 (May)		
1978 (Jan)		—
1978 (Dec)		—
1982		
1983 (Dec)		

Fig 11e

11.3 **Language practice**

11.3.1 **Degree**

When referring to numbers or figures, we often don't give the precise number. Instead we qualify it with one of the expressions below.

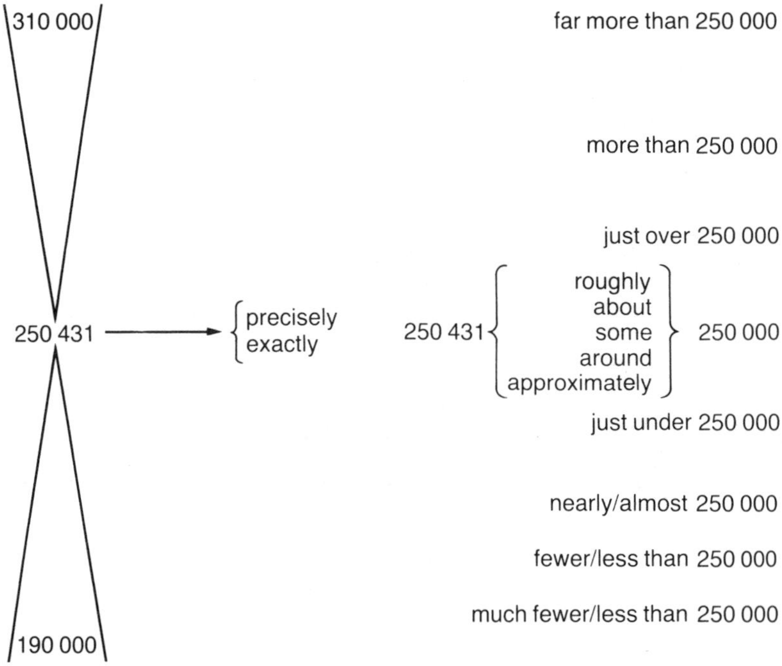

Now look at Figure 11a again. Use it to complete the sentences below.

a Paris has a population of . . . 2 300 000.
b Lyon has . . . inhabitants living in its suburbs . . . in its centre.
c Marseilles town and suburbs have a population of . . . one million.
d Grenoble has a population of . . . 170 000.
e Lille's town population is much . . . than its town and suburbs together.
f Toulon has . . . 185 321 inhabitants.
g Nice's population is . . . that of Toulouse.
h Lille, Grenoble and Toulon all have populations of . . . 175 000.
i Paris has . . . inhabitants living in the centre . . . in the suburbs.
j Paris' inner city population is . . . its total city and suburbs' population.

11.3.2 Describing change

Amount of change

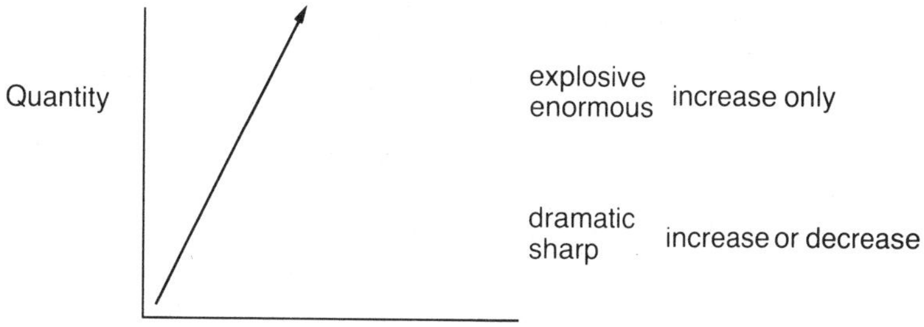

Speed of change

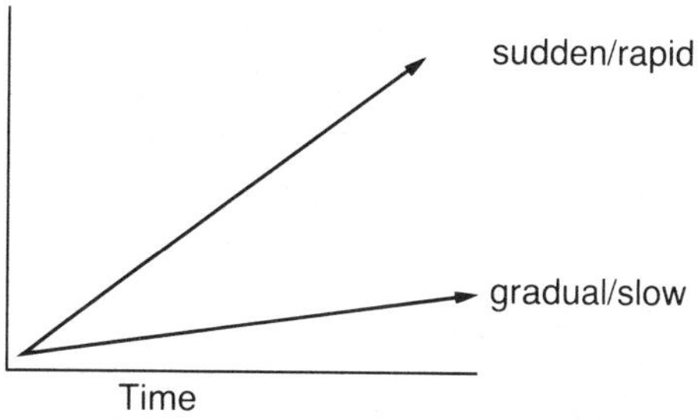

Significance of change

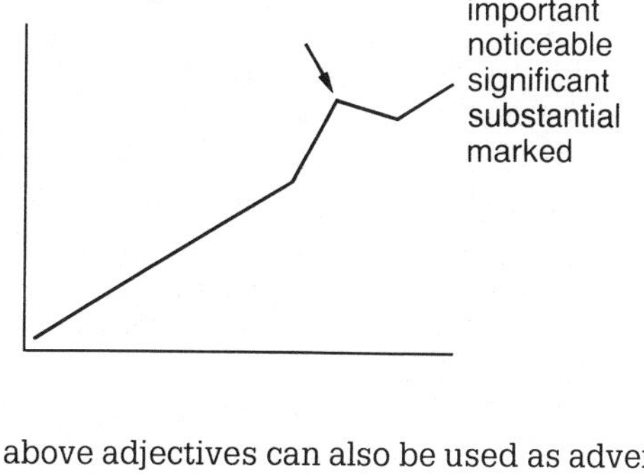

NB All the above adjectives can also be used as adverbs:
There has been an **explosive** growth in telecoms.
Telecoms has grown **explosively**.

Now use the two graphs below to complete sentences **a** to **h**.

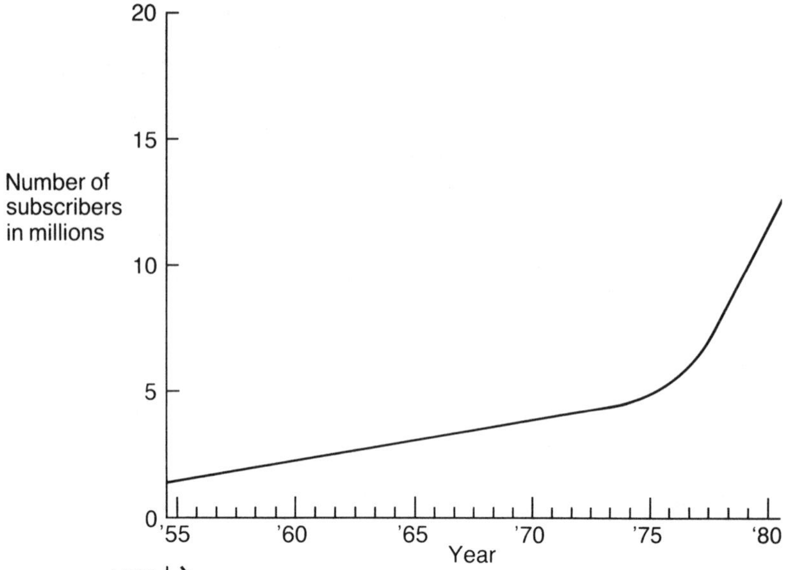

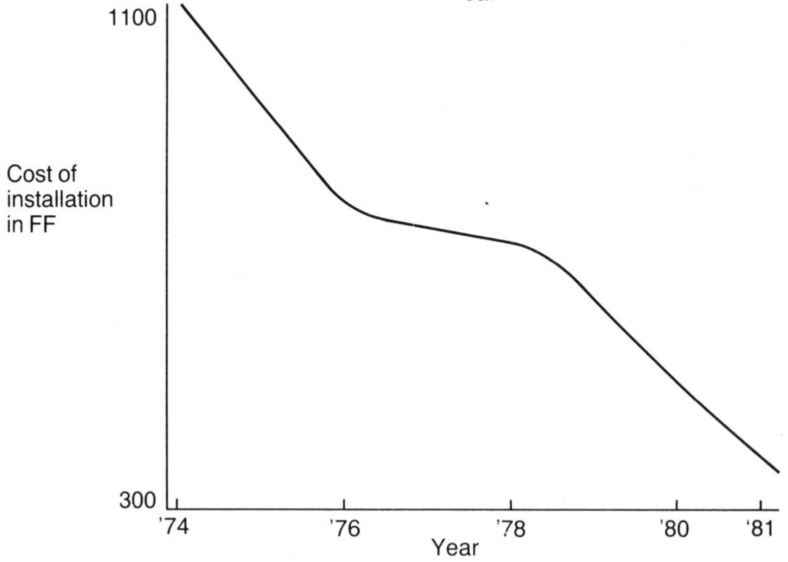

a There has been an . . . increase in the number of subscribers during the last ten years.
b In the eleven years from '54 to '65 the number of subscribers rose . . . .
c In the two years between '74 and '76 the number of subscribers increased . . . .
d During 1978 there was a . . . increase in the number of subscribers.
e In 1974 there was a . . . change in trend after 20 years of very . . . growth.
f Installation charges fell very . . . between '74 and '76.
g From '76 to '78 they decreased more . . . .
h In the following three years there was again a . . . increase in the rate of reduction in charges.

11.4 Reading 2

As you read the text, complete the systems layout diagram (Figure 11f).

Each user is connected to the Télétel computer centre via the public network. The centre then puts the user into direct contact with the various videotex services that are on offer. From a technical point of view, these services can be accessed in three different ways:

i) Through software installed in the Télétel centre itself.

ii) Through software installed in the geographical zone of the test, but not in the Télétel centre itself. The local computers in question are connected to the Télétel centre by leased lines.

iii) Through software installed outside the geographical area of the test. These remote computers are connected to the Télétel centre through TRANSPAC, a packet-switched data transmission network.

In groups ii) and iii) the user has the impression that he is in direct contact with the requested service, but the Télétel centre remains in control of the call and can intervene when requested to connect the subscriber to another service.

The Télétel computer centre in Vélizy uses a modular minicomputer system to handle both switching and database functions. The former involves switching subscribers' calls to the place where the software is actually installed. The main role of the centre is, of course, to act as an interface for the user, enabling him/her to get into contact with the exact service required, but it also stores statistical data concerning the use of Télétel necessary for activities such as billing. The centre has been designed to handle 300 simultaneous calls from the 2 500 subscribers.

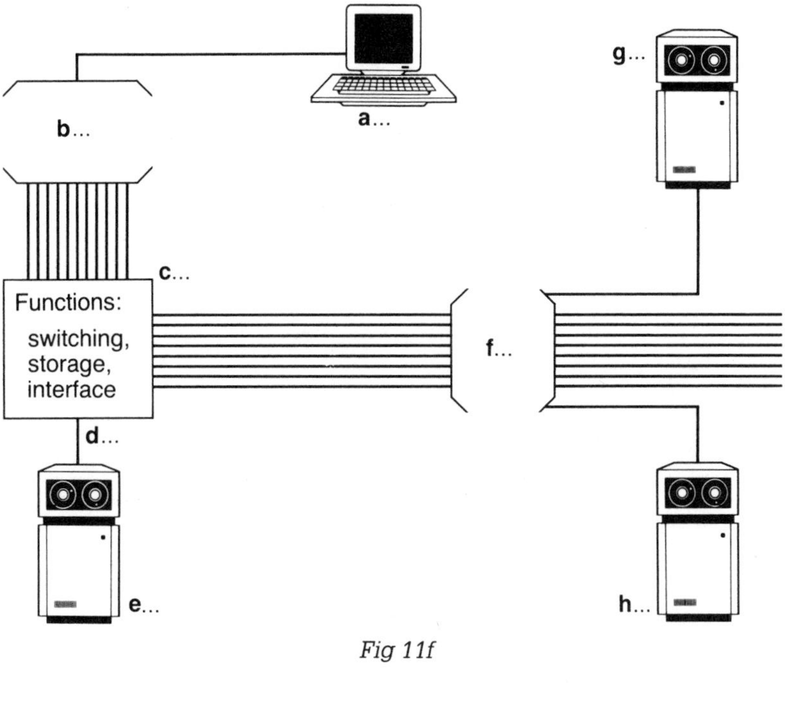

Fig 11f

11.5 Listening 2

You are one of a group of visiting engineers taking part in a discussion with a French engineer about the results of the Vélizy project. As you listen, make notes on the notepad below comparing the French results with the results of your experiment.

Notes for a comparison of our videotex experiment with the Vélizy project.

	Our project	Vélizy project
1. Users: domestic	60%	
public and institutional	10%	
information providers	30%	
2. Most frequent socio-economic group	Office workers	
3. Most frequent age group	30-39	
4. Calls per month (average)	18,000	
5. Average call: length	9 minutes	
services consulted	2.4 services	
6. Busiest days	Saturday	
	Sunday	
7. Peak hours / periods: weekday	4pm	
weekend	5pm - 11pm	
8. Most consulted service group	media info	
	local info	

11.6 Discussion

Choose one of the following themes for discussion:

a What role do you think systems like Télétel could, and should, play in our lives?
b Rather than making it easier to communicate, do you think videotex links could make people more lonely?
c What effects are videotex systems likely to have on the press?
d What use are these systems for children?

11.7 Word list

Experiments and projects

pilot scheme p. 142
to make funds available for p. 142 to provide money for.
a cross section of society p. 142

Evaluation and testing

to assess p. 142 to judge the value of, evaluate.
the switching centre was tried and tested p. 207(T)

Reporting

to summarize (summary) p. 142 to say in few words.
to draw conclusions about p. 208(T)

Miscellaneous

suburb p. 141
to deal with p. 208(T)
average duration of a call p. 208(T)
peak hours p. 208(T)
modular minicomputer system p. 147
bar graph/bar chart p. 208(T)

Unit 12 Telecoms in Britain

This unit looks at telecommunications in Britain and, in particular, the process of privatization of the TA.

12.1 Reading 1

12.1.1

Read the following introduction and complete Figure 12a.

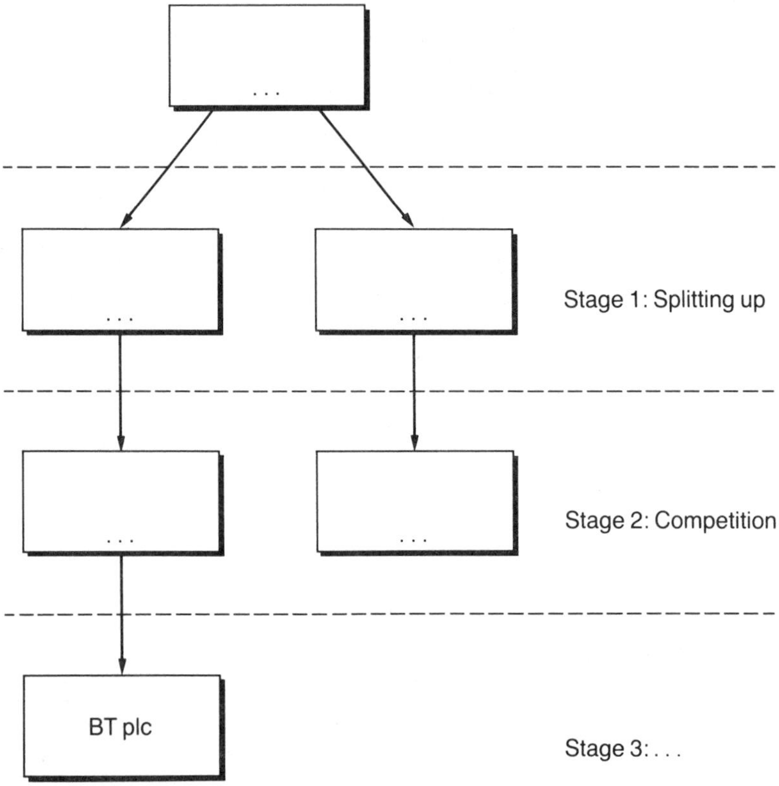

Fig 12a Evolution in telecommunications

Introduction

It is really not that long since control of communications between two different premises was a monopoly exercised by the British Post Office (BPO), but technology and policies have changed so fast that it already seems an age ago.

First came the splitting up of the BPO and the emergence of British Telecom (B.T.) and the Royal Mail as distinct operations with commercial objectives increasingly competitive with each other. Now legislation has changed the face of both and just as private delivery services are now franchised to compete with the Royal Mail, so Mercury (now owned by Cable and Wireless, who were originally one of three shareholders, along with Barclays Bank and British Petroleum) is emerging to compete with B.T. as a carrier. At the same time the monopoly control of peripheral equipment for the PSTN and the supply of exchanges is being liberalized gradually.

The next step in this process is privatization. The sale of B.T. started in October 1984. The government expects to raise about 4 billion pounds from selling 51% of the shares of B.T.

12.1.2

In the following extract two separate articles are mixed. One (**A**) expresses the Trade Unions' anxieties about privatization. The other (**B**) counters these arguments.

Read the extract and sort out the paragraphs (**1**–**8**) into either Article A or Article B:

1 The government was accused of pressing ahead with legislation to deregulate and privatize B.T. in the full knowledge that similar moves in the USA have trebled domestic telephone charges, disrupted telecommunication policy and caused legal and political chaos. This attack is based on a detailed study published recently, *The American Experience*: a report on the dilemma of telecommunications in the USA.

2 The study traces first how the privately owned monopoly American Telephone and Telegraph (AT & T) was forced to allow competitors on its profitable long-distance lines, how government attempts to regulate that competition were unsuccessful, and how AT & T divested itself of its local companies thereby freeing itself from having to subsidize unprofitable local residential users.

3 The report claims that calls will cost 300% more, installation costs will escalate and much of the country will end up with no service at all. It also claims to be 'as carefully researched as any document ever produced by the Trade Union Movement'. This tells us more about the standard of union research than it does about the real American experience.

4 The report traces how 'specialized carriers' were formed in the 1960s to compete with AT & T providing services to companies without assuming the 'common carriage obligation to serve the public in general'. The union committee claims that the specialized carriers represent an exact parallel to Mercury in Britain, which aims to cream off the more profitable inter-city business market.

5 The American Bell system (AT & T) is being broken up to be replaced with less regulation and more competition. Union arguments against this development fall back on the desire to continue to subsidize certain services. The report notes that for many years the Bell system used its monopoly position to overcharge for long-distance calls and use the extra revenues to subsidize the cost of local calls. But the unions are wrong to assume that such subsidies are a good thing, or that they simply ended because Bell lost its monopoly and had to compete.

6 The system had to end. When prices are set far above costs in any market, newcomers are tempted to enter and offer their services. In America, other companies such as MCI (a sort of British Mercury) appeared to provide cheaper long-distance calls than the Bell system. Other companies developed means of bypassing the telephone system altogether, using cable, satellite, cellular radio and paging to provide alternative services, especially for business users. If Bell was to survive in the face of this new competition for its lucrative long-distance calls, it had to cut its costs—which meant the end of the subsidy to local calls.

7 An internal AT & T report suggests that if price increases do double for the basic telephone services, as is now thought likely, the number of rural, very poor households will drop from 73% to 38%. The number of moderately poor people with phones will fall from 79% to 46%.

8 The result of this new technology and competition in America has been to enhance the telephone system even further. For some, costs will rise–but take scare figures of 300% with a pinch of salt. In many parts of America local calls are free so even a modest increase there produces a big percentage rise and is irrelevant to Britain, where local calls already make a profit.

12.2 **Listening 1**

12.2.1

Listen to this extract from a radio discussion about the effects of privatization of B.T. on private industry. As you listen, complete Figure 12b.

Opinions	Government	Tema
a The UK has the most liberal approach to telecommunications outside the US.		
b Liberalization has led to developments in the telecoms industry.		
c The Approvals Board is too slow.		
d The Approvals Board is too expensive.		
e B.T. will be in too strong a position after privatization.		
f Privatization will mean increased foreign competition.		

√ agree × disagree ○ no opinion expressed

Fig 12b

12.2.2

When you have listened once, listen again and find the words or expressions which mean the same as the following:

a free-market, non-government controlled
b additional service
c bureaucratic procedures
d institution/organization
e charges
f understand
g difficult
h enormous
i allow a great and sudden flow
j the responsibilities of
k allow things to continue as they are

12.3 **Language practice**

12.3.1 **Word study 1:** derivatives

Reading 1 and Listening 1 contained several word sets:
e.g. to compete competition competitor competitive

Complete the parts of the table below where you see three dots. You may need to check through Reading 1 and Listening 1 (you can use the tapescript at the back of the book).

	Verb	Abstract noun	Noun agent	Adjective
a	to compete	competition	. . .	competitive
b	to emerge	. . .		emerging
c	. . .	liberalization		. . .
d	. . .	. . .		private
e		politics	. . .	. . .
f	to install	. . .		
g	. . .	profitability		. . .
h	to subsidize	. . .		
i	to legislate	. . .		legislative
j	to approve	. . .		approved
k	to rely	. . .		. . .
l	. . .	. . .		regulative

12.3.2 **Word study 2:** trends and developments

Describing the direction of development:

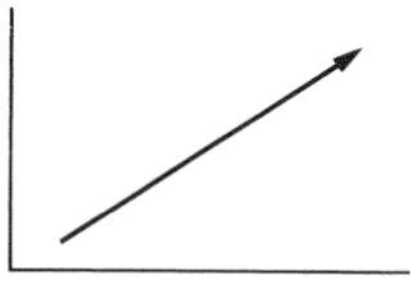

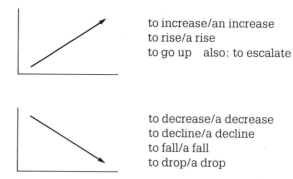

to increase/an increase
to rise/a rise
to go up also: to escalate

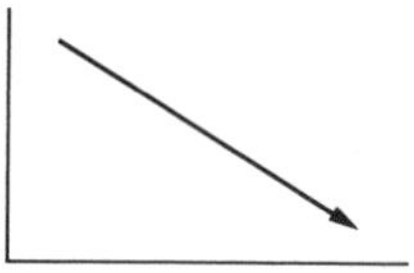

to decrease/a decrease
to decline/a decline
to fall/a fall
to drop/a drop

Describing the rate/speed of development:

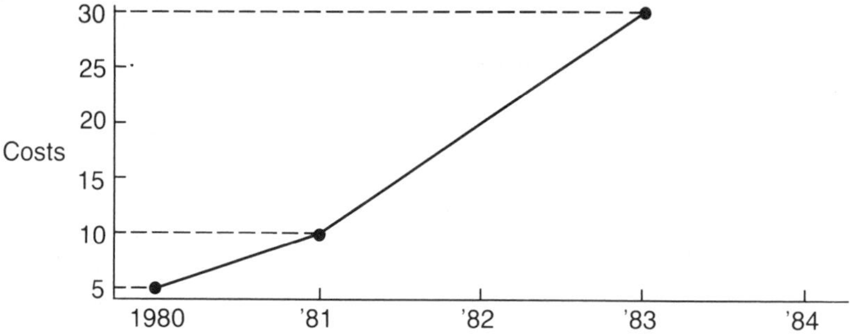

Costs **doubled** in 1980 (5 → 10)
Costs **trebled** between 1981 and 1983 (10 → 30)
Cost increases **speeded up/accelerated** between 1981 and 1983
Cost increases **slowed down** after 1983

Now use the graph below to complete sentences **a–h**:

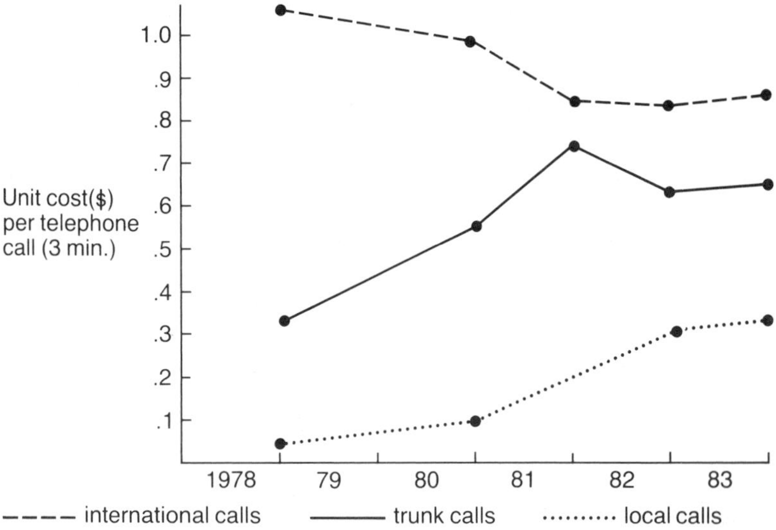

a The cost of local calls . . . in 1981.
b Between '80 and '82 local call charges. . . .
c Trunk call charges . . . dramatically from 0.3 to 0.5 in 1979.
d In the following year the rate of increase . . . .
e In 1982 the cost of trunk calls actually . . . by $0.1.
f International call charges . . . from '78 to '81.
g The decline in international call costs . . . in 1980 and then . . . in '81.
h During 1983 there was no . . . or . . . in the cost of any type of call.

12.4 **Reading 2**

12.4.1

Read the following article which looks at B.T.'s approach to meeting the competition.
As you read, complete Figure 12c.

TELECOMMUNICATIONS

BT set to compete in office

British Telecom is undergoing a slow and painful metamorphosis, from a safe monopoly untroubled by commercial pressures to a competitive organisation. BT Merlin is the latest in a series of commercial ventures launched by BT since the liberalisation of the telecommunications network early in 1981, and shows BT's determination to grab a chunk of the office automation market.

Merlin is the new name for what used to be British Telecom Enterprises' (BTE) Business Products and Services Division. It is also the brand name under which BT is to launch a new range of office automation products this Spring. "We intend to enter the office automation market in a big way and to compete directly with companies such as IBM," said a Merlin spokesman.

The first of these products, a series of communicating micros and word processors, are being made by ICL. BT is also talking to a number of other companies including Plessey and GEC about the supply of products to Merlin.

In its new role as a commercial organisation, BT has made what it calls a "commercial decision" to keep quiet about what other products Merlin has up its sleeve until the official unveiling in March.

The reason behind the creation of Merlin is the forthcoming liberalisation of Call-Connect systems (PABXs), in July of this year. The Business Products and Services Division was responsible for this area with products such as Herald and Monarch.

Merlin's office automation products will be centered around these, particularly Monarch, which is a digital system and therefore can handle data as well as voice. BT is gearing up to compete with other PABX suppliers by launching an office automation range to enhance its existing products.

Merlin reflects the spirit of BTE, which was formed in mid-1981 and described by BT as "our new competitive arm". BTE consists of four divisions, including Merlin. The other three are: Consumer Products and Services, which covers domestic telephone installations; Information Services, which is Prestel and Yellow Pages; and Spectrum which consists of add-on services; Tan, an answering service; and radio paging. All these are areas in which BT will have to compete increasingly as liberalisation proceeds.

Prestel, in particular, has seen the need to increase its domestic user base dramatically as it faces increasing competition in the business market from private videotex systems. It has recently set up two ambitious schemes to create a mass domestic market: Project Y and Club 403, both of which provide a selected group of homes with Prestel sets, either free or heavily subsidised.

Meanwhile, another commercial off-shoot of BT, Martlesham Enterprises, has just announced its first product. The company was formed a year ago in partnership with merchant bankers Lazard Brothers and three other organisations, to exploit spin-off ideas from BT's Martlesham Research Laboratories.

The product is a very specialised new method of making lasers for optical fibre systems and the Massachusetts Institute of Technology has already placed orders for it. Martlesham, like Merlin, is described by BT as "innovative", a word not usually associated with the organisation. It is however, part of a new language which BT is trying hard to adopt. □

Fig 12b

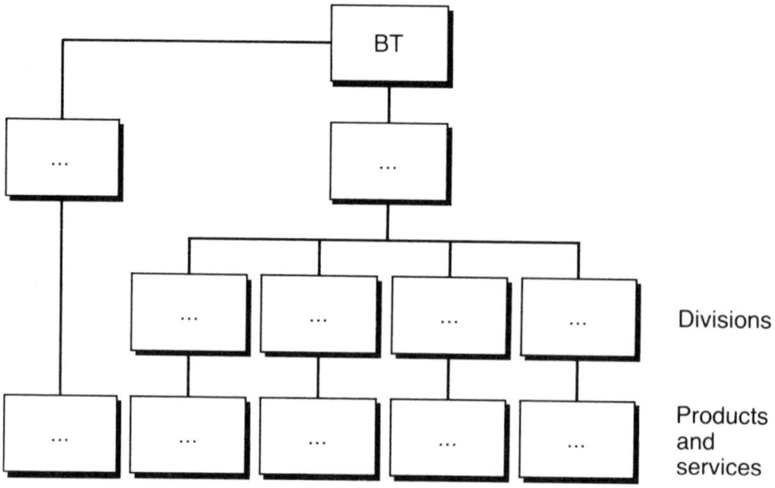

Fig 12c

12.4.2

When you have read the article, find the idiomatic expressions in the article which are visualized in Figure 12d.

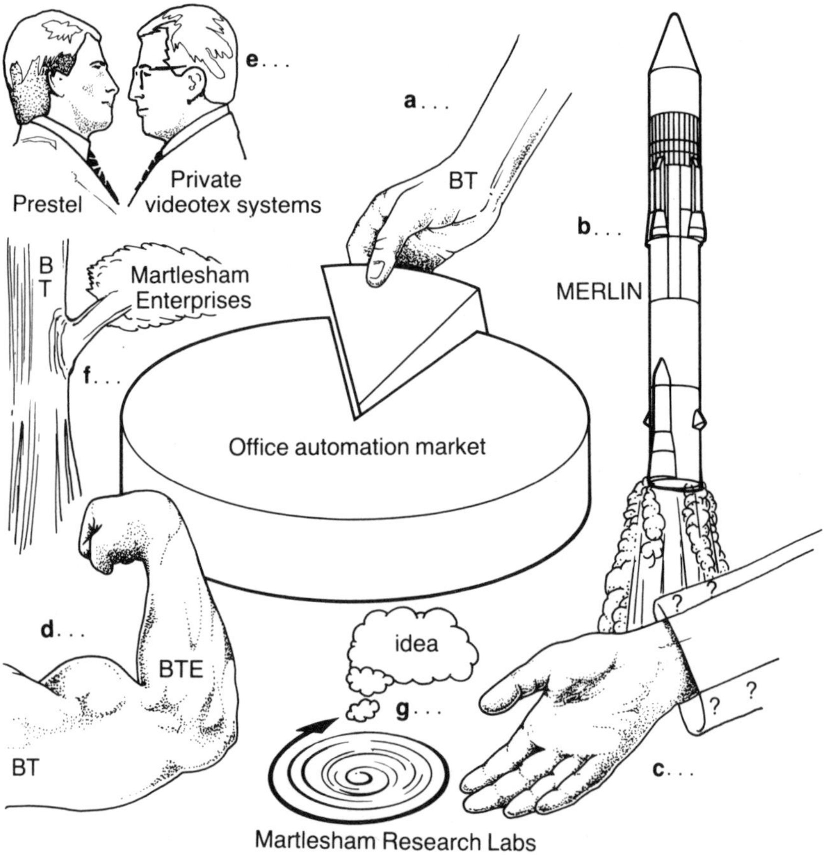

Fig 12d

12.5 Listening 2

12.5.1

In the following extract, you will hear part of a business presentation given in 1982 by a representative of Mercury Communications to a group of industrialists. As you listen, complete Figure 12e.

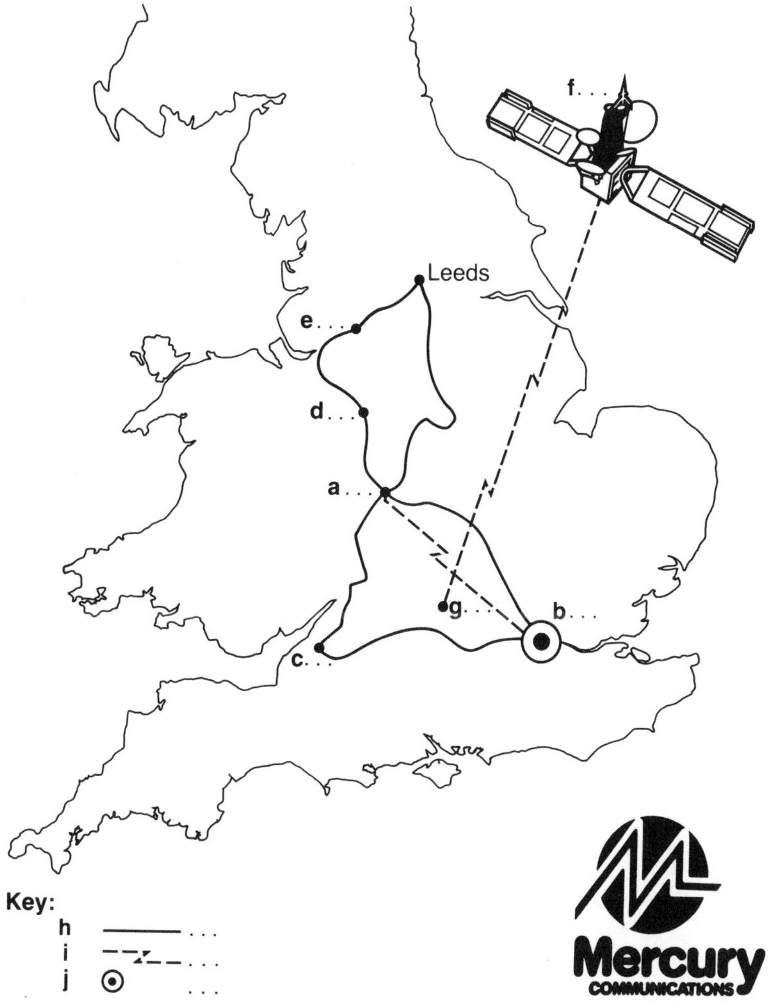

Fig 12e

12.5.2

Now complete the following minutes written by one of the industrialists who attended the presentation:

COMPANY: Mercury Communications
OBJECTIVE: alternative network between **a**) . . .
OWNER: Cable and Wireless
METHOD: Transmission means: **b**) . . . protected by **c**) . . .
Subscriber connection: **d**) . . .
DATE WHEN SERVICE AVAILABLE: **e**) . . .

12.6 Discussion/Role-play

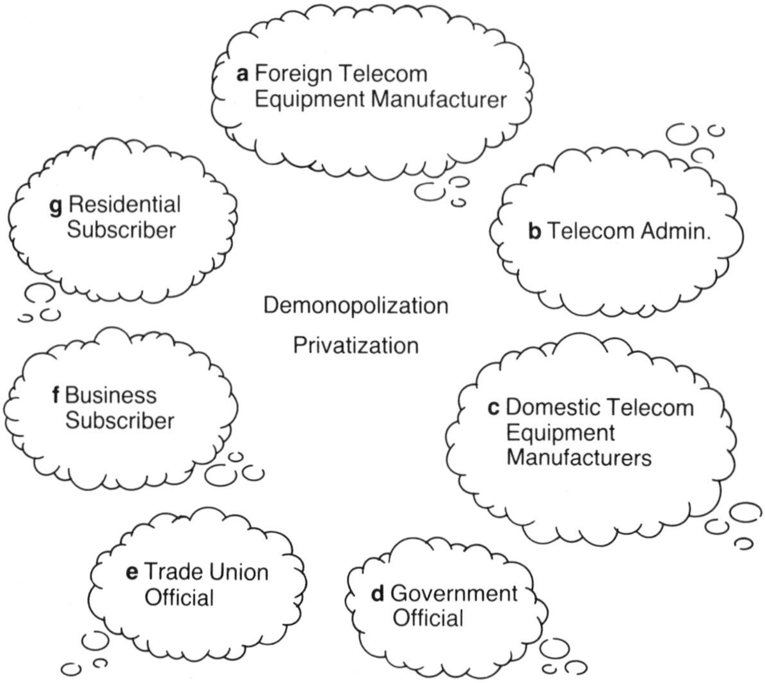

First choose a role (**a**–**g**). Then draw up a list of arguments in favour of or against breaking the monopoly and privatization.
Present these arguments to the group.

12.7 Word list

Marketing

to enter the market p. 155
to launch a product p. 155
to grab a chunk of the market p. 155 to capture market share.
brand name p. 155 name given to product for sales purposes.
domestic user base p. 155 the large residential market.
mass market p. 155 non-specialized, large volume market.
free market p. 209(T) non-government controlled, non-interventionist.
to establish oneself in the market p. 210(T) to get a significant share of the market.
to meet demand p. 210(T)
to meet the competition p. 155

Finance

to raise money p. 151 to get money, e.g. by selling shares.
to subsidize/subsidy p. 151 to support a product or service financially (often from other profitable products or services).
to cream off p. 151 to take the top end, most profitable, of a market.
to overcharge p. 151 to charge more than is profitable.
lucrative p. 152 profitable.
to franchise p. 151 to give permission to another person or company to sell your product or service.

Miscellaneous

peripheral equipment p. 151 terminals etc. (connection on the edge of the network).
to trace p. 151 to follow.
to divest oneself p. 151 to free oneself (of something one doesn't want).
to bypass p. 152 to go around.
to enhance p. 152 to improve.
to unveil p. 155 to uncover (e.g. present a new car which has been hidden by a sheet before launch).
call-connect system p. 155 PABX.
to gear up p. 155 to get ready for.
analogy p. 209(T) a similar case which helps understanding.
to take with a pinch of salt p. 152 not to believe entirely.
wayleaves p. 210(T)
uphill struggle p. 210(T)

Unit 13 **Telecoms in India**

In this unit we look at India and at the problems of developing a telecommunications network in a newly industrialized country.

13.1 **Reading 1**

13.1.1

As you read, complete Figure 13a to show total population and the ratio of rural to urban inhabitants. Also, complete the key to Figure 13b and indicate primary switching centres (pre-1985), and plot the graph in Figure 13c.

1 In 1951 India's population was 361 million. Thirty years later, it was 683 million, a startling increase of almost 90%. In the early 1980s, nearly 80% of the population lived in rural areas, the remaining 20% living in or around the main cities, Madras, Calcutta, Bombay and Delhi.
2 By the year 2000 there are likely to be 40 cities in India with a population of over one million and a projected 35% of the total population of around 1 000 million will be living in urban areas.

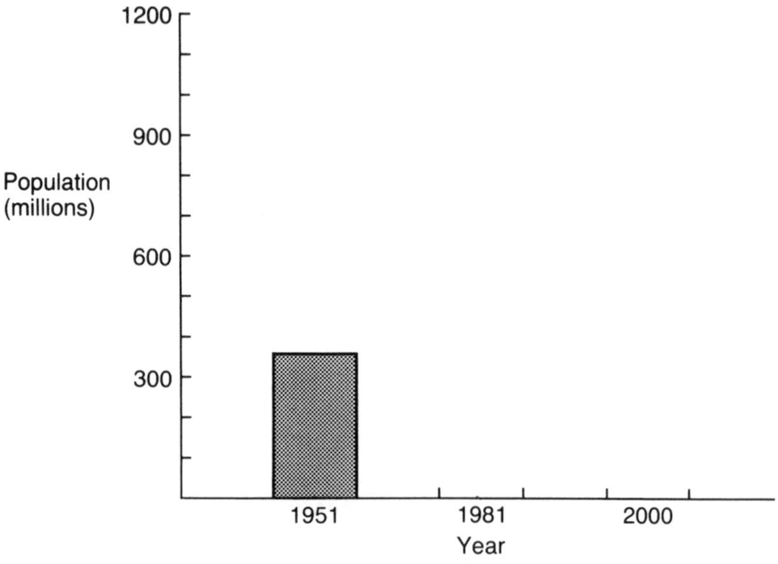

Fig 13a Population of India

3 The Indian Government's 6th Economic Plan, covering the period 1980–85, estimated that by the year 1985 there would be 45 million people unemployed, most of whom would be unskilled. Like most developing nations India is having to invest primarily in educating and training its youth rather than in job creation.

4 At the same time, however, India is one of the fifteen most industrialized nations in the world. She is a member of the group of non-aligned nations and also has close links with East and West. The USSR has provided a lot of heavy technology for Indian industry, while in the field of telecoms agreements have been signed with, for example, France. The latter provides for co-operation on the E10 exchange, notably the building of several factories in India for production of the latest high-technology equipment.

5 When India gained independence in 1947, there were only about 100 000 telephone lines in the whole country, together with 321 exchanges. This limited service had been designed to meet the needs of the colonizing power and no more.

6 Finding this situation unacceptable, the Indian government decided to embark on a series of five-year economic plans which, of course, included developing a better telephone network. In 1982 there were almost 2 400 000 telephones in India, but the population by then was over 700 million, which meant there was only one line for every 300 inhabitants. By comparison, Sweden and the US have almost one per inhabitant.

7 The main problems facing Indian economic planners have been the scarcity of resources and the size of the country and, above all, of its population. Allocating the budget between a large number of equally important projects, only some of which can be funded, and then only in part, is a classic problem faced by countries that have had a history of colonialism.

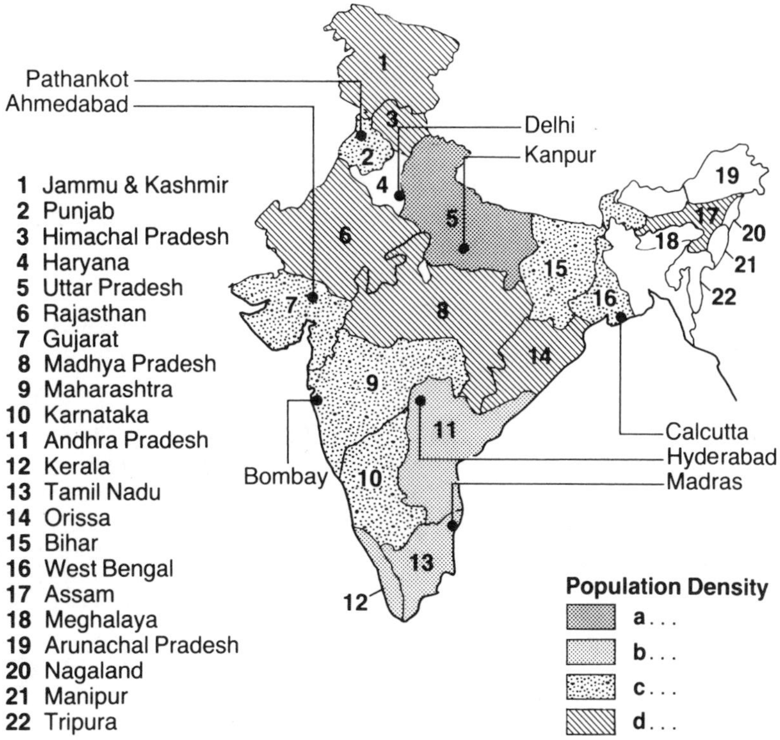

Fig 13b

8 If we look at the present state of the rural network in India, we can see that in the states of Himachal Pradesh, Madhya Pradesh, Orissa, Jammu and Kashmir, Assam and Rajasthan, eight out of ten villages have a population of less than 1 000 people. States like Bihar, Punjab, Karnataka, Maharashtra, Gujarat and West Bengal have varying densities depending on whether the farmland has access to water. In the southern states of Andhra Pradesh, Tamil Nadu and Kerala there are virtually no small or medium-sized villages, for the entire population is distributed in about 1 300 villages, each with a population of between two and ten thousand. At the other extreme, a state like Uttar Pradesh has a population of more than 100 million.
9 Out of the 600 000 villages in India, only about 15 000 had access to a telephone set in 1982. In fact, rural subscribers represent only 10% of the total number of subscribers.
10 Until 1976 the rural network suffered greatly from financial limitations as it has always been more profitable to install telephones in towns. Since 1977 an effort has been made to improve the service. The extra expense is justified in terms of the economic development of these country areas.
11 Looking at the urban and suburban areas, there are four main switching centres. These are situated, as might be expected, in the four main towns. By 1985 it is hoped that there will be 40 primary switching centres and more than 300 secondary centres throughout the country, connecting a total of four million lines. In India's main towns there are approximately three lines for every hundred inhabitants, while in the country there are about three lines for every thousand. By 1990 it is hoped that there will be ten million sets in the country.
12 The Indian P and T Department has outlined its main objectives for 1990 as follows:

- the completion of the intercity network between all towns with more than 50 000 inhabitants.
- the implementation of an automatic service between all the exchanges in each of the country's 300 secondary zones
- the elimination of all outstanding telex demands
- the provision of at least one telephone within five kilometres of any inhabited locality
- the extension of the network to ten million lines.

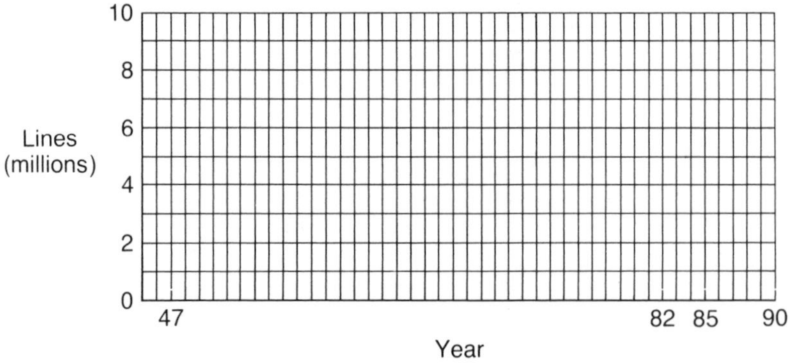

Fig 13c

13.1.2

Read through the text again quickly and place each paragraph (**1–12**) under one of the following headings:

a Demography **b** Industrialization **c** Telephone density
d Economic and telecommunication planning.

13.2 Listening 1

Listen to the interview in which George Haan, a personnel consultant, is talking to Ramesh Khan about recruitment and training in the Indian P & T. As you listen, complete Figure 13d.

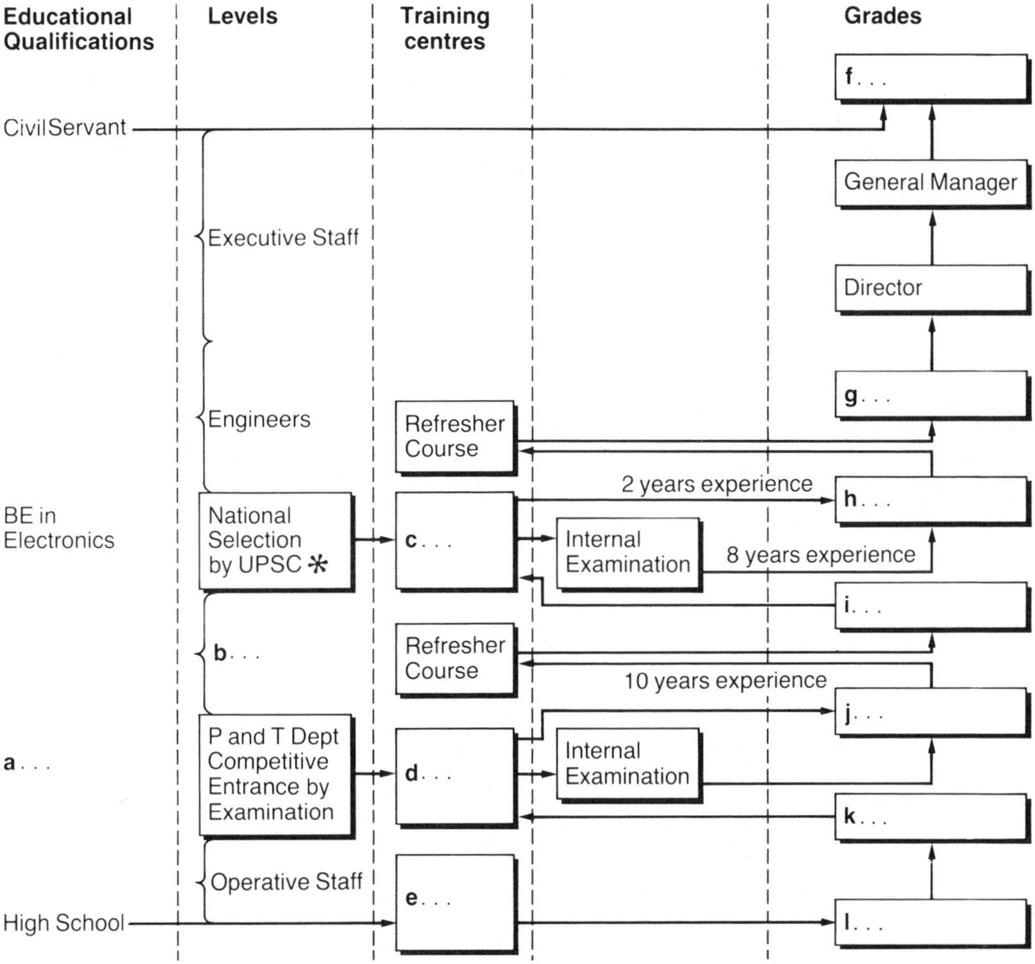

* = Union Public Service Commission, a State Body, which defines the conditions for recruitment.

Fig 13d Recruitment and training in the Indian Posts and Telegraphs department

13.3 Language practice

13.3.1 **Word study:** derivatives

Complete the table below:

1 agree	. . .		**11** implement	. . .	
2 allocate	. . .		**12** improve	. . .	
3 . . .	benefit		**13** invest	. . .	
4 collaborate	. . .		**14** . . .	maintenance	
5 complete	. . .		**15** produce	. . .	
6 . . .	co-operation		**16** promote	. . .	
7 develop	. . .		**17** provide	. . .	
8 eliminate	. . .		**18** . . .	recruitment	
9 . . .	estimate		**19** spend	. . .	
10 extend	. . .		**20** . . .	training	

Now complete the passage with words from the list above.

We have been **a** . . . a budget of £50 000 on the understanding that we **b** . . . our profitability. Any **c** . . . in profitability will only come if we can reach an **d** . . . with the trade unions about manning levels. The budget **e** . . . will be largely **f** . . . on **g** . . . in new machinery. One reason for this is that **h** . . . costs for our existing equipment are extremely high. We also plan to **i** . . . our present building so that we can **j** . . . better working conditions for our office staff. An additional five office staff have recently been **k** . . . .

13.3.2 **Written and spoken language**

Reading 1 presents typical written language—it is impersonal and distanced. Let us imagine changing Reading 1 from a written text to a speech given by an Indian P & T representative. Complete the spoken forms on the right.

Written	**Spoken**
There are likely to be 40 cities in India . . .	We are likely to have . . .
a By the year 1985 there will be 45 million . . .	. . .
b Agreements have been signed with France . . .	. . .
c There were only about 100 000 telephones . . .	. . .
d Finding this situation unacceptable, the . . .	. . .
e Since 1977, an effort has been made to . . .	. . .
f By 1985, it is hoped that there will be 40 . . .	. . .
g The Indian P & T has outlined its objectives as follows:	. . .
the completion of the intercity network . . .	We aim to/must complete . . .

Written	**Spoken**
h the implementation of an automatic service . . .	. . .
i the elimination of all outstanding telex demands . . .	. . .
j the provision of at least one telephone within five kilometres . . .	. . .
k the extension of the network to . . .	. . .

13.4 **Reading 2**

Read the text about Research and Development in the Indian P and T Department. As you read, complete Figures 13e and 13f.

Rather than taking the easy route of importing equipment, the Indians prefer to purchase know-how and technology so as to start manufacturing locally. Even more significantly, in many cases the products coming out of Indian factories have been locally designed and developed, and even the systems manufactured under licence have been adapted to the needs of the Indian network. To take an example, India produces a transformed version of the Pentaconta crossbar switching system. Compared to the original model, certain mechanical components have been improved and design modifications have been made to suit different approaches to traffic handling and maintenance. The first exchange of this sort was commissioned in 1978, and preparations are well under way for volume production at a rate of 200,000 lines of equipment per year. Similarly, Indian researchers and engineers developed an experimental Stored Program Control switching system (SPC 1) as early as 1974. They have also recently developed an 8 Mbit/s optical fibre transmission system.

These examples clearly demonstrate the Indian commitment to developing and manufacturing products locally, but without excluding recourse to foreign technologies. This policy would hardly be feasible without the country's impressive research and development resources.

The Telecommunication Research Centre (TRC), established in 1956 in Delhi with a team of 20 engineers and researchers, has played an important role in helping to achieve the aims mentioned above. It now has a total staff of almost 500 engineers and researchers and covers a wide spectrum of design and development activities. Apart from helping to adapt equipment manufactured under licence to local conditions, the TRC has independently developed systems for the Indian network. It is pursuing a major programme of research on new techniques and technologies, especially in electronic switching, digital data communication and transmission systems using microwave, satellites and optical fibres.

During the period 1980–85, it was allocated a budget of some Rs. 50 Crores.

Finally, the Technical and Development Circle (TDC), which has its headquarters at Jabalpur, tests telephone and trunk installations of all types (crossbar, Strowger, manual) as well as different transmission systems (coaxial cable, microwave, PCM and open-wire carriers) purchased by the P and T Department from the main Indian manufacturers, Indian Telephone Industries (ITI), Hindustan Cables Ltd and Hindustan Teleprinters Ltd. It also carries out development and design work which is not performed at the TRC.

Rs. 14 Crores were allocated to the TDC to meet its requirements in instruments and equipment for the 1980–85 period.

	R & D establishment	Location	2 main activities	Budget 80–85
1				
2				

Fig 13e R & D Establishments in India

Given the vast land area that India covers, there will also be a need to develop satellite-based telecommunications, and in order to begin providing satisfactory communication circuits to remote areas of the country, a quarter transponder was rented from the INTELSAT organization. India's first earth station was built at Arvi towards the end of the 1960s and seven others quickly followed, at Delhi, Madras, Leh, Aijal, Andaman and the Nicobar Islands (off the east coast of the country) (2) and at Lakshdeweep in the Laccadive Islands (off the west coast of the country).

The success of this experiment prompted the Indian P and T Department to design its own series of satellites, INSAT or Indian National Satellites, which now provide three services nationwide: telecommunications, meteorology and TV broadcasting. Five experimental satellites have been launched, three of which were manufactured locally.

The total INSAT network will be made up of 31 earth stations, five at main area locations (the four main cities plus Shillong), eight at primary area locations and fifteen at remote area locations. The three remaining earth stations are all transportable, two by air or road and one by road. They can be moved to any place where communication is badly needed during an emergency and can be set up at short notice.

The total cost of the INSAT operation will be about Rs. 120 Crores.

The INSAT scheme has also been designed to cater for one third of the total circuit requirement on the four main intercity routes: Delhi–Bombay, Delhi–Madras, Madras–Calcutta and Calcutta–Delhi. This will mean that more routes will become available over the traditional land links.

NB 1 Crore = 10 million Rs. 10 Crores = 100 million rupees.

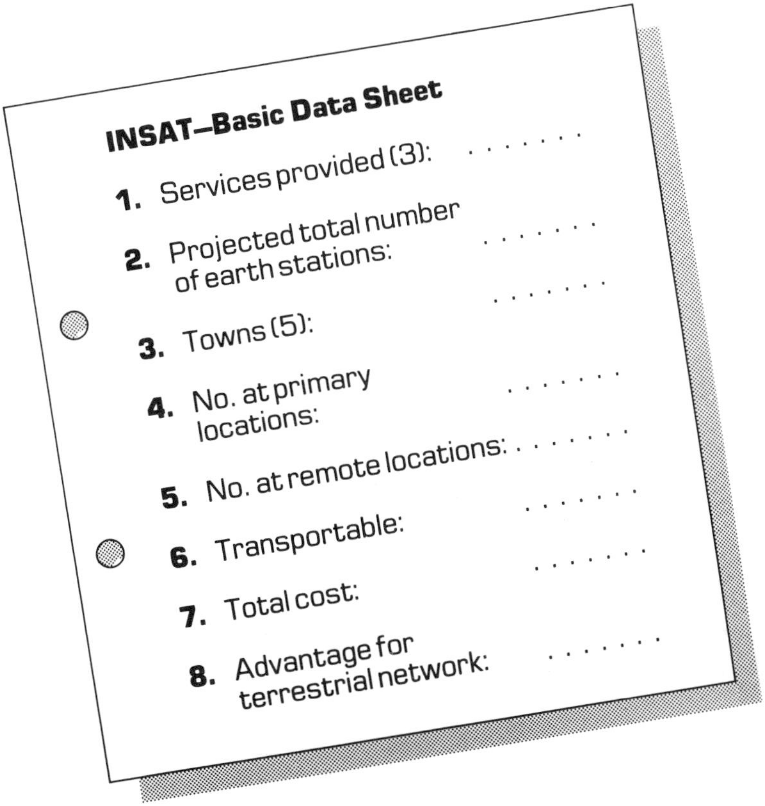

INSAT–Basic Data Sheet
1. Services provided (3): . . . .
2. Projected total number of earth stations: . . . .
3. Towns (5): . . . .
4. No. at primary locations: . . . .
5. No. at remote locations: . . . .
6. Transportable: . . . .
7. Total cost: . . . .
8. Advantage for terrestrial network: . . . .

Fig 13f

13.5 **Listening 2**

As you listen to the following discussion between three engineers, complete Figures 13g and 13h.

Contract	Details
1	
2	
3	
4	

Fig 13g

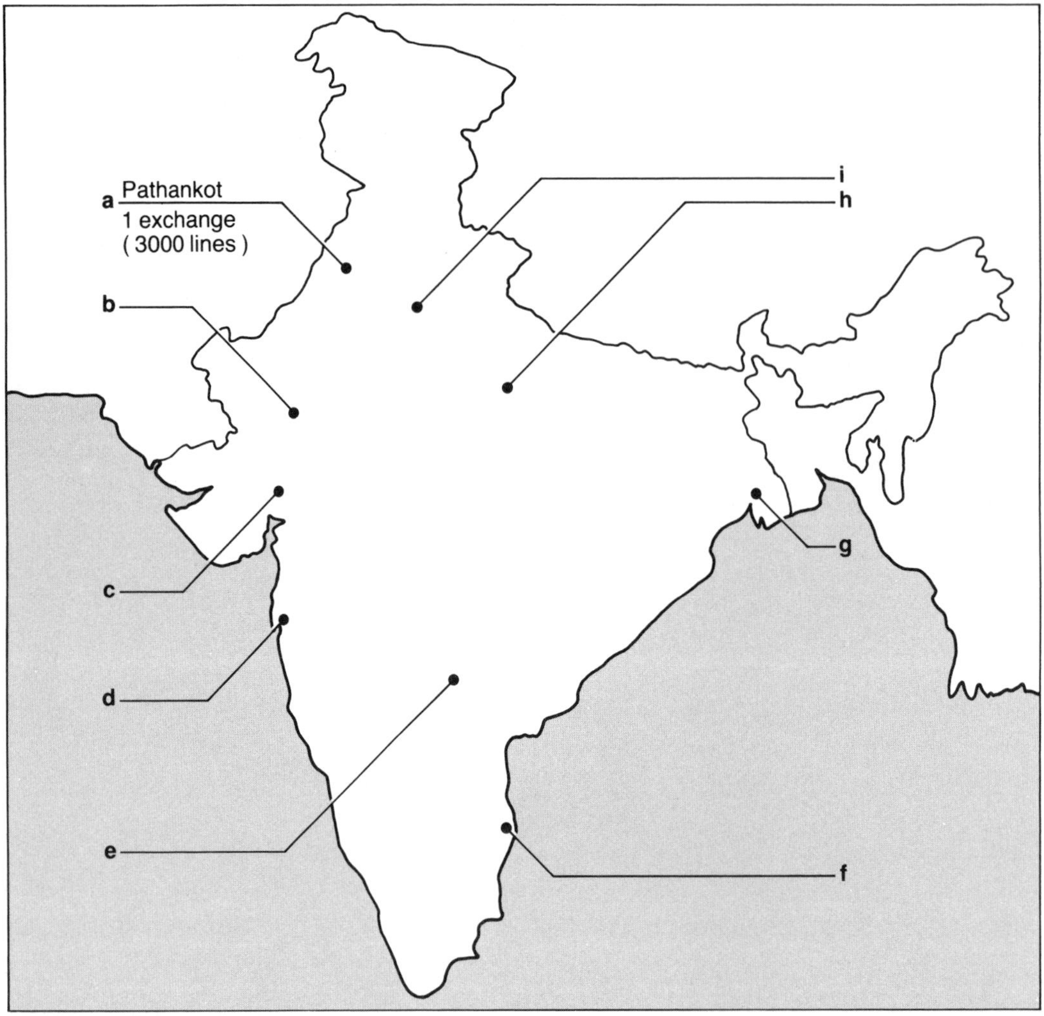

Complete the following table:

Town	**No of lines**	**No of E 10 exchanges**
a PATHANKOT	3000	1
b RAJASTHAN	3000	1
c		
d		
e		
f		
g		
h		
i		

Fig 13h

13.6 Discussion

a Discuss the following factors influencing the development of a telecommunications system: demography; politics; geography; finance; job creation; climate; national priorities; import policies. How do these factors affect your country? Compare your country with India from the telecommunications point of view.

b Are technology transfer schemes like the one between France and India really beneficial for both countries? Is your country involved in any such schemes?

c Compare recruitment and training in your telecom administration or company with the Indian system.

13.7 Word List

Planning and economics

five-year plan p. 161
civil servants p. 163 employee of government or state agency.
unemployed p. 160 out of work.
to outline the objectives p. 162
technology transfer p. 211(T)
decision maker p. 211(T)
growth area p. 210(T)

Training

initial training p. 210(T)
recruitment pattern p. 210(T)
promotion ladder p. 210(T)
rung (of a ladder) p. 210(T) grade.
to take on new recruits p. 210(T)
background p. 210(T)
to gain experience p. 210(T)
in-house training p. 210(T) internal training.
to acquire expertise p. 211(T)
a refresher course p. 211(T)

Miscellaneous

rural area p. 160
urban area p. 160
know-how p. 165

Unit 14 Telecoms in Sweden

This unit looks at telecommunications in another country—Sweden. It focuses on the organization of the industry.

14.1 Reading 1

14.1.1

Read the following description of Swedish Telecom and complete the organigram in Figure 14a.

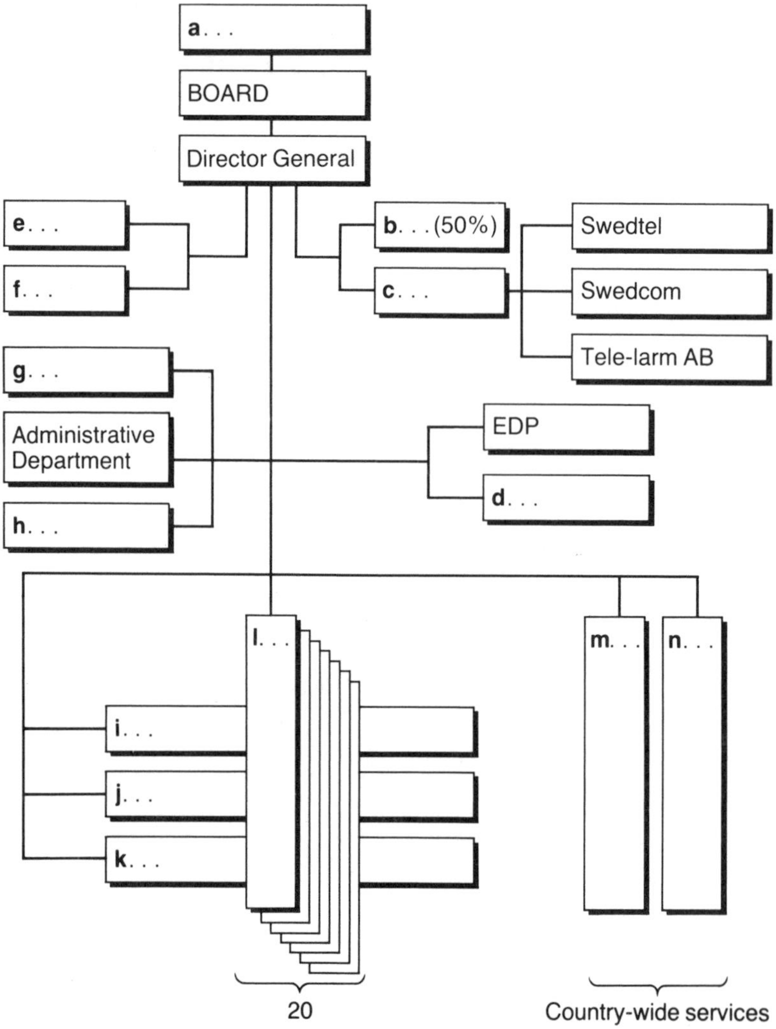

Fig 14a

Swedish Telecom is a state-owned public utility, operating on a commercial basis.

Swedish Telecom comes under the Ministry of Transport and Communications. All commercial public utilities such as the State Railways, Postal Administration and Civil Aviation Administration are headed in their respective fields by a Director General and a Board and their administrative, financial and technical affairs are separate from the Ministry. Some important principles underlying the organization of Swedish Telecom itself are given below.

1 Decentralization
The operational activities mainly take place in the twenty local 'telecommunications areas'. About 32 000 of the total 43 000 employees work in the 'areas', leaving about 4 000 at Headquarters level, and the rest distributed between other divisions.

2 Result orientation
Each of these areas are result-oriented units (profit centres), which have their own budgets and the responsibility for contributing to the surplus which Swedish Telecom is supposed to provide for the government.

3 Functional units
Nationwide functional staff units with matrix responsibility, namely the Marketing, Network and Materials Departments support the primary geographical units. The Network Department follows the allocation of investment in the national network; the Marketing Department has an overall view of the total income of the services. The Materials Department makes sure that the tied-up capital is minimized and includes the Central Store and Purchasing function.

The functional Service Units at H.Q. level are the Financial, Administrative and Technical Departments. Other such units are the EDP (Electronic data processing) and Management Services Department.

At HQ level there is another set of functions to help Swedish Telecom meet its responsibilities. Close to the Director General there is the Long-term Planning Unit working with aspects of strategic planning and the Internal Auditing function.

There are two country-wide services: the Industrial Division (TELI), which manufactures much of Swedish Telecom's own equipment including exchanges and telephone sets, and the Radio Division, which is responsible for transmitting radio and TV programmes and also maintenance and operation of radio links, maritime, aeronautical and other radio services.

Finally, Swedish Telecom set up Telinvest AB in 1981 to own and administer the share capital of subsidiary companies such as Swedtel and Swedcom (both consultancy companies) and Tele-Larm AB (dealing with the installation and marketing of alarm and security systems).

One other major joint venture is worth noting. This is ELLEMTEL, controlled equally by Swedish Telecom and Sweden's major telecommunications supplier, Ericsson. This company is engaged in research, design and development and is most well-known for the development of Sweden's digital exchange system—AXE.

14.1.2

Match functions/responsibilities with departments/divisions/ companies:

1	Rationalization and reorganization	**a**	Management Services
2	Operation and maintenance of telephone lines	**b**	Telecommunications area
		c	Materials Department
3	5-year national digitalization plan	**d**	Radio Division
4	Sales promotion of a new PBX	**e**	Marketing Department
5	Ground to air communication	**f**	Network Department
6	Advice on turnkey project in developing country	**g**	Industrial Division
		h	Tele-Larm AB
7	Manufacture of telephone sets	**i**	Swedtel
8	Research on new fibre-optic cable	**j**	ELLEMTEL
9	Marketing burglar alarm systems		
10	Central stock control		

14.2 **Listening 1**

14.2.1

In the following extract you will hear a representative of ELLEMTEL talking to some visitors at their laboratories in Älvsjö, just outside Stockholm.

Fig 14b

As you listen, match the acronyms on the left with their meanings on the right.

Ellemtel research projects

1 AXE	**a** very large scale integrated circuits
2 AXB 30	**b** printed circuit board testing
3 AXB 20	**c** digital exchange system
4 DIAVOX	**d** computer language
5 LSI circuits	**e** data communication system
6 PLEX	**f** telephone set
7 VLSI circuits	**g** telex exchange system
8 ISDN conversion	**h** integrated services digital network
9 PCB testing	**i** large scale integrated circuits

14.2.2 Writing task

Organize the following sentences and parts of sentences into a paragraph explaining the benefits of a small independent R & D unit.

a One reason is that routine technical work on established systems . . .
b offers a less bureaucratic and more creative environment to work in.
c These three factors contribute to a shorter time lapse . . .
d . . . from production and from administration.
e . . . can be separated from research into entirely new products.
f . . . thus eliminating duplication of work on similar research programmes.
g Another reason is that a smaller company devoted exclusively to development work . . .
h There are several reasons for separating research and development work . . .
i Finally the technical resources and expertise of the parent companies are merged . . .
j . . . between an idea being conceived and a marketable product emerging.

14.3 Language practice

14.3.1 Describing an organigram

A: Structure

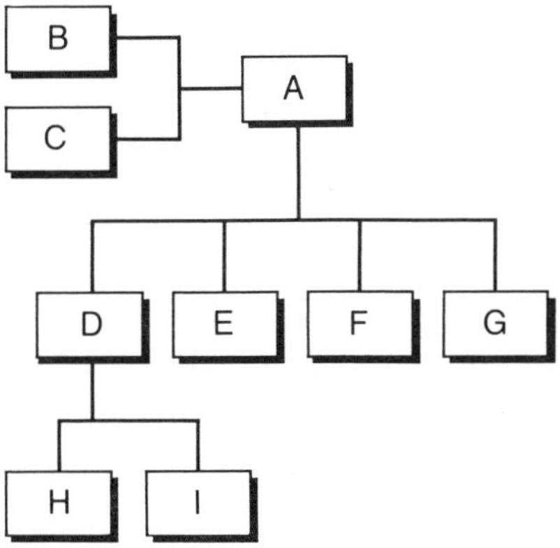

The company is headed by A
D,E,F,G report to A
Over/Above D,E,F,G is A
Under/Below A are D,E,F,G
Close to A, there are two departments B & C
B & C support A
A is supported/backed up by B & C
D is split into H & I
D is broken down into H & I.

B: Functions

A is in charge of . . .
A is responsible for . . .
D has responsibility for . . .
E is engaged in . . .
F is involved in . . .
G controls/is in control of . . .

Now use Figure 14c to complete the description of the marketing department.

MARKETING DEPARTMENT

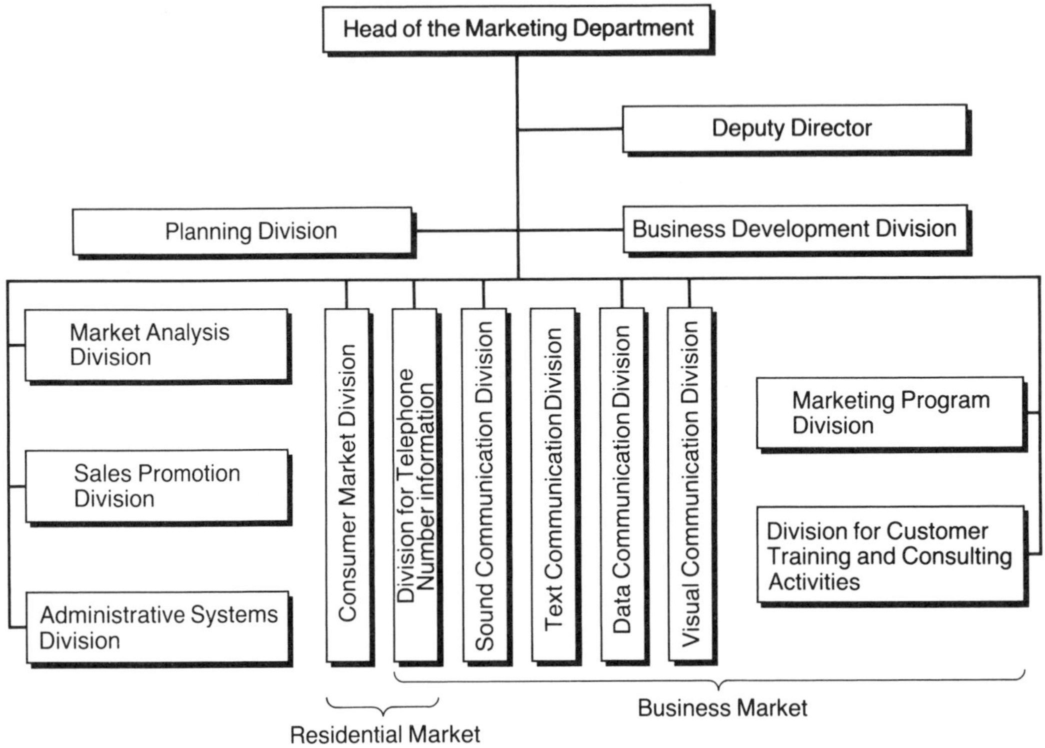

Fig 14c

In the Marketing Department there are **a** . . . product-based divisions which **b** . . . the Head of the Department. These six divisions **c** . . . into residential market and business market sectors. The two residential sector divisions have **d** . . . marketing products and services in this sector and for telephone number information. The other four product divisions **e** . . . according to medium. So there is one division each **f** . . . of sound, text, data and visual communication.
g . . . the Head of the Department, there is a Deputy Director who shares management **h** . . . with the Head. The Head is also **i** . . . two functional staff units—planning and business development.
The six product divisions are **j** . . . three divisions with **k** . . . market analysis, sales promotion and administrative systems. The business market divisions **l** . . . two additional services: Marketing Programs which **m** . . . in developing marketing campaigns for particular products and another division **n** . . . customer training and consulting.

14.3.2 Dealing with visitors

Welcoming
Welcome to . . .
I'm very glad to see you here at . . .
First, let me take this opportunity to welcome you . . .
Starting the tour
Let's take a look at . . .
Shall we walk round (the factory) . . .
I won't say any more. Let's see it in action . . .
Moving on
Shall we move on?
Could you come this way, please?
Pointing things out
Here you can see . . .
You might be interested in . . .
Keeping to time-limits
I'm sorry. We'll have to move on.
Time's running out . . .

Now listen to Listening 1 again and pick out the expressions used to do the following:

Welcome the visitors:
a . . .
Start the tour:
b . . .
Moving on:
c . . .
Pointing things out:
d . . .
e . . .
Keeping to time limits:
f . . .

14.4 Reading 2

14.4.1

The text below studies the reasons for Swedish Telecom's success as a national telecommunications administration.

As you read, decide where to place the following illustrative graphs/ tables in Figures 14d, e, f, g, h, i. (They can only be placed at the end of paragraphs and each illustration can only be used once.)

1 At the heart of Swedish Telecom's success is a highly saturated market. With a system size of more than 7 million telephones, the Swedish network is only a quarter of the size of the UK's, but Sweden has a telephone penetration of 850 telephones per 1 000 inhabitants compared with the UK's 550, and has recently overtaken the US as the country with the highest telephone density.

2 The reason for the Swedish success lies largely in the opportunities resulting from the highly penetrated market. Limited residual growth and low fault incidence has meant that the Swedes have recently been able to combine telephone area engineering installation and maintenance groups, pooling skills to make the best use of staff resources. This also results in increased job satisfaction, but is probably only viable in heavily-penetrated telephone networks where installation and maintenance work needs are low.
3 The delegation of responsibility for economy and performance to small groups has brought about a dynamic 'Productivity Results Scheme' (PRS) involving all local staff.
4 PRS allows Swedish Telecom to assess staff productivity in defined 'result units' and pay them according to their combined achievement. Result units are both geographical and functional with functions cross-related so that engineering wages can be affected by the performance of sales staff and vice-versa. The final productivity assessment takes account of many factors including customer service, quality of service, manpower performance and financial measurements such as improvements in the ratio of income to expenditure.
5 PRS relies on close co-operation from Swedish Telecom's 43 000-strong work-force as well as the three trade unions. Staff consultation is achieved through works councils at all levels which consider a wide range of issues including working environment, work organization and personnel management activities in general. Pay is negotiated centrally every year and a sum of money is allocated to each Telephone Area, but the Telephone Area Director has some freedom to negotiate adjustments to this with union branches locally.
6 Swedish Telecom has taken full advantage of the relatively stable environment in which it operates to increase efficiency and keep costs down. But in future, the company faces problems, particularly in relation to plant replacement. Existing plant, largely step-by-step or crossbar exchanges, has now largely been written off. Swedish tariffs are cheap because current account costs, especially depreciation and interest charges, are low, but now that the company is entering the electronic age, concern is growing about how it will finance future investment and replace this ageing equipment. Swedish Telecom has been largely self-financing in recent years but current funds are not sufficient to meet capital requirements for the era of digital telecommunications. As a temporary measure, Parliament has extended Swedish Telecom's revolving credit by 800 million Kronor.
7 Because the market is so well-penetrated, there is little scope for adding more subscribers to the network. The extra revenue to support increased investment will therefore fall on existing customers—either by encouraging greater telephone use or by tariff increases. Recognizing this, Swedish Telecom is promoting supplementary subscriber apparatus and stimulating higher calling rates through its marketing department which has chosen the residential sector as its prime target.
8 All calls used to be charged at the same rate throughout the day, but to encourage greater use of the telephone, Swedish Telecom has introduced an evening cheap rate period as well as at weekends and on public holidays. It has also started a special peak rate tariff during the morning to minimize use at that time.

9 Swedish Telecom is also relying on the expansion of growth areas such as data communication and the development of new products and services to consolidate its current healthy situation and ensure its future prosperity. The growing need for data communication is reflected in the number of modems installed, which has recently increased at a rate of 30 per cent per annum.
10 With a long history of co-operation between Swedish Telecom and Ericsson, telecoms in Sweden is much more closely and vertically integrated than in many countries. Indeed, Teli, the industrial division, often manufactures equipment for Ericsson on a sub-contract basis when production capacity is over-stretched.
11 Swedish Telecom's efficient organization, its background of success and stability, augur well for the next generation and place it in a good position to meet the challenges that lie ahead.

Leading countries as regards telephone density

Telephones per 1,000 inhabitants

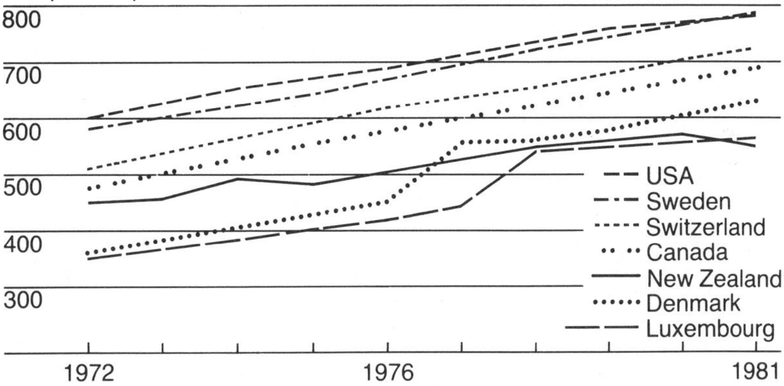

Source: Yearbook of Common Carrier Telecommunication Statistics Genève 1981 (ITU)

Fig 14d

Sales of subscriber lines

Index (1972/73=100)

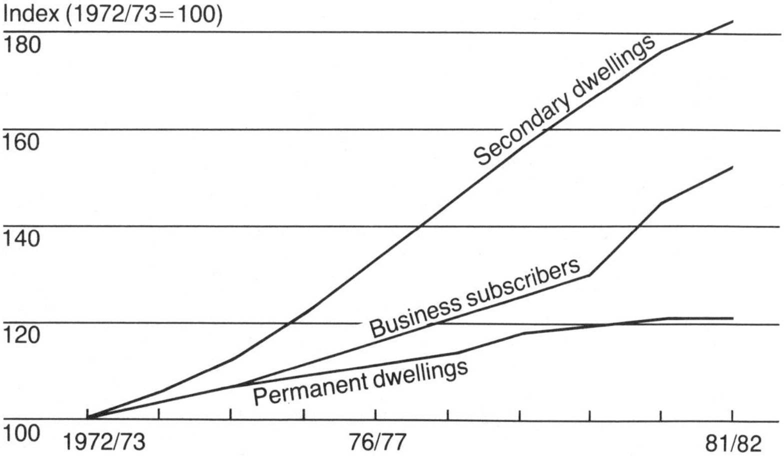

Fig 14e

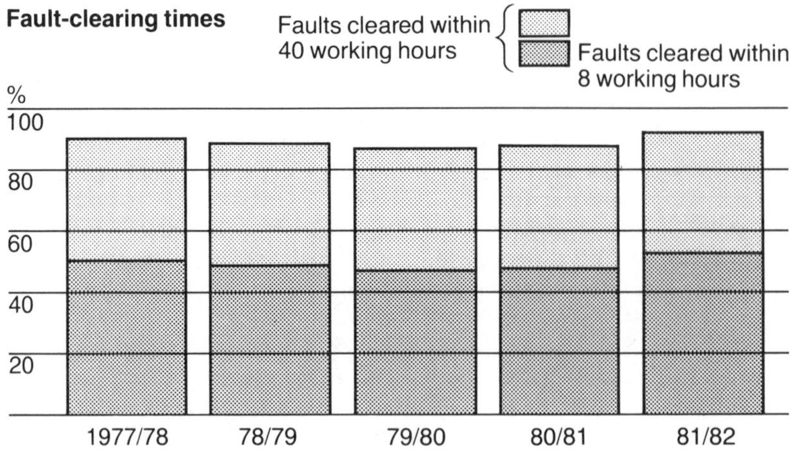

Fig 14f

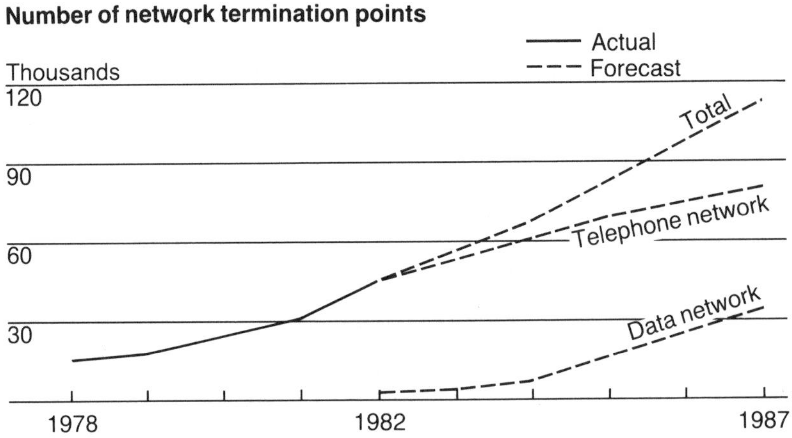

Fig 14g

Metered charge unit and rate/minute

Approx. distance \ Time	Weekdays 08-12	Weekdays 12-18	Weekdays 18-08 / Sat. Sun. holidays
Trunk call Max. 45 km	36 sec. 35 öre	45 sec. 27 öre	60 sec. 20 öre
Trunk call 45-90 km	19 sec. 65 öre	24 sec. 50 öre	32 sec. 38 öre
Trunk call 90-180 km	12 sec. 100 öre	15 sec. 80 öre	21 sec. 58 öre
Trunk call 180-270 km	10 sec. 120 öre	12 sec. 100 öre	18 sec. 67 öre
Trunk call More than 270 km	8 sec. 150 öre	10 sec. 120 öre	16 sec. 75 öre
Local call, i.e. call within one's own area	6 min. 20 öre		12 min. 20 öre

Fig 14h

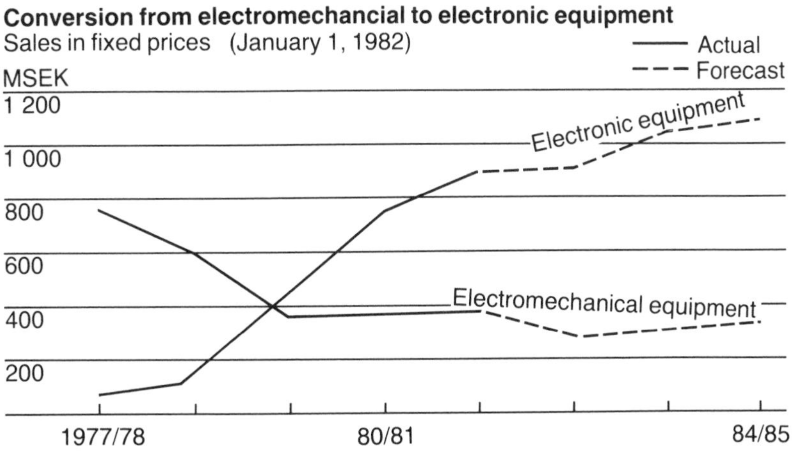

Fig 14i

14.4.2

To produce a summary of 14.4.1, place the following sentences under the following 4 headings: **1** Market, **2** Personnel/Productivity, **3** Financing, **4** Conclusions.

a Sweden has the most densely saturated telephone market in the world. (850 per 1 000.)
b Income has been maximized by introducing a 3-tier call charge rate.
c Low residual growth has meant it has been possible to pool installation and maintenance skills in the telephone areas.
d In the future, the company faces problems particularly in relation to plant replacement.
e For this reason, future growth can only come from promoting supplementary subscriber equipment (e.g. in second houses) and higher call rates in the residential sector.
f Involvement of staff has also increased since the start of a Productivity Results Scheme which relates pay to combined achievement.
g In the business sector, Swedish Telecom is relying on expansion in data communication.
h Swedish telecom's close co-operation with Ericsson ensures a very well-integrated telecom industry.
i This has resulted in greater job satisfaction.
j PRS is backed up by staff consultation in works councils which consider all aspects of staff working conditions.
k This factor, plus its own efficient organization, should ensure a bright future.
l Although Swedish Telecom has been self-financing recently, it is thought that current funds will not be sufficient to meet capital requirements and therefore credit has been extended to 800 million SEK.

14.5 Listening 2

14.5.1

In this extract you are going to hear a discussion between a representative of Teleskolan, Swedish Telecom's training centre, and a visiting administrator from the national telecommunications administration of a developing country.
They are discussing training courses aimed to transfer Swedish know-how to the developing world.

As you listen, complete the table below:

Title of course	Location	Length of course	Course dates	Type of participant	Course objectives & content
1					
2					
3					

14.5.2

Use the completed table and the following notes to write up the visitor's report on his return home. Use complete sentences.

Introduction

Benefits of Swedish Telecom training: experience (technical/managerial)
experience (manufacturing)

Advantages of courses vs. study visits.

Courses

See table.

Conclusion

IPTM course—too high level for our administration
Digital Networks—useful course, but wrong time of year (national holidays in June)
Opman—very useful—practical (field experience)

Recommendation

Send 2 middle-managers on Opman in August.

14.6 Discussion

In this unit several factors have been put forward as reasons for an efficient and profitable telecoms administration. The figure below illustrates these factors. Discuss the relative significance of these factors and any others which occur to you.

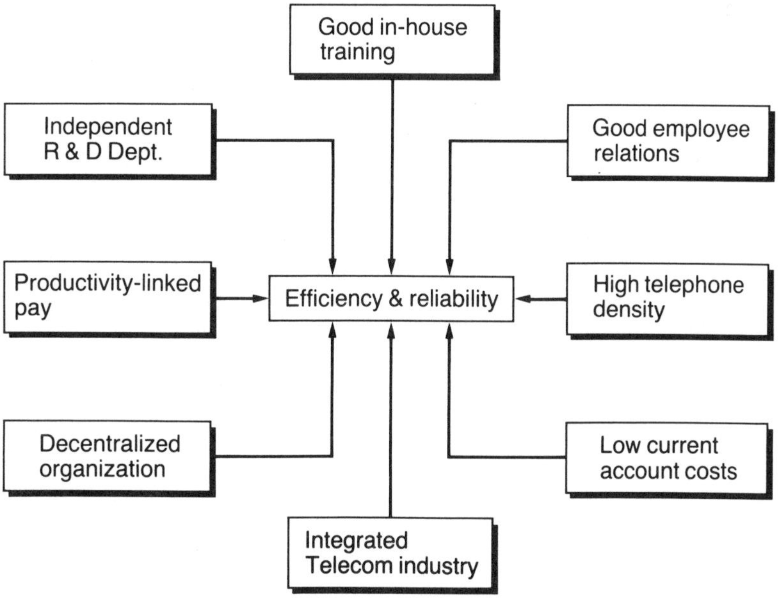

14.7 Word list

Financial

surplus p. 171
tied-up capital p. 171 capital, already used e.g. for purchasing stores, which cannot be used for investment purposes.
viable p. 176 workable, making business-sense.
auditing p. 171 financial control of accounts.
share capital p. 171 capital contributed by shareholders.
plant replacement p. 176 change, modernization of equipment.
to write off p. 176 to depreciate completely the capital value of a product, piece of equipment.
current account costs p. 176 non-capital costs.
depreciation p. 176 gradual loss of value of buildings and equipment.
interest charges p. 176 % charge made on borrowed money.
current funds p. 176 the money needed to run a business on a day-to-day basis.
revolving credit p. 176 a bank loan which is automatically renewed as soon as debts are paid off.

Marketing

saturated market p. 175 a market in which no further growth can take place.
penetration p. 175 share of sales in a specific market.
residual growth p. 176 growth which remains possible in the market.
prime targets p. 176 main objective.

Organization

matrix responsibility p. 171 responsibility for supporting a number of areas, departments or other company sections.
joint venture p. 171 2 or more companies working together.
middle-management p. 212(T)
to pool skills p. 176 to bring together different skills in a central pool.
delegation p. 176 sharing responsibility.
vertically integrated p. 177 closely linked e.g. as supplier and consumer.

Miscellaneous

public utility p. 171 nationalized service industry.
to foster (better relations) p. 212(T) to encourage.
tendering/a tender p. 213(T) asking for offers for supply of equipment or services.
to cater for p. 213(T) to be appropriate/useful for.
to augur well p. 177 indicate a positive future for.

Unit 15 International Telecoms

In this unit we look at the state of telecommunications in the 1980s throughout the world.

15.1 Reading 1

As you read, complete both parts of Figure 15a, and Figure 15b.

In the century since the birth of the telephone, the world telecommunications network has evolved both in size, slowly at first and then with astonishing speed, and in the techniques used to transmit information. The development has, however, been very uneven for, by 1983, three-quarters of the total number of telephone sets had been installed in just nine countries. These are the USA with 180 million telephones, Japan with 59 million, West Germany with 28 million, the UK and France with 27 million each, Italy with 19 million, Canada with 16 million, Spain with 13 million and Australia with 8 million.

In terms of continents, North America had 199 million telephones of all types in 1982 (38.1% of the world total), Central and South America 24 million (4.4%), Europe 203 million (39%), Asia 81 million (15.5%) with Japan accounting for 59 million (11.2% of the world total). Oceania had 1.8% of the total (10 million phones) and, finally, Africa had 6.5 million (1.2% of the world total).

The eastern block countries are not included in these figures, but at the beginning of 1982 the USSR is estimated to have had 25 million sets, East Germany, Poland and Czechoslovakia just over 3 million each and Yugoslavia a little over 2 million.

As the ITU declared when organizing 'World Communications Year: 1983', "Communications, which come immediately after food, housing and energy in the list of things which are indispensable for the survival of Humanity, make up the nervous system of today's world and constantly remind us that Humanity is one." As we can see from the statistics, some continents have an extremely small number of telephones, a fact that is likely to restrict socio-economic development, while in other countries telephones are so common that normal everyday existence without them seems unthinkable. Countries like Sweden and the USA have almost one telephone set for every inhabitant and their populations instinctively use the telephone in a very wide range of situations. The concept of the 'wired city' in which anyone can instantly talk to almost anyone else by using the telephone or some other form of electronic device has become a reality in countries such as these.

The importance of telecommunication services in the infrastructure of a country is universally recognized. But what is their internal order of importance? Arthur C Clarke, author of *2001 . . . A Space Odyssey* and the first person to conceive the idea of geosynchronous satellites, tried to answer this question in a recent address. He listed a number of services in the following order: the telephone, radio and TV, telex and, finally, data networks.

'A reliable telephone system must surely have the first priority,' said Clarke, 'for it affects every aspect of life . . . personal, business, government. It will be a long time, but not as long as you think, before everybody has a telephone. But with a telephone in every village we can have the next best thing.' He pointed out that with the introduction of International Direct Dialling in recent years, the power of the state to control news was broken. Private individuals can now speak to each other across frontiers.

Clarke placed radio next in his list of priorities because he considered it central to spreading information and establishing a national consciousness. He considered that radio was nowhere near the end of its development, an opinion which is confirmed by the rapid growth and enormous success of cellular radio. He saw at least two major developments in the field of radio technology: the use of built-in solar cells to replace batteries and the use of direct broadcasting satellites to give perfect signal reception all over the world.

He thought that telex equipment was still very expensive and thus limited to government and commercial use. He considered that it would eventually combine with data services. Dramatic reductions in the cost of computer equipment and the explosive growth of data communications mean that data services will, in the near future, be more widely used, and what is likely, as the technology advances, is that new high-capacity networks will transmit a number of different modes of information often, today, with separate transmission systems. It is, for example, technically possible to integrate telephone, telefax, video and data on a single line if optical fibres are used in the subscriber network.

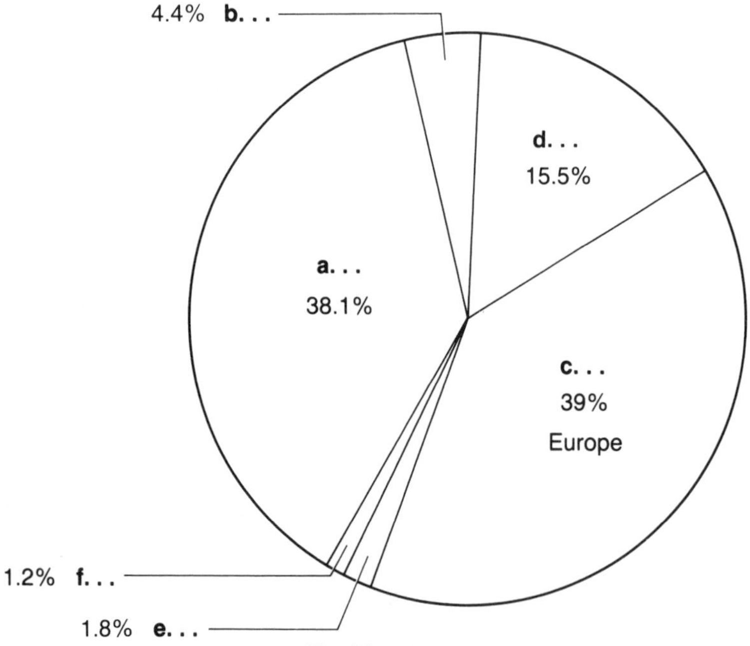

Fig 15a

Continent	Number of phones (millions)	% of world total
a		
b		
c		
d		
e		
f		

Fig 15a (contd.)

Service	Order of priority	Clarke's comments
a Telex	. . .	. . . . . .
b Telephone	. . .	. . . .
c Data networks	. . .	
d Radio	. . .	. . . .

Fig 15b

15.2 **Listening 1**

Listen to this interview between Diane Jansen, journalist on a Dutch newspaper, and Austin Eagle, an American transmission expert. They are talking about recent developments in optical fibre technology. As you listen, complete the following table and Figure 15c.

1	Locality : . . .	State : . . .
2	Locality : . . .	Country : . . .
3	Locality : . . .	Country : . . .
4	Bit rate	: . . .
5	Total cost	: . . .
6	Value of AT&T contract	: . . .
	Value of STC contract	: . . .
	Value of Submarcom contract	: . . .
7	No. of North American owners	: . . .
8	Largest European owner	: . . .

Type of cable	SW-MM	**c** . . .	LW-SM
Wavelength (nm)	**a** . . .	1300	**g** . . .
Mode	multimode	**d** . . .	**h** . . .
Attenuation dB/km	**b** . . .	**e** . . .	0.6
Typical repeater span (140 Mbit/s)	10	**f** . . .	**i** . . .

Fig 15c

15.3 **Language practice**

15.3.1 **Immediate past and immediate future**

Notice how we speak about the immediate past and the immediate future.

The Director General retired a few days ago.
→ The Director General **has just retired.**
The organization structure will be changed very soon.
→ The organization structure **is about to be changed.**

Now rewrite the following sentences in the same way.

a Their Teletex service will shortly be launched.
b The country's first long-distance optical fibre link was taken into service last month.
c They went over from a manual to an automatic mobile radio service last month.
d The capital city's tenth teleshop will be opened in a few days.
e Next week their fourth communications satellite is being put into geostationary orbit.
f The maintenance supervisors returned only a few days before the opening of the exchange.

15.3.2 Countries and nationalities

Complete the following table:

<table>
<tr><th></th><th>Country</th><th>Language</th><th>National adjective</th><th>Inhabitant</th><th>People</th></tr>
<tr><td>1</td><td>Sweden</td><td colspan="2">. . .</td><td>. . .</td><td>. . .</td></tr>
<tr><td>2</td><td>. . .</td><td colspan="2">. . .</td><td>A Finn</td><td>. . .</td></tr>
<tr><td>3</td><td>. . .</td><td colspan="2">French</td><td>. . .</td><td>. . .</td></tr>
<tr><td>4</td><td>. . .</td><td colspan="2">. . .</td><td>. . .</td><td>The Chinese</td></tr>
<tr><td>5</td><td>Italy</td><td colspan="2">. . .</td><td>. . .</td><td>. . .</td></tr>
<tr><td>6</td><td>. . .</td><td colspan="2">. . .</td><td>. . .</td><td>The Greeks</td></tr>
<tr><td>7</td><td>. . .</td><td colspan="2">. . .</td><td>A Japanese</td><td>. . .</td></tr>
<tr><td>8</td><td>. . .</td><td colspan="2">German</td><td>. . .</td><td>. . .</td></tr>
<tr><td>9</td><td>Spain</td><td colspan="2">. . .</td><td>. . .</td><td>. . .</td></tr>
<tr><td>10</td><td>. . .</td><td colspan="2">Norwegian</td><td>. . .</td><td>. . .</td></tr>
<tr><td>11</td><td>. . .</td><td colspan="2">. . .</td><td>A Russian</td><td>. . .</td></tr>
<tr><td>12</td><td>. . .</td><td colspan="2">. . .</td><td>. . .</td><td>The Dutch</td></tr>
<tr><td>13</td><td>England</td><td colspan="2">. . .</td><td>. . .</td><td>. . .</td></tr>
<tr><td>14</td><td>Great Britain</td><td>. . .</td><td>. . .</td><td>. . .</td><td>. . .</td></tr>
<tr><td>15</td><td>. . .</td><td>. . .</td><td>Australian</td><td>. . .</td><td>. . .</td></tr>
<tr><td>16</td><td>. . .</td><td>. . .</td><td>. . .</td><td>. . .</td><td>The Americans</td></tr>
<tr><td>17</td><td>. . .</td><td>. . .</td><td>. . .</td><td>An Algerian</td><td>. . .</td></tr>
<tr><td>18</td><td>Austria</td><td>. . .</td><td>. . .</td><td>. . .</td><td>. . .</td></tr>
<tr><td>19</td><td>. . .</td><td>. . .</td><td>New Zealand</td><td>. . .</td><td>. . .</td></tr>
<tr><td>20</td><td>Switzerland</td><td>. . .</td><td>. . .</td><td>. . .</td><td>. . .</td></tr>
</table>

Fig 15d

15.4 **Reading 2**

15.4.1

This article looks at the world market for telecommunications equipment suppliers. As you read, complete Figures 15f and 15g.

The stakes in this new global battle are enormous. This year (1983) nearly $59 billion will be spent on communications equipment alone, estimates Edgar A Graham, MD of Arthur D Little Inc's world telecom information program. By 1988, he predicts, the market will grow 50% to $88.4 billion. The lion's share of equipment purchases is being made by the PTTs for switching equipment, cable and other network gear.

But as deregulation opens up markets, selling directly to the users is becoming more important to the makers. This year, users will buy nearly $19 billion worth of equipment ranging from simple telephones and telex machines to sophisticated PBXs. In addition, Graham estimates that expenditure on calls, telexes and other transmission services will run three to four times the money spent on hardware.

Two Canadian manufacturers, Northern Telecom Ltd and Mitel Corp., will capture 28% of the $2.8 billion market in PBX systems sold in the US in 1983, while Japanese and European companies will grab an additional 22%, says Kevin J Sam, industry analyst for Northern Business Information Inc, a market research company.

Until recently, besieged US equipment makers were content to keep a smaller piece of the growing pie—sales of PBXs have doubled since 1977. But market saturation threatens to slow domestic sales of switchboards. One pessimistic forecast predicts that US sales of PBX systems will reach a high of $3.6 billion in 1984 and then slide back to $2 billion in 1987.

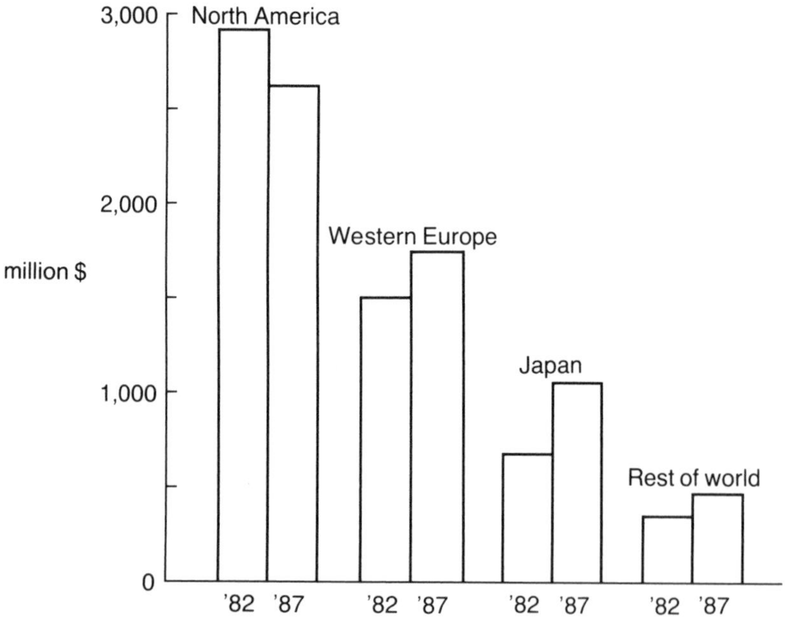

Fig 15e Growth and projected growth in PBX sales

So American companies are commencing a mad scramble for export orders, switching their focus to western Europe and Japan. However, here they will certainly encounter problems. For example in France, where CIT-Alcatel, Thomson and Jeumont–Schneider dominate the PBX market, the only foreign company able to sell switchboards is IBM, and that is allowed only because it makes them in France. In Japan, too, foreign companies still run into non-tariff roadblocks and bureaucratic snafus. Japanese makers still capture more than 95% of their home PBX market, estimates J Borden, a Yankee Group analyst.

In countries where trade rules have been liberalized, most of the TAs still require that products contain some locally manufactured pieces. Instead of fighting these local content laws many companies are opening foreign factories. 'Up to now we tried to manufacture 100% in Japan,' says Masaka Ogi, general manager of international operations at Fujitsu Ltd. 'But now,' he says, 'we will have to make 50% in Japan and 50% overseas or we won't be able to do business.'

The worldwide upheaval traces its roots to the US, the world's largest telecom market, which has been drastically deregulated over the past ten years, culminating in the split-up of AT and T. Liberalization has resulted in a plethora of new communications networks, services and products coming from such US suppliers as GTE, MCI Communications and Rolm. At the same time, long-established foreign manufacturers—Britain's Plessey, West Germany's Siemens, and Japan's NEC as well as Sweden's Ericsson—began attacking the wide-open US market.

Faced with this new competition at home, American companies, led by the world's largest, Western Electric Co., AT and T's manufacturing arm, began looking for their own export market. To keep pace in the race for export success, many switching equipment makers are looking outside their traditional markets and lining up new international business arrangements. One of the best examples is the co-operative venture by AT and T and the Dutch multinational Philips. The merging of telecommunications and data processing is prompting other joint efforts by such teams as Ericsson/Honeywell, IBM/Rolm and Plessey/Stromberg-Carlsson Corp. America's giant ITT, the world's second largest communications equipment maker, is also looking for business partners. The company is inviting more local ownership of some of its overseas subsidiaries. In 1982, it reduced its shareholding in STC, its British subsidiary, from 75% to 35%. And it is establishing joint ventures such as the one set up in 1983 with the National Postal and Telecommunications Industry Corp. of China to make switching equipment for the Chinese market. Such arrangements are necessary now because no company can afford to research and develop a new switching system without export markets. (See Figure 15f over page.) ITT, for example, has spent more than $750 million designing its System 12 digital switch. On paper, at least, the potential markets for switching systems are enormous for the simple reason that most of the world is still without a phone service. Although most developing countries attach a high priority to telephone networks, they lack the money at present to buy large numbers of multi-million dollar switches. And among themselves, ITT, Ericsson, Siemens and NEC (the 'gang of four') have divided up the rest of the world's markets.

To try to crack the new markets, the second-tier suppliers are teaming up. CIT-Alcatel plans to take over Thomson CSF's switching

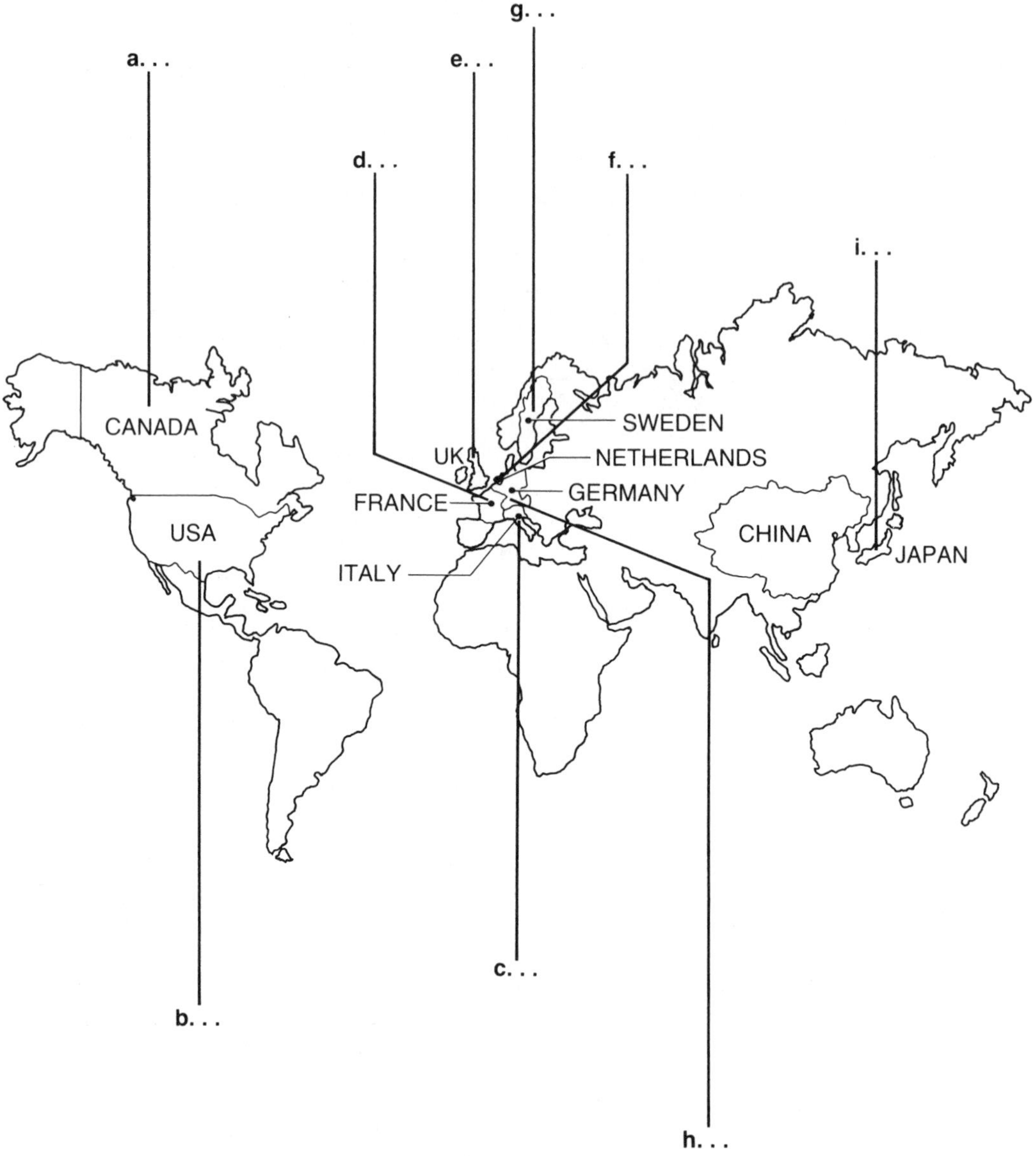

Fig 15f The world's principal telecommunications equipment manufacturers

business. Thomson and CIT-Alcatel were ranked ninth and eleventh worldwide in 1982. 'Together we will rank fifth,' says Georges Pébereau, Chief Executive of CIT-Alcatel. Two of Britain's switchmakers, Plessey and GEC, have co-operated for eight years on the development of System X, the British digital switching system. Similarly Italtel is teaming up with GTE to help fund development of a digital switch for the Italian network.

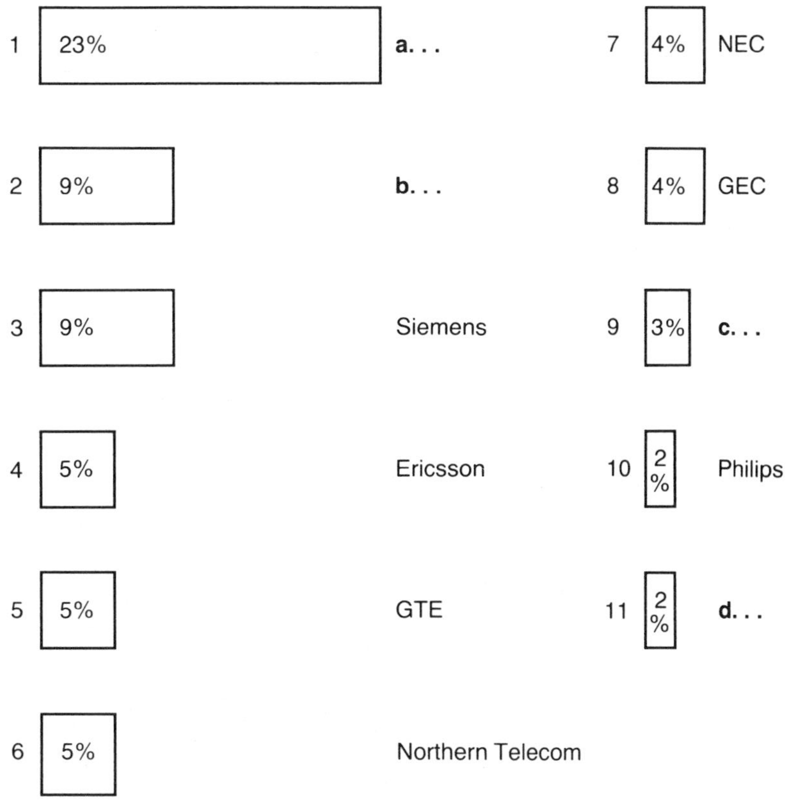

Fig 15g The world's leading equipment makers: 1982 sales $54.3 billion

The fight for the switching market will be fierce, says GTE's Gressens, because 'telecommunications has been looked upon as one of those essential industries a country had to have for itself—like steelmaking or airlines.' But the technology and resources that are necessary will be too much for most companies. In the long run switching will become an expensive game in which only the multinational players can compete, together or in partnerships.

15.4.2

Now link up those companies that have joint ventures or have merged.

1 GTE	**a** Honeywell
2 Plessey	**b** IBM
3 Ericsson	**c** Stromberg-Carlsson Corp.
4 Rolm	**d** NPTI Corp. of China
5 ITT	**e** Thomson CSF
6 CIT-Alcatel	**f** GEC
	g Italtel

Draw up a bar chart to show the growth of the world telecommunications market. Illustrate the following additional information for 1983:

A the size of the terminal equipment market.

B the size of the American PBX market.

15.5 **Listening 2**

In this extract you are going to listen to Geoff Peters, a communications consultant, talking to the editor of *Communications Weekly* about developments in telecommunications from the user's point of view. As you listen, use Figure 15h below to take notes about the users Geoff Peters mentions.

Company	Type of network	Hub of network (+ main centres)	Advantages
a			
b			
c			
d			

Fig 15h

15.6 **Discussion**

What impact is the tremendous growth of telecommunications going to have on society? Discuss the factors given below, whether they are effects or causes, and their relative significance.

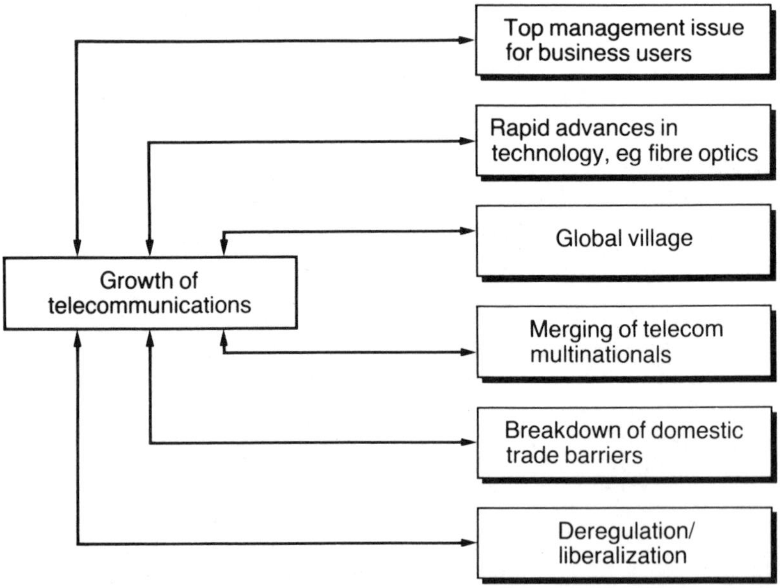

15.7 Word List

Marketing

to open up a market p. 188
besieged p. 188 unable to move because attacked from all sides.
a piece of the pie p. 188
market saturation p. 188 the market cannot be expanded.
to switch focus p. 189
to capture a market p. 189
to crack the market p. 189 to break into the market.
lion's share p. 188 largest part.
stakes p. 188 money at risk.

Developments/change

to evolve p. 183
to slide back p. 188
a mad scramble p. 189
upheaval p. 189
to keep pace in the race p. 189 to move as fast as your competitors.

Joining

to merge p. 189
a joint venture p. 189
to team up p. 189
subsidiary p. 189

Legal

snafus p. 189 complications.
local content law p. 189
fraudulent p. 214(T)

Miscellaneous

a threat—to threaten p. 188
a hub p. 214(T) centre of a wheel.
plethora p. 189 a very (too) large number of.
on paper p. 189
second-tier p. 189
to rank p. 189
turnover p. 214(T)
wired city p. 183
global village p. 192

Revision Unit C Growing Pains

In this unit you will practise the language presented in all units, particularly Units 11–15.
There will be three tasks to perform. Students working in a class should perform these tasks in groups or pairs, where necessary; those working alone will provide results in writing.

Task 1 Listening and note-taking: 'The C.T.A. in Perspective'

Mr. Nelson O'Higgins, Director-General of the C.T.A., gives a talk to the Costerutsi Telecoms Users' Association, entitled: 'The C.T.A. in perspective'.
As you listen, fill in the chart, map and graphs depicting the position a) 5 years ago b) today, and c) 5 years from now.

	5 years ago	**Today**	**5 years time**
Staff:	. . . . .	. . . . .	. . . . .
Organization:	. . . . .	transitional	. . . . .
Tel. stations:	. . . . .	. . . . .	. . . . .
Training emphasis:	technicians	. . . . .	. . . . .
Priorities:	STD	. . . . .	. . . . .
Status of C.T.A.	. . . . .	semi-liberalized	. . . . .

Transmission techniques

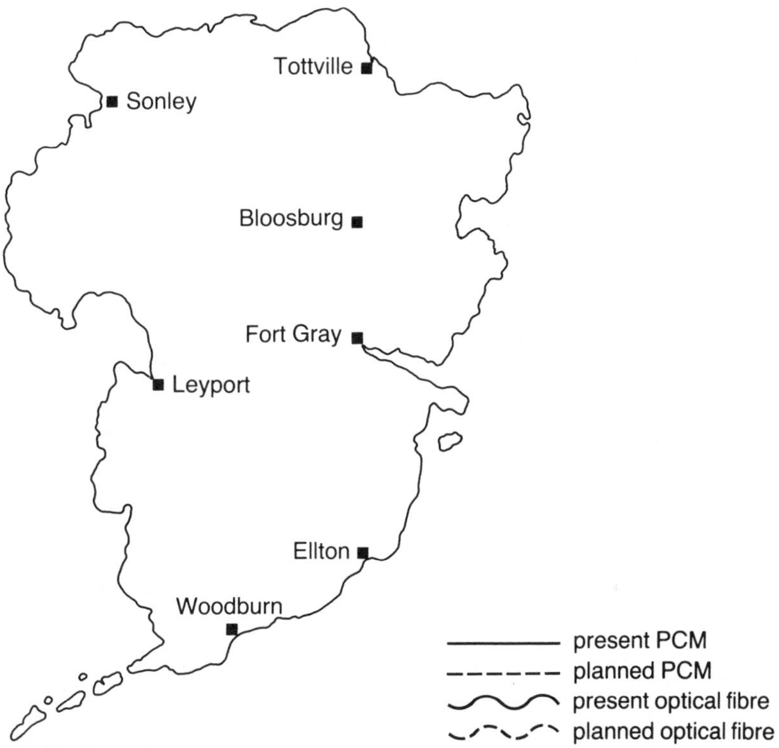

Installation Times (telephones)

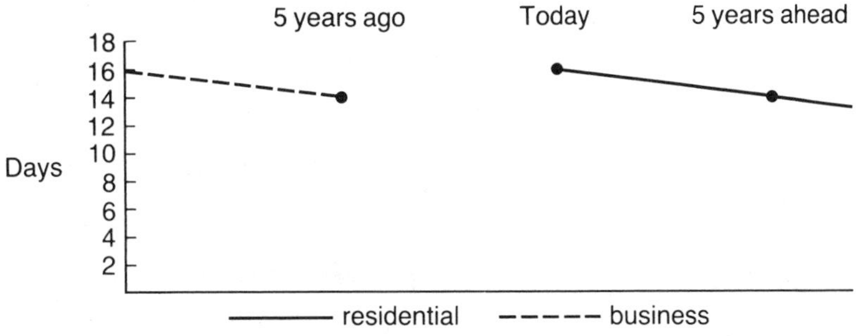

Fault repair times

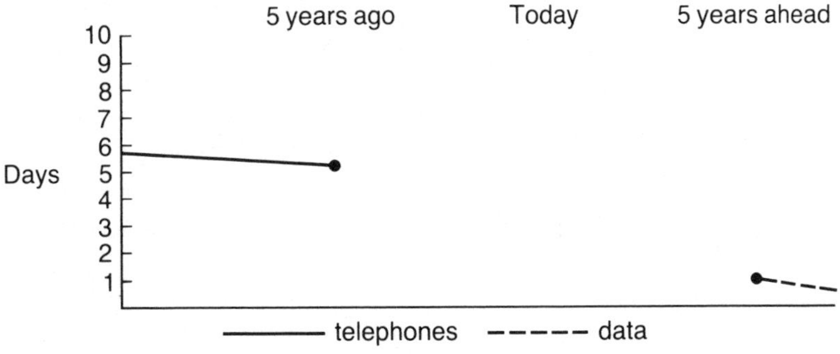

Task 2 Negotiating and report-writing: 'Trouble-shooting'.

Representatives of Reniat (Costerutsi) and C.T.A. meet to discuss problems which have arisen in the early stages of Reniat's development in Costerutsi.

Class Divide the class into a) representatives of Reniat and b) members of C.T.A. Each side studies only its own role-card, after which a meeting is held in order to get answers to key questions and to agree on future action. If desired, notes should be taken during the meeting and brief minutes written up afterwards.

Self-study Read the two role-cards carefully, then write two brief memos, under clear headings: a) from Reniat, stating their dissatisfaction and b) a reply from C.T.A., stating difficulties experienced and improvements likely in the future.

Reniat (Costerutsi): Notes for meeting with C T A

—— 3 months to fit extra PBX extension

—— 2½ weeks for some phone repairs

—— Call queueing, night barring facilities promised, not provided

—— Only Group 1 Telefax available. No competition to C.T.A. allowed.

—— 2 – 3 data faults per week

—— Poor reception MRT

—— Costs 11% up on budget

—— Good relations with Bill Wallace, Int.A/C manager

C.T.A.: Notes for meeting with Reniat (Costerutsi)

—— Delays caused by computerization of supplies. Imminent improvement.

—— Epidemic in fault repair teams.

—— Some special facilities impossible until digitalization - Leyport in 3 months

—— Telefax competition possible next year. Group 3, at competitive prices, from C.T.A. then.

—— Rationalization of radio frequencies last month

—— Data n/w teething troubles, now over

—— Installation charges up, call charges stable

—— Bill Wallace and Paul Bailey (Reniat Comm.Mgr.) worked well together. Future promising.

Task 3 Reading and Planning: 'Press Launch'

Reniat H.Q. have decided to launch their new model, the 'Coaster', in Costerutsi. They have invited 30 journalists to spend five days at the Sonley Beach Hotel, Sonley. (See map p. 195)
The exhibitions, trials and entertainments will need to be relayed to the world's press as quickly and efficiently as possible. A budget of C$50 000 has been allocated to provide a press telecommunications centre in the hotel.
Class Read the list of facilities and costs drawn up by the C.T.A., then discuss in pairs the best way of spending the C$50 000. Finally, hold a meeting in order to decide the best combination of facilities to be ordered by Reniat. If desired, write a brief memo of recommendation.
Self-Study Read the list of facilities and costs drawn up by C.T.A., then write a memo recommending the best way of spending the C$50 000.

Special facilities offered by C.T.A.

		C$
CCTV link with UK	installation costs	12 000
	cost per day	4 000
Telex: Operator	(per machine/per day)	400
Free-standing	(" " / " ")	100
Teletex	(" " / " ")	250
Telephones: Operator-assisted	(per machine/per day)	100
Phonecard	(" " / " ")	50
Electronic mailbox terminals	(" " / " ")	1 000
Advanced pagers	(" " / " ")	100
Facsimile machines	(" " / " ")	300

Tapescript

Unit 1 **Listening**

Lecturer Today we're going to consider local network development. In the case you have in front of you, the objective is to expand the existing local network and extend it into a new area.
In Figure 1d, you can see the traditional solution. The original central exchange is expanded in a new building and additional cables are laid and cabinets are installed.
Student A Sorry, what do you mean by cabinets?
Lecturer Ah yes, I should've explained that. We're only concerned here with the primary part of the network—that is, the lines between the exchanges and the cross connection points, or cabinets. Later we can consider the secondary and subscriber circuits.
Student A So cabinet is just another word for 'cross connection point'.
Lecturer Yes, that's right. Now, all they have done in this case is to build another electromechanical exchange in the new area and use analogue transmission for distribution in the network and the interexchange junction.
Student B So that means that there's no digital switching or transmission in the network?
Lecturer Exactly. In fact both exchanges are traditional electromechanical of the crossbar type. Very reliable but limited. Now, if we look at Figure 1e, we can see another solution to the problem. Here two SPC digital exchanges are installed. One to extend the central area, the other to serve the new area. The junction circuits between the exchanges use PCM, but analogue transmission . . .
Student B Sorry to interrupt again. I'm not sure I understand.
Lecturer Well, you can see that a new digital exchange is sited next to the old local exchange, and the connection to the other new SPC exchange in the new area uses digital transmission, normally called PCM, or pulse code modulation. Is that clear?
Student B Yes, I think so.
Lecturer Now, the rest of the network—that is the primary circuits from the exchanges to the cabinets—remain analogue. That's the big difference in the third solution shown in Figure 1f. Here the two areas, that is the central and new area, are served by one SPC exchange. This allows the use of remote subscriber switches, sometimes called remote concentrators, out in the primary network.
Student C Do these replace the cabinets?
Lecturer No, they are like remote parts of the exchange. They enable digital transmission, or PCM, to be used much further out in the network. In this solution, analogue transmission is only used for the lines between concentrators and the cabinets.

Unit 2 **Listening**

A I'd like to ask you some questions about PCM or pulse code modulation. Could you give me some background information to start with?
B Of course. As you know, in the simplest telephone system, speech, in the form of air pressure waves, in other words mechanical energy, is converted into electrical energy by the telephone microphone. This electrical energy travels along a pair of wires to a receiver which converts the electrical energy back into speech. Now, as you can see here in Figure 2g, in a traditional transmission system, the current is an analogue of the speech.
A Sorry, what do you mean by analogue?
B Well, that the current has the same waveform as the variations in air pressure. This is why we call this method 'analogue transmission'. As you can see on the graph, the vertical axis is either current or air pressure.
A So, what's the difference with PCM?
B Well, I was just coming to that. Let's look at this graph, Figure 2h. If the height of the waveform is sampled and these samples are transmitted, then the original waveform can be reconstituted at the receiver end.
A I see. How often does it need to be sampled?
B Good question. The sampling rate must be at least double the highest frequency component present in the waveform.
A So what's a typical sampling rate?
B For telephony, in which frequencies are limited to 3400 Hz, a sampling rate of 8000 samples per second is used.
A So that's what PCM is.
B No, that's not the whole story. This sampling process is known as pulse amplitude modulation. PAM for short. You'll notice the gaps between the pulses—these can be used for other channels. On this graph, Figure 2i, a second PAM channel, shown in black, has been inserted between the original PAM channels. This now forms a simple time division multiplex system, or TDM.
A So, how many channels can you put on a line?
B Well, the 24-channel system is widely used but you can have more. However, these PAM pulses are not transmitted directly over lines, since they would become distorted. Instead, the height of the pulse is measured and given a binary code. Each code is then transmitted as a train of pulses within the sample time or time slot. The process of approximating the sample value to a coded level is called 'quantization' and the whole process of sampling and coding is known as pulse code modulation or PCM.
A Thank you. That's a lot clearer. Could you now explain the 24-channel system in more detail?
B Yes, let's look at this block schematic diagram . . .

Unit 3 **Listening**

Gibbs Good morning, Mr Allison. Could you tell me how the user at any extension on our new PABX will benefit from its greater number of facilities?

Allison Of course. First you must make a clear distinction between internal and external calls. For internal calls, pick up the handset, wait for the dial-tone—which is almost instantaneous with this electronic system—then simply dial the four numbers of the extension.

Gibbs How do you obtain an outside number?

Allison You pick up the handset, wait for the internal dial-tone, then push button number 2, which will send you the dial-tone of the outside network. After that, you dial the outside number in the usual way, using the appropriate local, regional or international codes.

Gibbs In what way does the PABX make the switchboard operator's work easier?

Allison Well, you've probably noticed that each extension has four digits. The preceding two digits, which make up the full six-figure number, are the same for every extension in the company, in this case, 55. So anyone outside can dial 55 followed by the four digits of the internal number, and the call is switched directly to the internal extension without disturbing the operator.

Gibbs I see. So the operator isn't really necessary?

Allison Yes she is, because she can still be contacted directly—her own number is 552222—and, if the phone rings for more than 15 seconds at any extension without being answered, the call is switched automatically to the operator.

Gibbs How do you transfer your number to another extension if you leave your office for a long period?

Allison Pick up the handset, wait for the internal dial-tone, push button 8, and you'll receive another lower-pitched dial-tone, after which you dial the number of the extension in the office you're going to. You'll then get a short dial-tone informing you that your 'new' number has been recognized and stored in the PABX.
Now, when you come back to your office, don't forget to dial 8 followed by your own extension number, so that your own number is returned to your office. Do make sure you do that, or all your calls will continue to be transferred to the office where you were before! Well, let's make sure you've understood all that, shall we?

Gibbs OK. Pick up the handset. Internal dial-tone. Dial 8. Short recognition dial-tone. Extension number of the other office. On returning to my own office, I dial 8 then my own number.
Would you mind explaining how I can be called back automatically if my correspondent's line is engaged when I phone?

Allison Right. Don't forget this system only works if both you and your correspondent go through the same exchange. For internal calls, this is obviously the case with the PABX. You dial your correspondent and receive the engaged tone. Then, you simply press button 4 and hang up. When your correspondent hangs up, the phone will ring in your office, which, in turn, causes the phone in your correspondent's office to ring! Simple, isn't it?

Gibbs I suppose so! Could you also let me know what detailed billing facilities exist for the PABX?

Allison Of course. Each call is registered . . .

Unit 4 **Listening**

A B.T. Business Systems. Can I help you?

B Yes, we are interested in the Merlin Word Processing facility.

A Oh yes. Hold on a moment. I'll put you through to our Manager, Mr Binns.

C Binns speaking.

B This is John Dale of Dale Recruitment Agency.

C Good morning, Mr Dale. That's Dale Recruitment in York?

B Yes, that's right.

C OK. I gather you're interested in our M3300 Word Processing package.

B Well, maybe. At this stage, I'd just like to ask one or two questions.

C Of course. Fire away!

B Well, I've seen the brochure and I'm particularly interested in the integrated telecom facilities.

C Yes, we regard that as one of Merlin's principal advantages. Do you have a telex machine?

B Yes, we rent an old one.

C Well, that should be no problem. You'll have to change to an electronic telex machine, of course.

B Oh, what's the cost likely to be?

C Well, it won't work out much more than the existing telex rental, and with our new Puma, you'll be getting a lot of new facilities.

B What sort of facilities?

C For a start, it's much faster than a conventional terminal. You can store the information on both incoming and outgoing messages and then have them sent or printed whenever you want. You can use the screen to type in the message and then transmit it without any intermediate paperwork.

B Yes, that could be useful. We are certainly using telex more, and some messages are more urgent than others.

C Ah, so the Puma will suit your needs. If you're having a modem . . .

B Sorry, I didn't catch that.

C Well, for the telex interface you'll need a modem and I thought you might be interested in having access to data banks and Prestel, that's our viewdata system.

B I'm not sure about that. What's the availability like on the whole package?

C Well, we ought to be able to install the screen and keyboard within 3 weeks. There's no problem about the new telex, we've got plenty in stock. I'm afraid you'll have to wait a bit longer if you want the printer as well.

B How much longer?

C I can't tell you for sure. We are expecting new models in 3 weeks' time. What with processing the order, etcetera, it'll probably be four or five weeks before delivery. Is the printer vital to you?

B Yes, it is rather. You see we send out a lot of circulars to our clients, updating them on our candidate files.

C I see. If you don't mind me asking—how do you do that at the moment?

B Well, we photocopy standard letters and type on names and addresses. We've got a big mailshot coming up next month, I was hoping we could use the new equipment.

C I'm afraid that's a little optimistic. You see you'll have to key in client names and addresses first, index them with our software package Salesdesk and then use Wordstar, another software program, for the actual production of personalized circulars.

B Oh, why do you think it'll take so long?

C Maybe it won't. And, of course, once the system is set up, it'll all be pretty instant. But you've got to feed in the data and that takes time, especially if you've only got one terminal.

B Well, let's leave that. How about a demonstration? Could you arrange one soon?

C OK. We'll get someone over to you within the week. Actually, we've got a Business Systems Exhibition on in Harrogate next week. I could make an appointment for you to see our people on the stand and they could show you the whole system in operation.

B It's good of you to suggest that, but I'm afraid I'm away next week. I'd really like someone round this week to demonstrate it to myself and the office staff. Then we can go ahead and make a decision before I leave. Could you manage Wednesday?

C Well, it won't be me. It'll be our local Business Systems rep. I'll get him to give you a ring today to fix a time. Can you let me have your phone number?

B Of course. You don't want me to get in touch with him?

C No, no, don't worry, I'll give him a ring straight away, and he'll probably phone you before five to fix a time and a day.

B All right, my number is York two, eight, double four, Oh.

C Two, eight . . .?

B Double four, Oh.

C Thanks. He'll be in touch later today.

B Thank you, goodbye.

C 'Bye.

Unit 5 **Listening 1**

Peter Hello. Peter Needham speaking.

John Hello Peter. It's John Brown here. Where are you now exactly?

Peter I'm on the A 217 heading towards Greenwood. I've just gone past Chertsey windmill.

John Right. Well, I've got some good news for you. I've just had Swanford Tools on the phone . . . you know, the company over at Thurby. Apparently they're very interested in the RPH radiophone documentation I left with them about a month ago, and would like someone to visit them as soon as possible. On the phone I got the impression they're ready to bite.

Peter Good. We've had several inquiries about the radiophone recently. Our research is beginning to pay off. What do you want me to do then . . . deliver the equipment to Greenwood or get straight over to Thurby?

John I think it'd be a good idea to get straight over to Thurby.

Peter Can you give me some information on the best route?

John You said you'd just gone past Chertsey windmill, didn't you?

Peter Yes, that's right.

John Well, take the next turning on your right, the B 2378 to Slingdon. When you're in Slingdon, you'll see a pub on your left called 'The Bear Inn', and right opposite the pub you'll see the B 379 to Thurby. So turn right at the pub, and carry on for about 5 kilometres. Swanford Tools is on your left, just after the golf-course. It's very close to the A 19 which you can take to come back to Nutley.

Peter Fine. I'll be in Thurby in about 20 minutes. What's the name of the chap I've got to see there?

John Derek Salvage. He's in charge of their equipment modernization scheme. Oh, one word of advice. Don't mention the French contract to him. Few people know about it yet, and I wouldn't like it to become public knowledge.
Oh, and when you talk about the RPH radiophone, bring out all of the usual arguments: efficient businesses needing good communication, RPH's profit-making capacities, saving on fuel costs, and meeting the customers' needs. You know the sort of things I mean.

Peter Of course. I'll deliver the equipment to Greenwood first thing tomorrow morning. I should be back in Nutley by 4.30. The A 19 from Thurby's a fast road and a lot of people will be going the other way towards Slingdon at about 4. See you later at the office then. 'Bye John.

John 'Bye.

Revision Unit A **Listening**

'The Costerutsi Telecommunications Administration today': a brief address to the I.T.U. by the Director General of the C.T.A.

'As you are aware, the C.T.A. has only recently become a separate organization, previously forming part of the Post Office (C.P.O.).

We now have a monopoly of telecoms services—telephone, telex and data, and we regulate radio frequency usage throughout the country. The question of privatization of certain of these services is at present being discussed by the Government.

Statistically, telephone usage in Costerutsi is high: at 1.84 phones per capita, it compares very well with many of the more industrialized countries. One of our major problems, however, is that much of our switching equipment is old-fashioned: 71% Strowger; 25% Crossbar, with 4% of exchanges still being operated manually.

The system of charges now in operation is favourable to the private subscriber: 96% of all local calls are free, and although trunk calls are more expensive than in neighbouring Australia, private subscriber rental, especially when using a shared line, is considerably cheaper than business rental. This can be as high as CR $700 per annum, with an average cost of $560 p.a. (the exchange rate being approximately $2 to £1 sterling).
The trunk network now uses PCM, and optical fibres have recently been introduced into a small number of major lines. Microwave links are shared with radio services.
International Direct Dialling is available with 106 countries, (STD is available to 60% of all subscribers), and international phone and telex traffic has increased by 18% over the last year.
Data services offered are Datex at 2400 b/s which will eventually replace the 300 b/s Datel, using the switched telephone network. Leased data circuits, working at up to 9600 b/s are growing rapidly.
The private facsimile service is complemented by Bureaufax, which allows public access to the service at main post offices.
Mobile radio-telephone services are provided by 74 base stations, serving 4100 subscribers and 3500 radio-equipped vehicles.
Some international circuits are provided by satellite link, whilst the new undersea submarine cable link to Japan and Canada should increase the present undersea capacity from 105 to 2200 circuits.'

Unit 6 **Listening 1**

Student A I thought that LANs had been in existence for a long time.

Instructor Yes. You're quite right, of course, but it's only recently that there's been a heightened interest in the use of coaxial cable technology for office communications, the development of packet switching technology, and the advances in the field of optical fibres.

Student A So, according to you, the only reasons for the sudden interest in LANs are purely technical ones?

Instructor No, not at all. I think there are other reasons as well, mainly to do with marketing. For example, managers are now beginning to realize that office workers deserve greater capital expenditure on equipment which enables them to work more efficiently. Some people are suggesting that it's because executives have lost their fear of the keyboard that this has happened.

Student A Can you give me a definition of a LAN?

Instructor Well, LANs are used for interconnecting resources of various types in a local geographic area, for instance, minicomputers, data terminals, telephone sets, distributed data processors, printers, copiers, facsimile devices and word processors. This local area could include various desks in an office, floors in a building or buildings on a campus.

Student A Wouldn't it be more economical to have a PABX which is capable of carrying out all the functions you've mentioned rather than install a LAN?

Instructor Well, it's my belief that modern office systems are evolving towards a multimedia concept. In other words, the systems and equipment used in the office of the future must be able to handle information in a number of forms: voice, non-voice and even video. The bit rate required is enormous, too high, in fact, for most PABXs. It's here that a LAN ought to be useful, especially when optical fibres become operational.

Student B Yes, I see. What sort of network architectures are used in LANs?

Instructor There are several possibilities. The star, ring and bus topologies are generally thought to be the most interesting. In my opinion, the most efficient and cost-effective at the moment is the bus. Let's have a look at Xerox Corporation's Ethernet local area network. By the way, I'm going to the USA tomorrow to study this network in more detail for an article I'm writing for *Electronic Review*. As you can see from the diagram, this is a typical medium-scale configuration, in which a pair of coaxial cable segments, each up to 500 metres long, is joined by a repeater. The bus topology allows nodes to be tapped onto the cable through transceivers. Up to 100 nodes, or workstations, can be put onto any cable segment. The cable linking the node to the transceiver can also be up to 500 metres long. The maximum bit rate on this system is 10Mb/s, and the maximum length of any transmission between nodes is two and a half kilometres. A total of 1,024 workstations can be connected to this network.

Student A Systems like Ethernet require very high bit rates, don't they?

Instructor Yes, they do, of course, but I'm pretty sure that fibre optic cables, although at the moment they're more expensive than coaxial links, will offer much higher bit rates and wider bandwidth. Fibre optic cables don't generate electromagnetic interference, nor are they susceptible to it. This high voltage isolation means that a fibre optic LAN ought to work perfectly in hazardous environments, such as power stations or TV studios. They'll also be more secure because it'll be more difficult to tap them. Finally, optical fibre cables are smaller, lighter and easier to install than coaxial cables, which is perfect for an office environment.

Student A So you think that LANs in the future ought to be designed on a fibre optic system, do you?

Instructor Yes. I really do think that over the next ten years a lot of companies will install fibre optic LANs.

Unit 6 **Listening 2**

John Come in. Oh, hello Stuart. Do come in and take a seat. I've asked you to come up to tell me something about the Biarritz experiment. As you know Bromfield Equipment has just been named group leader for a similar project in this country. I ought to have read your report on Biarritz but, because of my illness, I haven't done so yet. I really must catch up on all the work that's accumulated while I've been off.

Stuart Well, John, I know you're familiar with what a typical local distribution network is in telephony. Well, the Biarritz experiment is based on a configuration with a primary centre and, for the moment, three secondary centres. What's so special about Biarritz is that all transmission between centres and from each centre to the subscriber is done over optical fibres.

John I see. So there's no coaxial cable, then?

Stuart No. None at all. Everything is transmitted over optical fibre: from the subscriber's premises to the secondary centres, and from the secondary centres to the primary centre.

John Why have they chosen optical fibres?

Stuart Mainly because of the type of traffic transmitted which requires very high bandwidth. I'm thinking of TV channels, stereophonic hi-fi channels and, of course, the videophone.

John Surely the whole town isn't wired up with optical fibres?

Stuart No. At the moment, there are only 1500 subscribers with a maximum figure of 5000 being aimed at over the next few years. Don't forget that Biarritz is an experiment. The objective of the whole operation is to master the technology of optical fibres and optoelectronic components in a real, working situation rather than in a laboratory.

John What's the maximum distance a subscriber can be from the nearest secondary centre?

Stuart At the moment between 300 and 1700 metres. Later on, the maximum optical loop length will be increased to 2200 metres. Each loop connecting the subscriber to the secondary centre consists of two fibres, one for each direction of transmission, for it's an interactive system. The main feeder cable linking groups of subscribers to the secondary centre is made up of seventy fibres, divided into seven units each consisting of ten fibres. Each unit has a central strength member. The seven units are protected in a metal casing, which is then coated in a plastic sheath. There are, of course, branching points between the secondary centre and the drop terminal.

John What services are offered?

Stuart Basically, there are two sorts of service. Firstly,.a switched service for point-to-point videotelephone connections between pairs of subscribers. Each connection has a sound channel and a picture channel for each direction of transmission. Images can be monochrome or colour.
Secondly, there are distributed services, enabling each subscriber to select one or two TV programmes out of a maximum of fifteen that can be offered. The number of TV channels may soon be increased to thirty.
Subscribers can also select any of the French or Spanish TV or FM radio stations that are received at Biarritz.

John Can a subscriber use his videophone on the national or international network?

Stuart Of course, but not with the picture, for the videophone has now become a normal telephone and has access to all the associated services of the public telephone network, such as directory enquiries, complaints and so on.

John I see. So to summarize the Biarritz project, we could say that new broadband services have been brought into the local distribution network using optical fibres as the transmission medium.

Stuart That's right.

John Very interesting. I think I'll have to go over to France to see it for myself. I have an old friend, Jean Dubois, who has just been transferred to Biarritz from Paris. I'll have to write to him to fix a date.

Stuart Fine. I hope you have a good trip. Goodbye, John.

John 'Bye, Stuart, and thanks for all the explanations.

Unit 7 **Listening 1**

Roberts Let me explain the position. We've got an office in London, but over the last few years, we've been doing more and more business in the Leeds area. Two years ago we took out a number in Leeds for our customers to ring and got the calls diverted to our London office.

Callan So you had an out-of-area line from London up to an exchange in Leeds?

Roberts Yes, that's right and it cost us something in the region of £400 a year to rent. Now this made sense at the time as we were getting a lot of enquiries. Things have quietened down recently—we're only getting about 20 calls a day, mostly orders from regular customers.

Callan I think I've got the picture. It sounds as if you should move over to our Remote Call Forwarding Service. Just hang on a moment, I'll get our Mr Philips to explain it to you. Caroline, could you ask Mr Philips to come up for a moment?

Caroline Right away?

Callan Yes, please. Yes, we've just introduced this system for customers like you. The big difference is that we use the Public Telephone Network for the diversion and not a dedicated circuit.

Roberts That sounds interesting.

Callan Come in. Hello, John. This is Mr Roberts from VIDEOTEC in London. He's interested in changing his out-of-area call diversion facility. I wondered if you could fill him in on the details?

Philips Of course. Well, at the moment, you're paying for a dedicated line. Is that right?

Roberts Yes, that's it. I was just saying we've got a number in Leeds for our customers to phone.

Philips I see. The big difference is that we would install some call-diversion equipment—we call it RCF—in the exchange in Leeds. This equipment automatically dials out a second call to your London number.

Roberts I see. So there's no need for a leased line between Leeds and London?

Philips That's right.

Roberts What about payment?

Callan I can answer that. The divert-a-call equipment in Leeds costs about £100 a year to rent. The calls themselves will be charged as before. That is, your customers will pay for a local to Leeds, you will pay for the trunk connection over the Public Network.

Roberts That sounds fine. How about delays? I mean, will the customer have to wait a long time to get through?

Philips No, not really. An average of 30 seconds, and while the call is being forwarded the caller hears an announcement something like 'hold while call is diverted'.

Roberts Oh, I'd prefer something different.

Philips No problem. You let us know what you want and we'll arrange it.

Roberts Good. How about quality on the line?

Philips This is improving all the time, as the network is updated. Also by installing RCF equipment in the exchange we've removed the weakest links—the local lines connecting the customer to the exchange.

Roberts So the quality's better?

Philips Well, certainly as good. We fit an amplifier in the RCF equipment to compensate for any transmission loss.

Roberts Great. Let's try to fix dates for the changeover, then.

Callan Certainly, I've got the installation times somewhere here. I was looking at them just before you arrived. Yes, we could switch over at the beginning of next month—December 1st. Would that be OK?

Roberts That would be fine. I was thinking . . .

Unit 7 **Listening 2**

Cornwall We've got a choice. We can either continue to have meetings here in London or we can start to use teleconferencing.

Mackintosh You mean discussion over the phone?

Cornwall No, we already do that when something important comes up. What I mean is using a studio here in London and one up in Glasgow. This will enable us to see each other and also to present material—graphs, figures, and so on. In other words both voice and picture transmission.

Mackintosh That would certainly save us time and money. It must cost a fair amount in travel each time we come down from Scotland.

Cornwall Exactly. I've got some bumph here from B.T. about their Confravision facilities. It seems we can have up to five people in each conference room.

Mackintosh That's plenty. Normally there are three of us from the Glasgow branch and I suppose three or four from your branch here in London.

Cornwall That's right. We don't need any cameramen or anything. We can just switch from one camera to another. We'll have a third camera for transmitting documentation.

Mackintosh What about the cost?

Cornwall Good question. I've got a model here which compares conventional meetings with a TV conference. The charge for a 3-hour meeting would be about £350.

Mackintosh That seems pretty high.

Cornwall Yes, I agree it does. But don't forget the savings. Flying down on the Shuttle from Glasgow costs us about £400 for the round trip for three of you and then we've also got the time to take into account.

Mackintosh It would be good to get a costing on that.

Cornwall Well, we can look at this example of a 3-hour TV meeting in London. In terms of manhours, that will take up about 11 hours for 3 of us in London—that allows a couple of hours to get to the studio—and 11 hours for you in Glasgow. If you fly down, it works out about 30 hours for you and, of course, just 9 hours for us.

Mackintosh How does that total up?

Cornwall Well, in total time saving, a TV conference saves us about 17 hours—that is, 22 as against 39. In cost, it works out about £50 cheaper.

Mackintosh So, not such a big difference in cost.

Cornwall That's true, but once we start quantifying the cost of time, it makes an appreciable difference.

Mackintosh Sure, but how do we do that?

Cornwall Well, it's artificial, but let's say we value one hour of your time at £15.

Mackintosh Only that!

Cornwall Well, let's not overestimate ourselves! Anyway, on that basis we save an additional £255.

Mackintosh Fair enough. So how do you think we should proceed?

Cornwall Well I suggest we give the teleconference a trial. We don't know how it will work out. We may find ourselves very nervous and very self-conscious in front of the camera.

Mackintosh True. The trial seems a good idea. Do you think you could arrange it for our next meeting in December?

Cornwall I doubt it, but I'll try. If not, I'll book the studio for our January meeting.

Mackintosh Good, I was just wondering . . .

Unit 8 **Listening 1**

John Peter, could you tell me something about the E 10 system? I believe it was one of the earliest electronic time division switching systems, wasn't it?

Peter Yes, it was and I'd be glad to tell you about it. To start with, the whole system has been developed with the idea of an integrated network in mind rather than in terms of individual exchanges.

John That'll mean using PCM techniques, won't it?

Peter Exactly. If we look at the network structure, we can see that each subscriber is connected to an electronic concentrator, which could be situated in the exchange itself, or which could be anything up to 50 kilometres away from the exchange. These are known as local and remote concentrators, respectively.

John I don't suppose the subscriber's line to the remote concentrator uses PCM, does it?

Peter No. At the moment, hardly ever. After arriving at the concentrator, the analogue signals are sampled and encoded to make up the outgoing PCM signals. These are transmitted to the exchange on a 2, 3 or 4-line link, depending on the number of subscribers in the area.

John I remember from my college days that each PCM line can handle 30 simultaneous conversations. If there is a 4-line link, that only means a total of 120 simultaneous calls. That seems to be rather a small number, doesn't it?

Peter Well, not really, because the maximum capacity of each concentrator is 1,000 subscribers. If 120 call at the same time, which is rarely the case although it can happen now and again, the ratio of one call for every eight subscribers is roughly respected. This figure is generally accepted as the norm in most switching systems.

John The fact that the concentrators can be so far from the exchange must be a great advantage, mustn't it?

Peter Of course, because it means that sparsely-populated areas with a low telephone density can be served just as well as urban areas.

John How many subscribers can an exchange handle?

Peter 45 000, although that figure's hardly ever reached.

John Let's come back to the network structure, shall we? How is the network supervision carried out?

Peter Well, we've seen that the network consists of concentrators, which are linked to the exchange by PCM techniques. All network supervision is done by an Operation and Maintenance Centre (an OMC) which handles 100 000 subscribers from as many as 6 different exchanges. Each exchange is connected to the OMC by a time slot in one of the network PCM links. Now every OMC has its own minicomputer as well as facilities for data storage—such as magnetic tapes and disks—and other pieces of equipment for man/machine dialogue.

John You mean high-speed printers, VDUs and teleprinters, I suppose?

Peter Exactly.

John I guess the centralization of all operation and maintenance functions means that fewer personnel are required to be permanently on duty at the exchanges, doesn't it?

Peter Right again. In fact, occasionally, there are no staff present at all. It's been calculated that the OMC has reduced operation and maintenance costs by 50% when compared to other types of exchange. That's a considerable saving, isn't it?

John It is indeed. Could you briefly describe the structure of an E 10 exchange?

Peter Well, it's made up of 3 main blocks, plus the OMC. Block 1 contains the subscriber connection units, from local and remote subscribers, as well as the multiplex connection unit which handles trunk lines. The multiplex connection unit is connected to other time and space division exchanges.

John With incoming signals from space division exchanges, it must be necessary to convert from analogue to digital. Is that right?

Peter Yes, always.

John From what I can remember, Block 2 houses the time division switching network (the TDSN) doesn't it?

Peter That's right. It provides 4-wire switching between the time slot allocated to the calling party and that allocated to the caller.

John And Block 3?

Peter Block 3 is the Control Unit which monitors all operations carried out by Blocks 1 and 2. It's made up of 3 main parts: the multiregisters (MRs), the translators (TRs) and the metering units (MUs).

John Detailed billing is provided on the E 10, isn't it?

Peter Yes it is, but only at the subscriber's request.

John Well, Peter, thanks very much for having explained the system so concisely.

Peter It's been a pleasure. 'Bye, John.

Unit 8 **Listening 2**

Subscriber Good afternoon.

Employee Good afternoon, sir. Can I help you?

Subscriber I hope so. I was interested to read your brochure on telematics which you enclosed with my recent telephone bill. Could you give me some more information about this new field, please?

Employee Of course. Did you find the brochure helpful?

Subscriber Well yes, I've read it and I'm very interested in the technical side of things, but I must say I find it difficult to keep up with all these new developments.

Employee I see. You know that the term telematics means the association of telecommunications and data processing, don't you?

Subscriber Yes. But what are the main applications?

Employee They can be divided into three main groups. The first group includes all the applications aimed at the general public, that's to say, designed for the ordinary subscriber. The term normally used to describe this first application is videotex.

Subscriber I'm familiar with the Prestel system in the UK, which, I suppose, could be put into this first group, couldn't it?

Employee That's right. Another interesting service in this group is what they call the electronic directory, which enables a subscriber to find out his correspondent's telephone number by using a home terminal linked to a data bank. This new service is likely to replace the telephone book in the near future.

Subscriber And the second group?

Employee The second group concerns consumers who have large numbers of terminals and other data processing equipment on their premises.

Subscriber You mean companies and businesses, I suppose?

Employee Exactly. Now, whereas most videotex services can use the existing analogue network, business users, who often have their own powerful data processing resources, frequently require more sophisticated services which cover a variety of uses. This sort of network is known as a multiservice network.

Subscriber You mean many business users need access to the public switched telephone network but also to high-speed data processing networks?

Employee Right. Now one excellent way of linking up such machines as computers, data terminals, videotex terminals, PABXs, telecopy machines and ordinary telephones, is to use a satellite linked to an electronic switching system.

Subscriber I read an article the other day about the Telecom 1 system in France, which seems to correspond to the description you've just given, because it links the E 10 switching system with a geostationary satellite, positioned above the Equator at a height of 36,000 kilometres.

Employee Yes. I read that article too. Very interesting, wasn't it? In this system, one single earth station serves an entire region. Each industrial location is connected to the station via high-speed data switches which also provide facilities for interconnecting other regions and other multiservice networks.

Subscriber There must be several hierarchical levels of exchanges in such a system, mustn't there?

Employee No. Only two. Level 1, with its 2 Mbit/s PCM signals, provides the interface between premises connected to it on the ground network, while Level 2 controls the data links between each earth station and between other networks.

Subscriber And what about the applications of the third group?

Employee Oh, yes. Well, the third group is designed for specialized uses, such as cellular radio telephone networks, which aim at extending the public telephone service to mobile users.

Subscriber What are the principles of such a network?

Employee The geographical area served is divided up into cells, each of which has a transceiver station equipped with directional antennae.

Subscriber I suppose the radio stations are linked to a switching centre?

Employee That's right. Several stations are linked to one switching centre which then switches the calls onto the public switched telephone network, or PSTN.

Subscriber I see. I think I now understand a little more clearly what the term telematics means. If I have any more questions, I can always call in again, can't I?

Employee Of course, sir. Goodbye.

Subscriber Goodbye.

Unit 9 **Listening 1**

I'd like today to summarize the international developments in videotex. It all started in the early 70s when Britain launched its Prestel system which, as you know, is now offered as a regular service by British Telecom.

However, as you would expect, other countries were quick to take up the challenge, and recently, tests have been carried out with different technical solutions in most industrialized countries. Still, for our purposes today, I shall confine myself to 3 services: Prestel in the UK, Télétel in France and Telidon in Canada.

Let me start with Prestel. This service now has 250,000 pages of information stored in data banks. The system, unlike the Canadian's Telidon, uses alphamosaic graphic techniques, which, as you can see, give rise to the building block effect. The central data banks are owned and operated by B.T. Information Providers, or IPs, as they are sometimes known—that is, companies, authorities, service agencies and so on—buy capacity in the data banks, and then, in some cases, charge Prestel users for access to the information. Prestel also offers Micronet 800, a telesoftware facility and a home-banking service, Homelink.

This brings me to the French system. In contrast to Prestel, Télétel is open to independent companies, which can set up their own data bases. A special part of the Télétel equipment is the electronic telephone directory. Here, instead of the usual paper telephone directory, the user has a simple display and keypad from which he can obtain information from a data base directory. Another service which Télétel offers is electronic mail, but more about that in a minute.

First, a few words about the Canadian system. In Canada, the Department of Communications has developed and controls Telidon, which, as you'll remember, uses a different graphic display technique to Prestel. This alphageometric system allows the IP to draw smoother curves and use more colours. For this reason this system is proving popular in the export market.

Well, before I finish, I think the use and evolution of videotex raises some important questions. For example: 'What effect will it have on traditional media, especially newspapers and postal services?' Télétel, as I mentioned, already provides electronic mail facilities: messages can be typed in on one keyboard for display on another set. Prestel, on the other hand, has been slow in offering this service to the general public, partly because of the impact it could have on traditional postal services. Another question being asked in some countries is: 'Should advertising be allowed on videotex?' In fact, interactive videotex, such as Prestel's Homelink service, already makes advertising an integral part of the service. Finally, and perhaps, the most important question: 'Who has the responsibility for the information provided?' In Britain, for example, there is no control of information and anybody can become an IP.

Well, these are just some of the questions raised. Whatever the answers, videotex is here to stay and we must adapt to it in an appropriate way.

Unit 9 **Listening and Reading 2**

a Can I use the Homelink services twenty-four hours a day?
b I understand that I can use it for normal banking services like account statements and transferring funds. What other financial services does it offer?
c Besides the financial services, what about travel? I believe there's something on offer here?
d How much does it cost to advertise something through Homelink—my car, for example?
e If I join, will I get all the Prestel information services?
f Now, coming to the equipment. Do I have to buy a special TV?
g Do I need a special adaptor for the Home Deck?
h What about training? I suppose I'll need some training on how to operate the Home Deck?
i I'm worried about other people getting access to my bank account. What safeguards are there to prevent this?
j Finally, the cost. How much do I have to invest with the Nottingham Building Society?
k How much do I have to deposit in the Bank of Scotland account?
l So, £1000 with the NBS, nothing with the Bank of Scotland. Are there any other charges?
m I see, so there's a £5 rental a quarter and local telephone charges each time I use it. Anything else?
n Right, thanks very much. That's all for now. I'll be in touch soon.

Unit 10 **Listening 1**

Clayton It's very kind of you to agree to come and discuss the Tele-X project with me, Mr Leijonflycht.

Leijonflycht It's a pleasure to be here, Mr Clayton, and I shall do my best to answer your questions. I must say at the beginning, though, that many aspects of the project are not yet finalized, and I may not be able to give you answers that are as complete as you would wish.

Clayton Right, well let me tell you what I know and then we can start from there. Tele-X is an experimental direct broadcasting, video services and high-speed data satellite due to be launched in 1986.

Leijonflycht That is correct.

Clayton And the project is a joint one including the telecommunications administration, space authorities, broadcasting and private industrial companies in Norway, Sweden and possibly Finland. When will Finland finally decide if it is going to join the project, do you think?

Leijonflycht Well, I'm not really in a position to be able to comment on that. We hope there'll be a decision in the near future.

Clayton The Finns are said to be unhappy about the size of the financial contribution they'll be asked to make. Could you comment on that?

Leijonflycht Sorry, I'm not really the person to answer that one. I act as adviser on the technical organization of the project.

Clayton Then perhaps we should move on to that.

Leijonflycht Fine. Well, as I'm sure you know, overall responsibility is held by the Swedish Board of Space Activities. It has appointed a Steering Committee for the project with members from Norway, Finland and Sweden.

Clayton What will happen to the composition of the committee if Finland decides not to join?

Leijonflycht We'll come back to that in a minute, if you don't mind. I'll describe the general organization to you first.

Clayton OK.

Leijonflycht The principal parties involved, apart from the Swedish Broadcasting Corporation (the SBC) which I'll come back to in a minute, are Swedish Telecom and the Swedish Space Corporation (SSC). The definition work is being done by them under the general influence of the SSC/ST Co-ordinating Group which reports direct to the Steering Committee. The SSC is responsible for maintaining links with industry. It does this through its Contracts Division and through the Satellite Group, one of three technical groups that come under the Project Team.

Clayton How does the SBC fit into this?

Leijonflycht Well, let me just tell you about the Swedish Telecom organization before we get on to the broadcasting corporation's role. Swedish Telecom has two management groups, DASAT for the data and video experiments and RASK, for the radio parts of the project. Subordinate to these two groups there is a working party called RATEX.

Clayton Does RATEX liaise direct with the space corporation at all?

Leijonflycht In fact it does. One of the three technical groups in the corporation that I mentioned earlier deals with earth stations. This group is in direct contact with RATEX since Swedish Telecom is responsible for operating the earth stations.

Clayton OK. Now what about the SBC? They must be pretty worried about the possibility of dozens of TV channels raining down on you from space?

Leijonflycht I'm sorry, I can't really answer that. All I can say is that they're following developments with great interest. In the Tele-X project, the SBC liaises with Swedish Telecom in a Contact Group which is parallel to the SSC/ST Co-ordinating Group.

Clayton Is there no direct contact between the two?

Leijonflycht Yes, at a lower level, the broadcasting corporation is in direct contact with Swedish Telecom's RASK group.

Clayton Does it report to the other Nordic broadcasting corporations too?

Leijonflycht Yes, its other principal role is to lead an informal working party of the other Nordic BCs to make sure that everyone is informed.

Clayton OK. Could I come back now to the private companies you mentioned? Which companies are we talking about here?

Leijonflycht Well, I can't give you the full list. As you can imagine, it's extremely long. But the most important contractors are Aerospatiale, which is the prime contractor for the satellite, Ericsson which is supplying the payload and Saab Scania which is providing the . . .

Unit 10 **Listening 2**

. . . well, now that we've taken a look at the satellites and the programming that's up there, it's time to come back down to earth and check out just how the Homearth Mark II receives them. Now, as you know, the microwaves transmitted by the satellite are very weak when they finally get to our back gardens and this is why we need a fairly large dish antenna, in the case of the Homearth, two metres across. This dish captures as much of the signal as possible and reflects it to a point above the centre of the dish called the focal point where a metal object called the feedhorn is located. This helps to gather up all the reflected microwave signal and conduct it back to the first stage of electronics with a minimal amount of signal loss. This first stage, the low noise amplifier, or LNA as it is also called, consists of several microwave amplifier circuits in series. These multiply the incoming microwave signal, which is probably not more than a millionth of a volt, by a factor of 100,000. This amplified signal is then sent out of the LNA on a large coaxial cable to another electronic box called the downconverter. This reduces the 4 GHz signal to a much lower frequency, called the intermediate frequency (or IF). A microwave mixing circuit inside the downconverter combines the incoming satellite signal with a second signal generated by the voltage-tuned oscillator (or VTO). When these two signals are heterodyned together, the IF signal is created. It is then amplified and filtered before being sent to the indoor receiver via a length of coaxial cable. We often say that the IF is 70 MHz, but what we really mean is that it's a band of frequencies centred on 70 MHz. This band needs to be around 30 MHz wide in order to be able to carry all the information necessary for one satellite TV channel. The incoming signal is amplified and then, after being filtered, this IF signal is fed into another circuit called a discriminator. The discriminator's job is to strip off the video and audio signals. These are contained in the 70 MHz IF in the same way as they were in the original 4 GHz signal. We may have stepped the frequency down in order to handle it more easily, but that doesn't affect the video or audio information at all. For this reason the original 4 GHz frequency is called a carrier. After leaving the discriminator, the separated audio and video signals are sent to another unit called the Radio Frequency (or RF) Modulator. This may be contained within the receiver or, in some cases, it comes as a separate unit. This modulator acts as a miniature transmitter and hooks up directly to the TV's cable input, if it has one, or through a CATV transformer to the TV's antenna terminals. All receivers have a means of selecting which channel to see. The cheaper ones have a variable tuning knob like those used on radios. The basic Homearth has a channel selector knob with 24 positions, rather like a CB radio. The Homearth Deluxe has a digital channel display with up/down scan tuning and remote control. Whichever method is used, a voltage signal is sent back to the downconverter along a wire cable. This adjusts the VTO and causes the mixer to produce the desired satellite channel. Well, that's the basic design of the earth station. This would be a good point to stop for any questions . . .

Unit 11 **Listening 1**

Until the mid-1960s, when the first crossbar exchanges were installed in Paris, there had been very little interest in anything to do with telecommunications in France. Then, at about the same time as the new exchanges were installed, French telecoms researchers began exploring the subject of electronic switching, and in 1970 the world's first electronic switching centre connected to the public network and handling real calls was tried and tested. Three years later, in 1973, it was taken into use in some areas of Paris. More money was then allocated for telecoms. In the Seventh Economic Plan, for example, telecommunications became the number one priority for the French government. This enabled a period of explosive growth and innovation to take place.

1978 was an extremely important year for French telecommunications, firstly because the 10 millionth subscriber was connected in January, and secondly because the government informed the Telecommunications Authority that funds would be made available for the following projects:

First, 2500 subscribers in Vélizy, a suburb of Paris, would be linked to a data-bank through their telephone lines, in a pilot project similar to Prestel in the UK.

Second, the electronic directory would be tried experimentally in the Rennes area. The sudden, enormous increase in the number of subscribers had led to a similar increase in the number of telephone books that were required. The price of paper had also just risen significantly, and this seemed a good opportunity to try out a new system. The applications of this new system would probably spread far beyond simply providing domestic subscribers with information about telephone numbers.

Third, high-speed facsimile (or Téléfax) would be developed nationally, enabling modified photocopy machines to use the telephone network to send messages anywhere in the country.

Fourth, a French domestic satellite system would be developed (Télécom 1) enabling companies to transmit data at high speed between computers. The system would also be capable of handling high-speed facsimile as well as containing a number of telephone channels, and would also include facilities for teleconferencing and for the videophone.

And fifth, a pilot scheme using optical fibres for a variety of purposes would be undertaken in Biarritz.

How have all these changes affected the ordinary subscriber? Firstly, of course, the number of subscribers has risen dramatically over the last 10 years. In 1954, there were only 1.75 million telephones in France, or, put another way, there were 4 subscribers for every 100 inhabitants. In 1965, there were only 3 million lines and in 1970 only 4 million. By December 1974, the figure had reached 6.2 million and in May 1976, there were 8.4 million subscribers, or 16 subscribers for every 100 inhabitants. January 1978 saw the connection of the 10 millionth subscriber and the 12 millionth could use his telephone by the end of that same year. By 1982, the figure had reached 19.3 million, or 35 subscribers for every 100 inhabitants, or, again put another way, 60% of all households in France had their own telephone. By the end of 1983, there were 21 million subscribers, or 38.5 subscribers for every 100 inhabitants.

So, we can see that in terms of quantity, the figures are most impressive. In terms of quality and value for money, a consumer organization, the AFUTT, which represents the ordinary subscriber, noted that during the period 1978 to 1981, there were fewer wrong numbers, the waiting-period for the phone to be installed was much shorter than before, and, most important of all perhaps, connection charges had fallen sharply. These were 1,100 francs in 1974 (a fantastically high sum), 800 francs in 1976, 700 francs in 1978, 500 francs in 1980 and 400 francs in 1981, the date of the last fall.

Well, I hope you haven't been too bored and that when you visit Vélizy later in the week my talk will help you to put everything into an historical perspective. If you have any questions, I'll deal with them over coffee in about 5 minutes.

Thank you very much.

Unit 11 **Listening 2**

French Welcome to this short discussion in which we'll look at some of the results of the Vélizy experiment before trying to draw some conclusions about its usefulness. You should all have a little brochure in front of you which contains a statistical analysis of what we at French Télécom consider to be the most important points of the test. Figure 1 shows that an average of 25 000 calls were made each month during 1982.

Indian How many subscribers were involved in the experiment?

French Just under two and a half thousand.

American They weren't all domestic users, were they?

French No. The information providers and some schools used the system, and there were also terminals in public places such as Town Halls and Post Offices. Domestic users, in fact, accounted for about 54% of the traffic, except during the summer months. The 57 terminals in schools and public places accounted for about 16%, which means that the information providers made about 30% of the calls.

British What about the average duration of a domestic call?

French Well, this was just under 15 minutes which represents three call units. Another interesting feature is that the number of services consulted during the 15-minute period hardly varies throughout the year, averaging about 3.3.

Indian Were there any days in the week that were particularly busy?

French Yes, generally speaking Saturday was the busiest day all year with Wednesday the second most popular day. French children don't go to school on Wednesday and . . .

Indian . . . so you think that a lot of children used the system during their day off?

French Yes, that's what the figures seem to suggest.

British What about the peak hours?

French An interesting question because they varied on weekdays and weekends. During weekends the heaviest period was around 3 p.m. and then again at around 5 p.m. The low points were during mealtimes and between 8.30 p.m. and 10 p.m. when there's often a good film on TV. For weekdays the profile was rather different. Instead of the relatively even traffic that you get at the weekend, weekday traffic was heavily concentrated between 5 p.m. and 11 p.m., with a little trough between 8.30 p.m. and 10 p.m., again probably because of the TV.

Are there any more questions about this section or shall we move on? No questions? Fine. Let's move on to the distribution of the calls by sector.

American Is that the information that's summarized here in this bar graph?

French That's right. We've taken October '82 as a sample month. The figures show that the most consulted service group was the one that covered radio, the press and TV, closely followed by some of the local services such as the electronic mailbox. This is a service that enables any subscriber to contact any other subscriber or group of subscribers and leave a message. In fact, if you take all these local services and put them in one group, then they were consulted more often than the radio, TV and press group.

Indian What you're saying is that the local services were consulted more than any other category, in fact.

French That's right. It's an interesting point because in future projects it could lead to a special emphasis being placed on local questions and events. In this way the community spirit might be improved by videotex rather than harmed, as many people fear may happen.

British Yes, that could be very significant. What other social information do you have? I'm thinking of socio-economic data, age-groups and so on.

French Well, you won't be surprised to hear that retired people used the system least. In terms of age, the 40 to 49 year-old group made the most calls, closely followed by the under thirties. The professional group that made most calls were the senior office executives, who came just ahead of office workers.

American OK, and what about the future? Where do you go from here?

French Well, the last terminals are to be connected in June 1984 and soon after that a decision will have to be made about how to continue. I'm not sure what that will be but I guess we'll be planning . . .

Unit 12 **Listening 1**

Interviewer We're going to be looking this evening at the question of privatization of British Telecom and will be hearing the views of both government and private industry. In the studio this evening we have Mr Johnson, Undersecretary of State at the Department of Industry, and Mr Simons, a representative of TEMA, the Telecommunications Equipment Manufacturers Association. Let's start with Mr Johnson.

Johnson Thank you. In the international context I think we'd all agree that the UK now has the most liberal approach to network access outside the U.S. And it's this liberal approach which is encouraging new enterprises to produce new levels of the most advanced telecommunications technology available in the world.

Interviewer Would you agree with that Mr Simons?

Simons I think it's true that liberalization has enabled the development of alternative value-added networks such as Mercury . . .

Interviewer Excuse me, what do you mean by a value-added network?

Simons Well, simply a network which gives the subscriber additional services on top of the ones provided by B.T. Mercury is a value-added network which provides the user with a wider degree of choice and flexibility. However, I don't think any of us are happy with the red tape which slows down private industry's attempts to compete against B.T.

Interviewer What do you mean by red tape?

Simons Well, our main concern is the British Approval Board for Telecommunications—BABT. This was set up by the government to test and approve equipment for connection to B.T. networks.

Interviewer That seems fair enough. Surely you've got to have a body like that?

Simons Yes, of course, but the problems are the delays in getting approval and the cost, especially for smaller suppliers. The fees for approval are between two and five thousand pounds.

Interviewer So you're saying, in a sense, that B.T. is still in a protected position.

Simons Yes, I think many of our members feel that.

Interviewer Mr Johnson, what's your response to Mr Simons's concern about BABT?

Johnson Well, to take his point about the cost of approval first. I think you'll appreciate that approval involves substantial costs in testing equipment and time for testing. BABT has a responsibility to the customer to make sure all equipment is well-made and reliable. As far as the delays are concerned, I think we're dealing with that, and the process should speed up over the next few months.

Interviewer Some critics say that privatization will just change B.T. from state monopoly to a public monopoly. In other words, B.T. will continue to be in such a strong position as to make it very hard for the private sector to really compete. What's your view Mr Simons?

Simons We would certainly like to see more competition allowed. Mercury is the only licensed alternative network at the moment and B.T.'s massive resources put it in a strong position to dictate developments in the market.

Johnson I agree B.T. is in a strong position, and that's why we've set up OFTEL—Office of Telecommunications—to regulate it, both in the interests of consumers and the free market.

Interviewer Right. One last question. Isn't there a danger that liberalizing telecoms in the UK is going to open the floodgates to foreign competition? American companies have already set up in the UK. Isn't this a sign of things to come?

Simons That's probably right. But it's up to British manufacturers to compete even more effectively. Large and small manufacturers can't sit back any more and that's a good thing for all concerned.

Interviewer Thank you gentlemen. I'm afraid that's all we've got time for . . .

Unit 12 **Listening 2**

A First, gentlemen, a little background to Mercury. Back in February 1982 we received a licence to build a privately owned national network competing with B.T. When I say 'we', I mean the shareholders—Cable and Wireless and British Petroleum with 40% each, and Barclays Merchant Bank with the remaining 20%.

Now people thought at the time that we were only interested in large business users but as you'll soon see the picture is very different. In fact, we'll be able to offer much more than leased lines from one company location to another. We aim to extend the service to the private telephone user and become a true alternative to B.T. as a national carrier.

Now you may well ask why you as subscribers need another network. The answer is that the speed of growth in information technology means that the customer needs choices. We believe we can provide a network at equivalent or lower costs which will be very attractive to you. Now before I go on to describe the network and how it will work, are there any questions?

B Yes, just one. It's been said that a telephone network works much like a road network. In other words there's no more point in having two telephone lines from A to B along the same route as there is in having two roads.

A I don't think the analogy is a good one. As I've just said, there is a lot of point. B.T.'s own programme of conversion to a digital network is going to take time and even when it is available, demand, especially for data communications, will be high enough to support two networks.

So, shall I go on? On this map you can see the proposed network. Our plan is for a figure of eight network centred on Birmingham. The Southern loop will have London and Bristol at its two corners, the Northern loop will connect Leeds, Manchester and Stoke-on-Trent.

C We've heard that you're using British Rail track for laying optical fibre cables. Is that right?

A Yes, we'll be using monomode fibre, which gives a better all-round performance than multimode, laying it in concrete ducts along the side of railway tracks. With this fibre we've got a carrying capacity of 565 megabits per second and regenerators or repeaters only every 25 kilometres.

B Excuse me, what's available to the user at the moment?

A Well, we're meeting demand in London with microwave radio. We've already got roof-top dishes for line-of-sight communications and we've linked up Birmingham in the first place with a chain of six microwave sites.

C So, no optical fibre transmission yet?

A True, but we reckon that the initial network will be finished by mid-1985 linking up London, with its own optical fibre ring, to Birmingham and Manchester via Stoke-on-Trent.

B And what about the connections to the user?

A We'll be using cellular radio because of the shortage of frequencies in the first place. In the longer term we hope to connect city subscribers by a cable network using wayleaves such as the London Underground.

C One thing concerns me. No company is going to be interested unless you offer international connections.

A Of course, you're right. We signed an agreement with BTI—that's British Telecoms International division—in December '82, giving us access to space segments on satellites. But since then we've got capacity on Intelsat V and also on the French Telecom I satellite. Our first ground station should be somewhere in the Oxford area.

B I hope you don't mind me asking, but why will Mercury be the only alternative network available in the UK?

A The short answer to that is that the government has limited network licences over the next seven years—that's up to the end of the 80s—to just one carrier. I don't mind admitting that we have an uphill struggle to compete with B.T. in a market where they've long held a monopoly position. It's hard enough for one company to establish itself. I think the government rightly feels that Mercury needs time to do this. After that, things may well change.

Any further questions? No? Well perhaps we could take a look at some of the facilities which will be offered by Mercury . . .

Unit 13 **Listening 1**

Ramesh How do you do? Ramesh Khan is my name.

George How do you do? Very kind of you to see me. My name's George Haan. I'm over here on a job for the Indian P and T. My brief is to look at personnel recruitment and training within the telecom administration and to make recommendations for changes in the system where necessary.

Ramesh Fine. Where would you like to start?

George Well, it would help if you could give me some idea of the promotion ladder and recruitment pattern in the P and T. I know that telecoms in India is one of the priorities and handling personnel is always important in a growth area.

Ramesh Yes, that's right. We've been increasing our staff levels by about 5% a year for the last ten years, and plan to continue at that rate until 1985. You should look at this rate in relation to the expanding network. As far as I remember, in the period '62 to '80 the number of lines increased by 90% while personnel in the P and T found it hard to keep up at around 63%.

George I see. So at what levels do you take on new recruits?

Ramesh Oh, there are three broad levels. The lowest is for what we call Operative Staff who come in after high school as Assistant Operators or Telephone Inspectors.

George Yes, and what do they do?

Ramesh Well, basically, they check telephone sets, perform simple maintenance and repair work.

George So what sort of training do they get?

Ramesh They're trained at one of our 26 Circle or District Training Centres that are spread all over the country.

George I see. And what would be the next rung on the ladder for them?

Ramesh Well, the next grade is Technician.

George And what's their background?

Ramesh No different really from the operatives. Any operative who works well and gains experience can expect to move up to Technician.

George Right. So what comes next?

Ramesh The next step is to so-called Junior Engineer. A Technician who wants to move up to JE will have to attend in-house training at one of our 13 Telecoms Training Centres. Similarly, new entrants at this level will attend a one-year initial training course at a TTC.

George What sort of qualifications would a new entrant have?

Ramesh Well, he'd probably have a B.Sc. in Maths or Physics, and would have passed the P and T Entrance Exam.

George You mentioned three broad levels. I suppose Junior Engineer is the second level?

Ramesh That's correct—Junior Supervisory Staff. Someone at this level would expect to spend about ten years as a JE before moving up to Assistant Engineer after the refresher course at our Advanced Level Telecom Training Centre near New Delhi.

George How about new entrants at this level?

Ramesh They mostly come out of Engineering school with BEs, that is Bachelor of Engineering degrees in electronics. Then, having passed a national selection board—that's the Union Public Service Commission—they go to the ALTTC for one or two months. Is that clear?

George Yes, yes, please go on. I'm just noting it down.

Ramesh Well, we've now reached Engineer level and the next step is Assistant Divisional Engineer which a Bachelor in Electronics Engineering would expect to reach after two years' experience.

George And now we're reaching the upper echelons?

Ramesh Yes, indeed. The final engineering level is Divisional Engineer and then we move on to where, right at the top, that is the Directorate, civil servants are recruited direct.

George Well, thanks very much. That's given me a good overview. There are just a couple more things while we . . .

Unit 13 **Listening 2**

American I know that India and France recently signed a series of agreements to collaborate in the field of telecommunications. What do the agreements cover?

Indian Well, as you've just said, there were several different agreements. The first goes back to February 1980 and was a simple protocol for co-operation between the French PTT and the Indian P and T. It entered a more active phase in December 1981 when another agreement, to co-operate on the E 10 system, was signed.

American I see. So you're going to install the E 10 in India?

Indian That's right, but we'll come back to that in a moment. Four agreements were signed between the French company, CIT-Alcatel on the one hand and the Indian government, the Indian P and T Department and the company ITI (Indian Telephone Industries) on the other.

French That's right. A further two agreements for co-operation were signed between the Indian P and T and another French company, Sofrecom. The final agreement was signed between the Indian TRC and its French equivalent, the CNET.

American That seems rather a lot of contracts, doesn't it? What fields do they cover?

French Well, let's take the four signed with CIT-Alcatel first, shall we? The first contract will enable ITI to manufacture the E 10 system under licence in India. The second contract covers the building of a factory at Gonda, in Uttar Pradesh; this factory will be sold to ITI and, when full production is reached, it will produce 500 000 lines per year. The third covers the development of a new time division switching system by the Indian TRC in collaboration with CIT-Alcatel, while the fourth contract covers the delivery and installation of 23 E 10 exchanges to India, providing a total of about 200 000 lines.

American And what about the contracts with Sofrecom?

Indian These two contracts will help the Indian administration to plan and control the growth of the network more efficiently. It will involve using modern engineering and management tools, as well as other methods developed in France. It also includes training, because engineers from India will be trained in France and also locally at the ALTTC. After a period of theoretical instruction on E 10 design, engineering, administration and maintenance, the Indian engineers will be assisted by French experts in applying their knowledge to their everyday work.

French Sofrecom will help with network planning, but also with the creation of a component-reliability monitoring centre.

American This whole scheme is an example of what you call 'technology transfer', isn't it?

French Right. But for technology transfer to work correctly, the two partners must work hand in hand. For example, in the new switching system which is to be developed on a collaborative basis between CIT-Alcatel and its Indian partners, the latter have decided to 'indianize' digital exchanges, drawing on the know-how of Indian researchers and engineers, combined with the expertise acquired under the E 10 technology transfer agreement.

American You mentioned that 23 E 10 exchanges are being installed. Where exactly?

Indian The short answer to that question is all over the country, in nine different areas, in fact. Calcutta will have four exchanges with a total capacity of 32 000 lines. Madras will have two, with 12 000 lines, Hyderabad one 10 000-line exchange, Bombay seven with a total of 60 000 lines, Ahmedabad one 10 000-line exchange, Rajasthan one 3 000-line centre, as will Pathankot. Kanpur will also have one 10 000-line exchange, and finally, Delhi, the capital, will get 5 switching centres with a total capacity of some 50 000 lines.

French Decision-makers in India are convinced that electronics can accelerate the development of their country, but, at the same time, they are determined that India will not lose its independence. In France, we hope to be able to show that our know-how in advanced telecommunications can be made available through real, far-reaching technology transfer schemes.

American Well, gentlemen, thanks for explaining the situation to me. I hope the whole project is a big success and that soon India will have a system worthy of such a great country.

Unit 14 **Listening 1**

Rep I am very pleased to welcome you to Ellemtel. As you probably already know, Ellemtel is a Research and Development company jointly owned by Ericsson and Swedish Telecom.

I think there are good reasons for separating Research and Development work from the production and administration of telecommunications. One is that you can draw a clear line between continual technical work, done on established systems, and research into entirely new products. Another is that a smaller company—and we are just 700 employees—compared to Swedish

Telecom's 43 000 and Ericsson's 40 000, offers a far less bureaucratic and thus more creative environment to work in. Finally Ellemtel benefits from the technical resources and expertise of two highly-advanced organizations and avoids the danger of duplicating research programmes.

So, what does all this add up to? Well, I think these factors mean a shorter time-span between an idea and a marketable product.

English woman We've certainly heard about the success of AXE, your digital exchange system. What other products have you developed?

Rep There is the AXB30—a data communication system being used for the first time in the Nordic Data Network. Then there is the AXB20, our new telex system with stored control. Also, you may have seen the Diavox telephone. That's some of the hardware. On the software side we developed a new high-level language for use in the AXE systems—we call it PLEX. We're using CAD—computer aided design—in designing LSI circuits and printed board assemblies.

Indian So what are you working on at the moment?

Rep Of course, new applications and equipment for AXE. We're also studying ISDNs and doing some work on very large scale integrated circuits—or VLSIs as they are called. Anyway, can I suggest we take a look round our laboratories and perhaps we can see some of our staff at work.

Indian Yes, that would be very interesting.

Rep As I was saying earlier, we've got about 700 employees. Most of them are engineers—working in teams of 4 to 8 persons.

English man So, each team has its own project?

Rep No, not necessarily. Normally each member of the team works independently, but has the opportunity to discuss his work and solve problems with other team members. Now in this lab, they're setting up a complete test plant for testing some PCBs . . .

English woman Sorry?

Rep Printed circuit boards, I mean. We do a lot of testing—especially mechanical parts in any assembly or rack.

English man What's over there?

Rep I'm afraid I couldn't tell you. Just a moment, I'll try and find out.
I'm sorry, none of the engineers are around.

English man Doesn't matter.

Rep Shall we move on? Right, here you can see a model of the AXB30 system. I mentioned it earlier. And now actually someone doing some work. Sven, what are you working on?

Sven Well, I'm feeding some test results into the computer. We've been working on some new PCM equipment and we've just finished a series of reliability tests.

Rep Ah, this you might find interesting. We've had one or two problems with the operation of AXE exchanges during thunderstorms—the build up of electricity can cause circuits to fail. Here they're testing some new housing for the circuits.
Sorry to hurry you. What about visiting the canteen for a coffee?
This way . . .

Unit 14 **Listening 2**

Rep We have got a few minutes left to consider our international training programme for 1984. As things stand, we'll be running 3 courses: that is, the IPTM, our top management course starting mid-August; Digital Networks, that's the introduction to digital techniques for four weeks in June; and Opman, our middle-management course to run concurrently with the IPTM.

Visitor Yes, I'd be interested in hearing about all three of these, but before that, what's the background to these courses? Why did you decide to run them?

Rep A good question. We started about six years ago. At about the same time, the Swedish Commission for Technical Co-operation, an independent government agency, was set up to support technical training programmes for developing and newly industrialized countries.

I suppose this factor, plus our experience and available facilities for training, made it an obvious step. From an organizational point of view, we ourselves have gone through a series of re-organizations, forced on us by changing circumstances—especially the digitalization of the network. This experience we can share with other administrations and, hopefully, solve their problems more quickly and efficiently than we did ourselves!

Visitor I can see that. But all developed countries have a similar experience.

Rep That's true, but Swedish Telecom, unlike its counterparts in other countries, manufactures equipment as well as handling the construction, installation and maintenance of the network and subscriber equipment. This broad experience has given us a lot of know-how in the whole area of telephony.

Visitor I suppose also it's in your interests to run such courses?

Rep Yes, that's true, in the sense that it fosters better relations with the developing world. We found that we were already receiving a lot of students on study-visits. These visits were often difficult to arrange and only partly of benefit to the visitors. As an alternative, regular courses can produce better results for both the students and ourselves.

Visitor So, you mentioned the facilities. Where do you run these courses?

Rep Mainly at our training school in Kalmar in southern Sweden, but all the courses involve visits and field-study in the telecom areas in other parts of Sweden.

Visitor I see. Who should I send on the different courses, then?

Rep The first one, the International Programme for Telecommunications Management—that's a bit of a mouthful so we just call it the IPTM—is designed for senior managers. We don't cover purely technical aspects.

Visitor What do you cover then?

Rep Well, a lot of time is spent on analysing methods and approaches to the most efficient telecom administration. We also deal with planning and programming for future network growth.

Visitor Anything else?

Rep I'll let you have a copy of the course programme, but purchasing—in other words, looking at tendering and evaluation of tenders—plays an important part as well.

Visitor Thank you. What was the second one called?

Rep That's our Digital Networks Course—really designed for senior engineers and managers with a good knowledge of switching and transmission systems.

Visitor So this is a more technically orientated course?

Rep Yes, that's right. The objective here is to give the participants a good understanding of their administrations and plan efficiently for their digitalization process.

Visitor What do you mainly look at then?

Rep We start with network structure, costs and distribution, and then move on through present equipment available, route plans, transmission media . . .

Visitor What form do the lessons take?

Rep There are some traditional lectures, but we use case-studies a lot during the workshops. Here the participants work in small groups on models. In fact, case-studies play a very big part in all three courses.

Visitor So, how long does the Digital Networks course last?

Rep Nearly four weeks, whereas the IPTM is a full nine weeks. The third course, Operational Management or Opman for short is the longest, lasting a full 12 weeks. However, in this case, 7 of these weeks are spent in the field attached to one of the local areas.

Visitor That sounds interesting. Who are you catering for here?

Rep Well, one of the things we noticed during the IPTM course was that some of the management ideas discussed during the course would be valuable at a lower level—so-called middle-management. However, in these cases the students would have much closer and more frequent contact with the actual work in the field.

Visitor I see. What are the objectives then for this course?

Rep Briefly, to clarify and demonstrate an operational management control system which will improve network performance. The participants have to work out operational systems suitable to their own administrations which will then be implemented on their return.

Visitor Thanks very much. I'm afraid that's taken more than a few minutes. Anything else I should know?

Rep No, I don't think so. You'll find it all in the documentation. Oh, yes, perhaps one thing. All the courses are run in English so the participants must have a reasonable level of that language.

Visitor I don't think that should be a problem. I hope not, anyway.

Unit 15 **Listening 1**

Journalist I wonder if you would tell me something about TAT 8. There's a lot of interest in it in Holland.

Engineer Sure. Well, as I guess you know, it's the eighth transatlantic cable but it's the first one to use optical fibres. It'll link Tuckerton, New Jersey with Widemouth Bay in England and Penmarc'h in France.

Journalist This must be the first time that optical fibres have been used over such a great distance.

Engineer That's right, and another unique feature is that it'll have a Y configuration. When it gets near Europe it'll divide into two with one part going to England and the other to France. This represents a considerable development in undersea cable technology because, as you know, the existing coaxial cables cannot be connected in this way.

Journalist What about the cost?

Engineer Well, the co-owners have placed orders to the value of $335 million.

Journalist Which companies have won the contracts?

Engineer AT & T Communications will design and construct the largest part of the cable. That contract's worth $250 million. Standard Telephones and Cables, ITT's British subsidiary, will construct the British section for $52 million and Submarcom, which represents CIT-Alcatel and Cables de Lyons will lay the French section at a cost of $33 million. AT & T also has the job of co-ordinating the connection of the three parts.

Journalist Who are the owners of the cable? Presumably it's a consortium?

Engineer Yes. AT & T will have the largest share, 37% in fact, and, together with seven other American companies and Teleglobe of Canada, own half the cable. The other 50% will be owned by twenty European telecom administrations. The three largest shares there, 16%, 10% and 6% will be held by British Telecom and the French and German PTTs respectively.

Journalist This must be a really significant breakthrough for optical fibres?

Engineer It certainly is. And as the market expands and the technology is perfected, costs will continue to fall. The market has developed very fast and it's expected to grow at almost 50% per year. To start with, it was mostly city junction networks, but it's now evolved in two directions: one towards long-haul large capacity systems like TAT 8 and the other towards subscriber networks. The technological advance that has made the former possible is the use of longer wavelengths, what we call the second window, that is wavelengths around 1300 nm. These can be used on both multimode and single mode fibres.

Journalist What's the advantage of these longer waves?

Engineer I can answer that in two words. Less attenuation. You have to reckon with a loss of 3 dB per kilometre on short wave multimode fibres. So, at 140 Mbits per second, these 850 nm fibres can't be used with repeater spans above 10 kilometres. That's why they are mostly to be found in urban networks. Multimode systems operating at 1300 nm allow for much greater distances between repeaters, about 25 kilometres, because the attenuation is far lower, about 0.8 dB per kilometre.

Journalist You mentioned single mode fibres too.

Engineer Right. These are even better. The loss is only 0.6 per kilometre so you can get 35 kilometre spans or more at 140 Mbits. It's this that has made TAT 8 possible.

Journalist And where do we go from here?

Engineer Well, they're working on 565 Mbit systems now with over 30 kilometre repeater spacings. So in the medium term I think we can look . . .

Unit 15 **Listening 2**

Peters We were just talking about the joint ventures and mergers which have been forced on telecom manufacturers. What's interesting is that this same trend towards multinational activity can be seen in some of the users of telecoms.

Editor What sort of users are you thinking about?

Peters Well, take Ford, for example. In developing their world car, the Escort, they have built up a whole network of manufacturing and selling operations around the world. Now a few years back, Ford had a system where each region—Europe, Latin America, North America and Asia Pacific—was responsible for its own communications. That won't work any more, so they've linked up a worldwide communications network with its hub in England.

Editor So that they can co-ordinate manufacturing and selling activities?

Peters Yes. Now previously telecoms were considered by many companies as just another utility, like electricity. But what they're finding is that telecoms can be an important strategic means of competing effectively.

Editor Could you be a little more concrete?

Peters I'll try. The latest communications and computer technology enables businesses to deliver information more quickly. For example, the First National Bank of Boston is installing a data communications network linking its offices in Boston, New York, London and Hong Kong. Loan applications, for instance, can now be approved in a couple of minutes whereas previously it would have taken several days. So immediately you have savings in time, but ultimately much more.

Editor In what way?

Peters Well, telecoms has the power to change the way people work. For example, Atlantic Richfield has just installed a $17 million video conferencing system that will connect its Los Angeles headquarters with offices in Philadelphia, Denver, Houston, Dallas and Washington. Now, instead of travelling to meetings, executives can speak to and watch one another on a TV link without leaving their offices. Arco reckons it can save $10 million in travel expenses each year with this system. Perhaps an even more startling example is the American Express company. It's estimated that they spend $300 to $400 million annually—that's 4–5% of their turnover—on information processing. They've built up a worldwide network linked to their computer centre in Phoenix which now handles about 250 000 credit card transactions a day, at an average speed of five seconds or less.

Editor That's pretty impressive.

Peters Yes it is, but even more impressive from the company's point of view is that they've saved a lot of money through introducing this system. Their business—that is, the number of credit card holders—has gone up by about 50% over the past five years but they've managed to hold losses from the fraudulent use of cards at the same level. So the system is not only quick, which is good for the customer, but also secure, which is good for both customer and company.

Editor So the capital investment in these systems always pays off?

Peters If it's well-planned and the right decisions are made, yes. As I said earlier, telecoms used to be considered just another service. It's now becoming a top management issue in all large companies—or if it isn't, it certainly should be.

Revision Unit C **Listening**

Ladies and gentlemen: it is my purpose in this brief talk to illustrate the rapid developments taking place in telecommunications in Costerutsi today. I shall do so by contrasting the position in a number of key areas of activity at different points in time: 5 years ago; today; and the projected position 5 years from now.

Firstly, some statistics about C.T.A. staff. The rapid expansion of C.T.A. has seen an increase in overall numbers of staff, but rationalization and mechanization restricted that growth. From the 8500 employees of 5 years ago, we have grown to 8700 today, but in 5 years time it is anticipated that this number will have increased by only 100. At the same time, the centralized nature of our organization 5 years ago is now undergoing a transition which will lead to a much more decentralized system in the future. As equipment becomes more automatic, the accent on training, which was almost entirely for technicians in the field, will concentrate on problems of management; at the present time, the area of operational management is our biggest concern.

As the amount of telephone traffic grows with the increase in the number of telephone stations (1.01 million 5 years ago, 1.34m today, 1.75 projected) the question of transmission techniques becomes increasingly important. PCM techniques, unknown 5 years ago, are at present used between Leyport and the towns of Sonley, Fort Grey and Woodburn. In the near future they will be extended between Woodburn and Ellton, and Sonley and Tottville. The present optical fibre between Fort Grey and Bloosburg will be extended from Fort Grey to Leyport.

Whilst optical fibres increase radically the amount of traffic carried by one line, the expense incurred by the priority we have recently put on this technique is prohibitive. In the next 5 years we shall concentrate on research into techniques allowing ordinary copper pairs to carry increasing amounts of traffic.

However important the new technologies may be, the contact which most customers have with C.T.A. is through the installation and repair of telephones. Here our record is good, and improving. The average time necessary for installation 5 years ago was 18 days for residential and 14 days for business. These figures are now 16 and 13 respectively, and in 5 years time each should have dropped by 2 days more. Our fault repair service is equally impressive in the improvement it has shown: 5 years ago it took 5 days on average to repair a telephone fault, and 2 for a data fault. These figures are now 4 and 1.5, and should drop further to 3.5 and 1.2.

Increasingly, this kind of improvement must be our target. The reason is very simple: from the position of monopoly that we enjoyed 5 years ago, we are moving towards the age of liberalization, in which competition will be strong. Our present semi-liberalized position is preparing us for this, but we need to continue to set high standards if we are to maintain our share of the market.

Thank you for your attention.

Answer key

Unit 1

1.1.1

Fig 1a **a** local **b** junction **c** main/trunk **d** subscriber **e** primary centre/tandem exchange **f** secondary centre/GSC Fig 1b **a** open wire line **b** multi-pair cable **c** multi-unit cable **d** telephone set **e** distribution point **f** cabinet/CCP **g** main distribution frame **h** local exchange **i** the subscriber circuit **j** the secondary circuit **k** the primary circuit Fig 1c **a** 6% **b** 24% **c** 70% **d** Transit Network **e** 24 **f** 11 **g** International Gateway Exchange.

1.1.2

a Group Switching Centre **b** District Switching Centre **c** Main Switching Centre **d** distribution point **e** cross connection point **f** Transit Switching Centre **g** the trunk network **h** a tandem exchange **i** a Group Switching Centre **j** a District Switching Centre/Main Switching Centre **k** a cross connection point **l** a pair (cable pair) **m** a multi-pair cable **n** a multi-unit cable **o** a coaxial cable **p** a radio link **q** overflow traffic (from the normal trunk network) **r** international traffic.

1.2.1

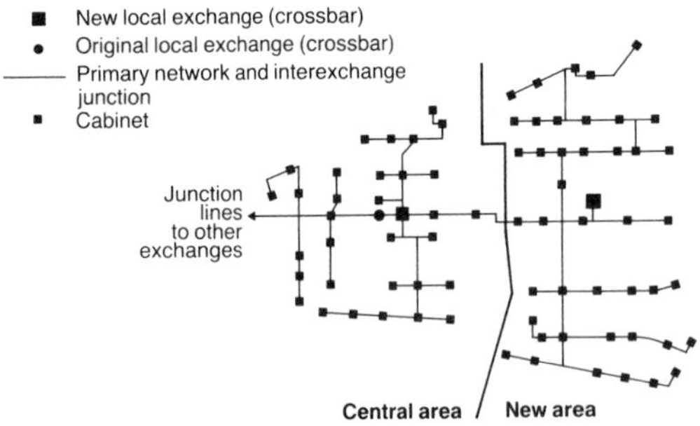

Fig 1d Solution 1

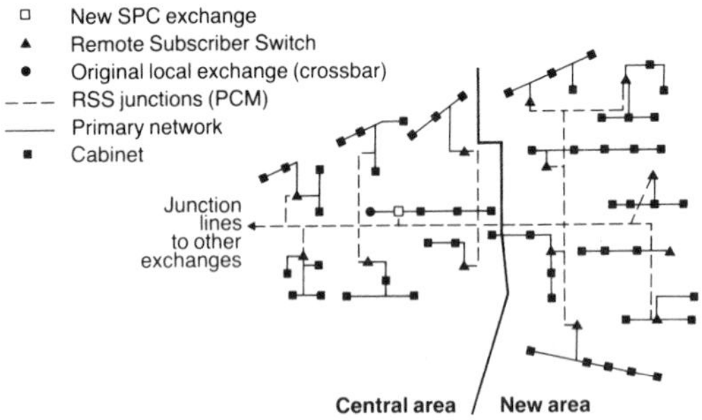

Fig 1f Solution 3

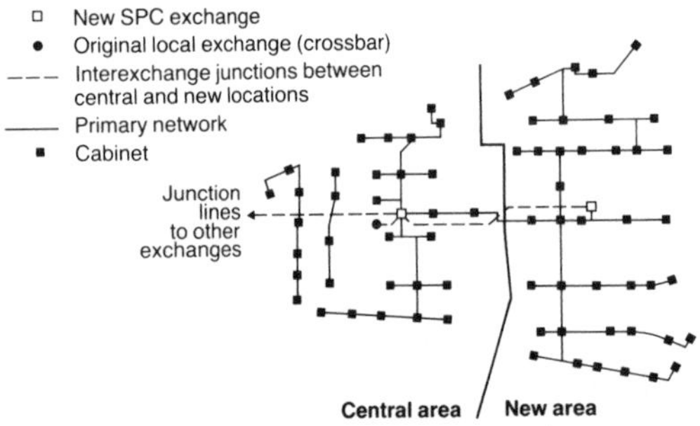

Fig 1e Solution 2

1.2.2

a to expand the existing local network and extend it into a new area **b** the primary part **c** analogue **d** electromechanical (crossbar type) **e** i) to extend the central area ii) to serve the new area **f** next to the old local exchange **g** the junction circuits between the exchanges **h** 1 **i** No **j** the lines between the concentrators and the cabinets.

1.3.1

a The Newtown telephone network *consists of* 2 secondary centres and *4 local exchanges.*
b The Area is divided into 3 sub-areas; North, *South and Central.*
c There *are* two secondary centres. *Both are* connected to the DSC in Sisley by radio link.
d There *are two* junction routes between the secondary centres: *one* direct, *the other* via a local exchange.
e Routing from *one* local exchange to *another* can be direct or via *other* exchanges.
f *Both* Northern and Southern areas are served by *two* local exchanges.

1.3.2

a The central exchange is expanded.
b The Junction circuits use PCM mainly.
PCM is used mainly on the Junction circuits.
c SPC exchanges serve both areas.
Both areas are served by SPC exchanges.
d Cabinets are installed in the local area.
e Traffic is routed direct to a GSC.
f An open-wire line connects the subscriber to the DP.
The subscriber is connected by an open-wire line to the DP.
g All non-local calls are set up via a GSC.
h The road is dug up in order to lay a cable.
i The exchange is sited near the old exchange.
j The RSS switches the call to the designated cabinet.
The call is switched by the RSS to the designated cabinet.

1.4.1

a SSC **b** TDM **c** DCC **d** TDM **e** DMX **f** DCE **g** DCE **h** DTE

1.4.2

a 1c 2d 3f and **h 4g 5a 6e 7b**
b It provides a means of fast, synchronous data transmission. **c** 100 calls per second **d** a printing or alphanumeric visual display terminal or a computer.

1.4.3

a 1e 2a 3c 4d 5b 6g 7f.

1.5 Model answer

The subscribers *are connected to* a switching part. This *consists of* wires and contacts over which signals and speech connections are established *i.e.* the switching network. It also *contains* circuits for simple telephoning functions *such as* tone generators and circuits for hook and key set signals. The control part is *made up of* circuits and programs which take care of the more intelligent functions in the exchange *such as* identification and interpretation of state changes in the switching part. The techniques *used* in the switching part are mainly electromechanical *whereas,* in the control part, they are electronic. This difference in technique *means* that there must be an interface part in *order* that the switching part can communicate with the control part. The interface part *consists of* electronic circuits whose function is *mainly* signal transfer.

Unit 2

2.1.1

Fig 2a open wire lines
Fig 2b underground cable
Fig 2c **a** number of channels **b** intermediate repeaters
Fig 2d **a** line of sight **b** radio relay links
Fig 2e **a** modulator **b** receive side **c** transit exchange.

2.1.2

a Because of demands on operating reliability **b** coaxial cables **c** line amplifiers **d** reception, amplification and transmission of signals **e** the diameter of the parabola in relation to the wavelength **f** transmission as a group to the receive side **g** demodulation of signals **h** extraction of conversations **i** transmission to another transit exchange **j** i) aerial cable ii) underground cable iii) satellite iv) radio relay links.

2.2.1

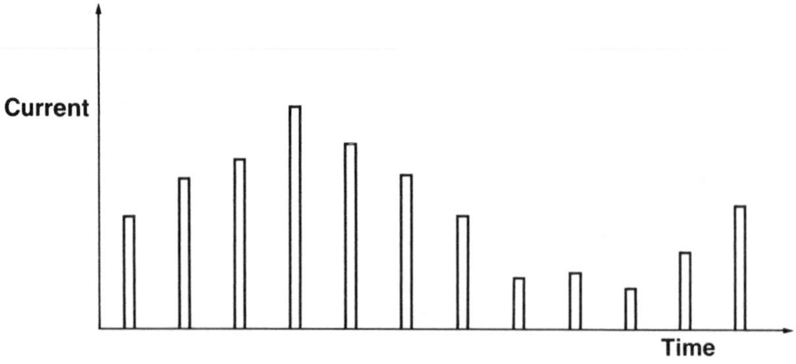

Fig 2h

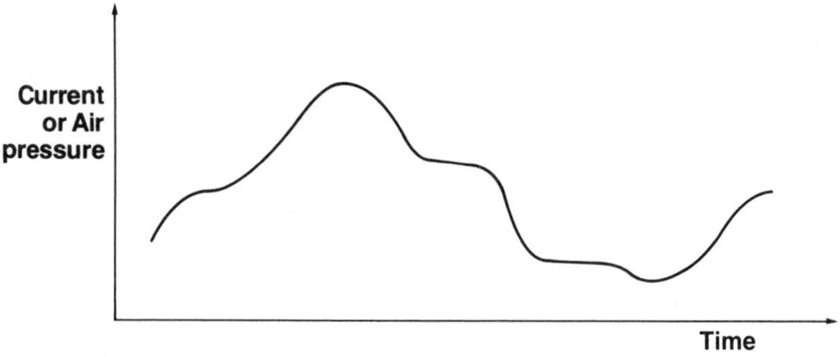

Fig 2g

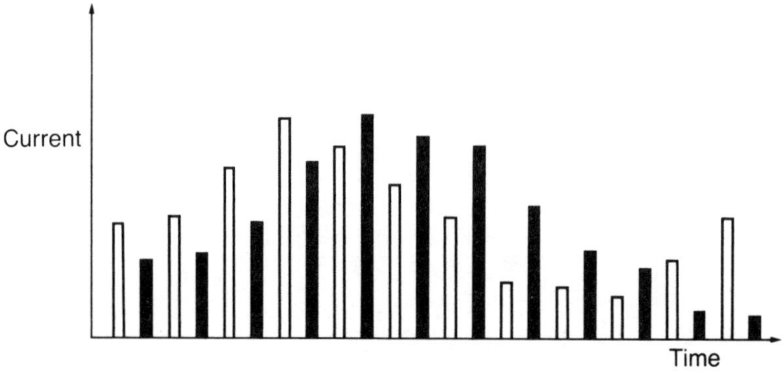

Fig 2i

2.2.2

a mechanical energy **b** electrical energy **c** ii) **d** ii)
e No **f** Because they would become distorted **g** iii).

2.3.1

a Model answer

First subscriber A lifts the handset and waits for the dialling tone. Then he dials the number and hears the ringing tone. Next subscriber B picks up the receiver and the conversation takes place. Finally, the two subscribers replace the handsets.

b Model answer

When the handset is lifted, a signal is sent to the exchange where a dialling tone is sent back. Then the number is dialled and subscriber B's number is selected in the exchange. Next subscriber A's number is connected to subscriber B's number and the conversation takes place. Finally the handsets are replaced before the connection is broken.

2.3.2 Model answer

a The higher the frequency, the higher the number of samples.
b The greater the number of channels, the lower the cost of transmission.
c The greater the degree of network digitalization, the fewer the exchanges.
d The higher the degree of automation, the lower the number of manual operators.
e The return on investment is four times the original investment.
f The new system has double/two times/twice the number of channels.
g 1980 cable costs per kilometre were a quarter of the 1985 costs.
h The new distance between repeaters is a third of the old distance.
i The pulse rate is half the capacity.

2.4.1

Fig 2j stepped-index multimode **a** core **b** cladding
Fig 2k graded index multimode Fig 2l stepped-index monomode.

2.4.2

Table 2a **a** core **b** cladding **c** graded index multimode **d** progressive transparency **e** **
f stepped-index monomode **g** very narrow core, no pulse spreading **h** ***
Table 2b **a** LEDs **b** less powerful, cheap, durable
c lasers **d** closely-defined wavelength **e** monomode
Table 2c **a** silicon pin photodiode **b** less sensitive, cheaper **c** silicon avalanche photodiode **d** sensitive, expensive.

2.4.3

1d 2a 3c 4e 5b.

2.5

a Sentence order: **C**, **F**, **A**, **E**, **D**, **B**.

b Model answer

To illustrate the principle of a time division multiplex (TDM) system, consider the simple case of transmission of one audio signal, of bandwidth 300–4800 Hz, over a PCM line.
The audio signal cannot be transmitted directly over the line. First it is passed through a low pass filter which restricts the upper frequency to 3400 Hz.
Next, a clock pulse is synchronized with the audio signal at the AND gate so that the output is a PAM waveform. The PAM waveform is then converted to a quantized PCM waveform by the encoder. The waveform can now be transmitted directly over the PCM line, regenerated at intervals as necessary.
At the receiving end, a decoder converts the PCM back to PAM which finally is passed through a filter to restore the original audio signal.

Unit 3

3.1.1 Fig. 3a Model answer

1880 Manual system.
1892 Strowger system. First automatic exchange, step-by-step, patented 1889.
1940s Crossbar system. Common control system, cheaper and less noisy than Strowger.
1948 Semi-electronic system. Beginning of process of miniaturization of components (transistors).
1970s Electronic system. Cheaper, smaller, easier to procure and install, more reliable than previous systems.

3.1.2

a A switching centre or central office.
b A.G. Bell, Boston, 1876.
c They connected calls manually.
d He invented it to make his business more profitable.
e A series of vertically and horizontally crossed bars.
f It is cheaper and less noisy.
g The invention of the transistor.
h Electronic exchanges.

3.2.1

Fig 3b
a ii) Wait for the dial tone
b ii) Wait for the internal dial tone iv) Wait for the dial tone of the outside network v) Dial the outside number
c iii) Push button 8 iv) Wait for the lower pitch dial tone v) Dial other extension number
d ii) You receive the engaged tone iv) Replace your handset
e F **f** T **g** F **h** T **i** T **j** F.

3.3.1

a the greatest **b** noisier than **c** as reliable as **d** worse than **e** the most important **f** more (and more) profitable **g** faster than **h** better than

3.3.2

a spoke **b** have begun **c** became **d** has lived/lived **e** went **f** has worked/worked **g** have just undergone **h** patented **i** have already seen **j** connected

3.4.1

a High cost of installation **b** Lower installation cost **c** Replacement of wear-prone exposed moving parts **d** Reliability and easy replacement of printed circuit boards **e** interference **f** slow connection speeds **g** virtually no transmission loss **h** less interference than previously **i** greater network flexibility **j** fewer wrong numbers **k** much faster connection speeds **l** data-processing techniques used.

3.4.2

a 1b 2c 3d 4a.
b Greater speed, easier maintenance, smaller size.

3.4.3

a 1f 2c 3a 4e 5b 6d.

3.5

Gibbs How do I transfer a call to someone else?

Allison Well, obviously you answer the phone when it rings, let's say on line 1. When you find out the call's not for you, but for your colleague at extension 3, say, you should push the 'HOLD' button. You'll see that the held exchange line lamp will then flash. Then you simply call the required extension in the normal way, by pressing button 3. When your colleague answers, you can transfer the held call in one of 2 ways. You can either simply replace your handset, in which case extension 3 takes over the original call from line 1, or your colleague at extension 3 can press the exchange line button and he is automatically connected to line 1.
If no one answers at exchange 3, you should press the exchange line 1 button, to be re-connected to the caller. You can then take the caller's message or ask him to call back later.

Fig 3e Instructions for call transfer: Model answer

1. Lift handset when phone rings
2. Push HOLD button
3. Push button 3
4. **a** Replace your handset
   OR
   b Push exchange line button 1
   i Take caller's message
   ii Ask him to call back later

Unit 4

4.1.1

a Teletex **b** Telefax, groups 3 and 4 **c** Videotex **d** Electronic mail **e** Viewdata **f** Teletext.

4.1.2

a D, A, D, A, D. **b** iii) **c** Memory to memory transmission and faster transmission speed **d** Because of the complexity of Japanese script (i.e. it is not suitable for conventional typewritten text communication)
e Viewdata is interactive, Teletext is broadcast (one-way) **f** Because they will have to live side by side for many years.

4.2.1

a Mr Binns **b** John Dale **c** Dale Recruitment Agency **d** York **e** York 28440 **f** M3300 **g** Puma Telex Machine **h** circulars, mailshots **i** conventional telex machine **j** SALESDESK and WORDSTAR programs **k** not discussed **l** Yes **m** No **n** Phone York rep. to arrange demonstration this week.

4.2.2

a Not much more than the existing telex rental
b Electronic telex, videotex and access to data banks are available **c** Screen—3 weeks, keyboard—3 weeks, electronic telex—immediate, printer—4 to 5 weeks **d** By having more than one terminal **e** Because he is away.

4.3.1

d will **e** could **f** likely to **g** won't **h** the signs indicate **i** should/ought to **j** won't.

4.3.2

The order is: **6**, **18**, **16**, **3**, **12**, **21**, **1**, **10**, **11**, **13**, **5**, **2**, **20**, **15**, **14**, **4**, **9**, **8**, **22**, **19**, **7**, **17**.

4.3.3

a Videotex is a service enabling a subscriber to obtain alphanumeric and/or graphic information over the PSTN.
b Lasers are light sources producing light of a closely defined wavelength.
c PCM is a means of transmission involving the sampling and coding of analogue signals.
d Electronic mail is a new service enabling videotex subscribers to send messages directly and instantaneously to one another.
e Telefax is a service providing for the transmission and reproduction of still pictures and printed matter.
f CCS is a method of signalling using one pair for performing all the signal functions of one route.
g SPC is an electronic system using data processing and computer techniques for switching.
h Datex is a packet-switched network providing a means of asynchronous data transmission.
i Remote concentrators are remote parts of an exchange enabling PCM transmission to be used further out in the local network.

j The Nordic Public Data Network is a circuit-switched network providing a means of synchronous data transmission.

4.4.1

a 8 **b** 1 **c** 5 **d** 3 **e** 2 **f** 7 **g** 4 **h** 6.

4.4.2

1 2500 words **2** approx. 25 telex nos. **3** 400 characters (66 words) per minute on line/1800 characters per minute local mode **4** 7 × 5 dot matrix **5** 69 characters/spaces per line **6** Standard single or multi-ply paper **7** Standard black/red nylon **8** 240 v **9** 480 mm **10** 546 mm **11** 151 mm **12** 18 kg.

4.4.3

Advantages to operator: automatic operation; abbreviated address codes; keyboard calling; ease of editing and correction; simple typewriter keyboard; quiet. These features will save time, be less complicated than conventional telex and improve office working conditions.

4.5 Model answer

83 – 11 – 1 10.45
743321 DALERECY
054321 BS LEEDS G

Tlx.No: 2543

ATTENTION: MR.DALE

REF. YOUR TELEX NO 1148 RE M3300 WORD PROCESSING PACKAGE PLS FIND BELOW ANSWERS TO 4 QUESTIONS:

1. YES
2. YES
3. NO, IT IS OPTIONAL
4. NO, IT IS OPTIONAL

PLS CONTACT US RE FURTHER ENQUIRIES.

REGARDS,
MR.BINNS

054321 BS LEEDS G
743321 DALEREC Y

Unit 5

5.1.1 Model answer

Fig 5a **a** a satellite link **b** to link 2 subscribers in different parts of the world.
Fig 5b **c** ship-to-shore radio **d** warning that the ship is in danger.
Fig 5c **e** radar **f** following the flight path of a plane from take-off to landing.
Fig 5d **g** radio-paging **h** calling to warn Doctor Jones to return to the hospital at once.

5.1.2

a A method of sending or receiving sounds, pictures and data through the air by means of electrical waves.
b ship-to-shore radio; broadcasting (TV and radio); mobile radio services; radio-paging; satellites; radar.
c Because you don't need hundreds of kilometres of wires and cables.
d A pager (bleeper).
e In his pocket.
f Underground.
g It improves their competitive position; it allows them to be more responsive to their customers' needs; it increases company efficiency (e.g. saving on fuel costs).
h To be contacted quickly in emergency cases.

5.2.1

a Chertsey windmill **b** Swanford Tools **c** The Bear Inn **d** 5 km **e** A 19 **f** Golf-course.

5.2.2

a In his car on the A 217 heading towards Greenwood.
b Because they were interested in the RPH radiophone produced by Bradfield Electronics.
c He must take the B 2378 and turn right opposite The Bear Inn.
d He's in charge of their equipment modernization scheme.
e He must not talk about the French contract. John Brown doesn't want it to become public knowledge.
f Efficient businesses need good communication; its profit-making capacities; it saves on fuel costs; it meets the customers' needs.
g ii) 4.30.

5.3.1

a i) No ii) A few iii) Many/A lot of iv) Most v) All
b i) No ii) A little iii) Much/A lot of iv) Most v) All
c i) a lot of/much ii) Little; piece of iii) a few iv) A little/some v) Many; a little vi) A piece of; a lot of/many.

5.3.2

a on **b** from **c** to **d** over/across **e** past **f** in; towards **g** into **h** out of; on.

5.3.3 Model answer

1 Good morning. Could I speak to Chris Bradley, please?
2 Hello Tom. How are you?
3 Oh yes. What would you like to know exactly?
4 Does the user need a lot of equipment?/Is there a lot of equipment in the system?
5 Where does the user keep the pager?
6 How small (is it) exactly?
7 How is the user contacted?
8 How much does the call cost?
9 Does it work if the user's underground?
10 Is it expensive for the subscriber?/I expect the quarterly rental's very high, isn't it?

11 What's the availability like?/Do you have many in stock at the moment?
12 Would you mind giving me a demonstration as soon as possible?
13 Yes. That would be fine.
14 Will you be alone/on your own?
15 Would you mind giving me your phone number?/Could you remind me of your phone number?
16 Shall I come straight to your office?

5.4.1

a local exchange **b** trunk exchange **c** MTX **d** base station **e** traffic area **f** lines **g** telephone area **h** mobile telephone exchanges **i** radio network.

5.4.2

a In the MTXs.
b It is the distance between the base stations in a traffic area.
c One.
d The MTX assigns the mobile station a traffic channel.
e When the mobile subscriber is in a traffic area not belonging to his home MTX.

5.4.3

a Country and Service Area **b** Frequency (MHz) **c** Number of subscribers **d** Date service started **e** Number of cells **f** Switch **g** Operated by.

5.5 Model answer

Tel: 0432–53260
Ext: 208

Swanford Tools Ltd.,
Slingdon Road,
Thurby. TH2 SY3.

16th May, 19—

Mr. C. Bradley,
Bradfield Electronics,
Nutley, NU6 SR7.

Dear Mr. Bradley,

Following the most interesting demonstration of your radio-paging equipment at Bradfield Electronics on 26th April, I should like to confirm that Swanford Tools intend to buy ten pagers for their salesmen.

In order to finalize the exact details of this order, Mr. Davies suggests you visit him at Swanford Tools on Wednesday, 29th May at 3.30.

I hope that the date and time are convenient for you.

Yours sincerely,

Ms. J. Whitfield
(Secretary)
p.p. Mr. T. Davies

Revision Unit A

1 a

a is divided into **b** two, both, one, the other **c** Another, also **d** is supported by **e** Each, is divided into, Sales.

1 b

a 75 cc **b** 125 cc **c** 250 cc motorcycles **d** assembly **e** distribution **f** sales **g** Japan **h** Leyport **i** East of Leyport **j** Leyport **k** Ellton **l** Woodburn **m** Fort Gray **n** Sonley **o** Bloosburg **p** 5 **q** 30 **r** 585 **s** HQ in London **t** Costerutsi National Bank.

1 c

will be manufactured; shipped; will be transported; in; will be assembled; in; have been assembled; will be taken; by; to; in; From; will be distributed to; in; with; comes; will be: will liaise with; on; to.

2

Situation

than; long/wide; highest; above; on; most/many; near.

Communications

between; a few; Most; from; to.

Population

has risen; took place; was; under; has increased; over; biggest; almost; as; as; has been; less; fewer.

Products

was discovered; was set up; replaced; forms; was extracted; taken; exported.

3 a

a Yes **b** telecoms services and radio frequency regulation **c** telephone, telex and data **d** 1.84 **e** Strowger (71%); Crossbar (25%); Manual (4%) **f** 96% **g** more expensive than in Australia **h** $560 p.a. **i** PCM, optical fibres and microwave **j** 18% for international phone and telex traffic **k** Datex, Datel and leased data circuits **l** 300, 2400 and 9600 b/s **m** private and public services **n** 74 **o** 4,100 **p** 3,500 **q** yes **r** 105 circuits **s** 2200.

Unit 6

6.1.1

Fig 6d **Level 1**: within a group or department of a company; a few metres to about one hundred metres; 50% (with level 2); LAN.

Level 2: between other groups or departments of the same company; a few hundred metres to 2 or 3 kilometres; 50% (with level 1); LAN.

Level 3: between branch offices of the same company in different geographic areas; a few dozen to hundreds of kilometres; 20%; PABX.

Level 4: with the outside world; any distance; 30%; PABX.

6.1.2

a Transmission and switching systems that provide high-speed communication between devices located on a single site.

b An office complex; an industrial estate; a college campus; a closely linked group of buildings.

c Ring and bus.

d Replacing old electromechanical PABXs with modern electronic ones.

e Familiarity of most users with a PABX; can be easily upgraded through software modifications; full access to all national telecommunication services; single wire connectivity; customers prefer tried and tested systems.

f High-speed data transfer; less cabling required; offers distributed control, making the LAN more powerful and flexible than a PABX; easier to share specialized resources with a LAN; terminals can be connected more economically; frees PABX for other functions.

g Central processing unit; office automation; distributed data processing.

6.2.1

Fig 6e **a** 1 = nodes **b** 2 = transceivers **c** 3 = coaxial cable **d** 4 = repeater **e** 100 **f** 1024 **g** 10Mb/s **h** 2.5 kilometres **i** maximum of 500 metres **j** maximum of 500 metres.

6.2.2

a Increasing use of coaxial technology in office systems; the development of packet switching technology; advances in the field of optical fibres.

b Managers realise that office workers deserve greater capital expenditure on good equipment; executives no longer fear keyboards.

c Minicomputers, data terminals, telephone sets, distributed data processors, printers, copiers, facsimile devices, word processors.

d That information will come in many forms: voice, non-voice, video.

e Because they have high bit rates.

f Higher bit rates; wider bandwidth; does not generate electromagnetic interference; not susceptible to electromagnetic interference; greater security; smaller, lighter, easier to install.

6.3.1

a he's working **b** arrives; he's arriving **c** he's flying **d** Do you like; love **e** does she live; she's living **f** work **g** are losing **h** is opening up **i** are moving towards **j** What does OA stand for? It stands for office automation.

6.3.2

a Possibility/Ability **b** Advice **c** Ability **d** Probability **e** Obligation **f** must/has to **g** should/ought to **h** may/can **i** should/ought to **j** can
Model answer **k** can/could (Possibility) **l** should/ought to (Advice) **m** should/ought to (Probability) **n** can/may (Permission) **o** should/ought to (Probability)

6.4.1

Fig 6f **a** primary centre **b** secondary centre **c** branching point **e** subscriber **g** main feeder cable **h** two-fibre subscriber loop Fig 6g **1** plastic sheath **2** metal casing **3** ten fibres **4** central strength member

6.4.2

a Because Bromfield Equipment has just been named group leader in a similar project.

b Because the traffic using it requires a very high bandwidth.

c To master the technology of optical fibres and optoelectronic components in real conditions rather than in a laboratory.

d Switching (videophone) and distribution (TV and hi-fi stereo).

e New broadband services have been brought into the local distribution network using optical fibres.

f To go to Biarritz and to write to Jean Dubois.

6.4.3

Technical = **1**, **3**, **6**, **9**, and **11**. Commercial = **2**, **4**, **7**, and **10**. Industrial = **5** and **8**.

6.5

Ref: 374/JB/85

Bromfield Equipment,
24, Conway St,
London EC4
England

Mr Jean Dubois,
Primary Switching Centre,
18, rue du Vieux Moulin,
Biarritz
France.

14 February 19__

Dear Jean,

I hope that you are well and that your work on the Biarritz project is progressing satisfactorily.

I am writing to you about this most interesting experiment, for, as you may know, Bromfield Equipment has been asked to lead a group of British companies in a similar optical fibre scheme.

If convenient for you, I should very much like to pay a two-day visit to Biarritz in the week 12–16 May. The aim of this visit would be to look at your network design, especially the role of the primary and secondary centres. We could also discuss questions to do with the number of subscribers, the types of equipment that you use and the frequencies that you apply on different parts of the network.

Bromfield Equipment is prepared to finance a three-day seminar for a small group of British engineers in London later in the year. The theme will be 'Local Optical Fibre Networks', and I should be delighted if you could attend all or part of the seminar. Bromfield Equipment would, of course, meet all of your travelling and other expenses.

I do hope that you will be able to participate in our seminar and I look forward to hearing from you as soon as you have decided which two days in the week 12–16 May are the most convenient for you.

Best regards,

John Baker, Marketing Manager

Unit 7

7.1.2 Model answer

a i) **D** ii) **C** iii) **E** iv) **A** v) **B** **b** ii) **c** ii) **d** ii)
e Continuous monitoring is necessary in order to identify when B-subscriber's phone becomes idle and to check that A-subscriber's phone is idle at the same time. **f** ii)

7.2.1

Fig 7e **a** out-of-area line **b** RCF **c** public telephone network
d ______ **e** – – – – – – – **f** ______

7.2.2

a £400/year **b** £100/year **c** local call **d** trunk call
e 30 seconds **f** **

7.3.1

a If remote call forwarding cost £400 a year, we would not subscribe to the service.
b If the caller paid for the diverted call, this service would not be used.
c If the customer phones the Leeds number, the call will be diverted to London.
d If CCS was available nationwide, new services would be available nationwide.
e If a subscriber receives fewer than 20 calls a day, an out-of-area line will not be economic.
f If you subscribe to RCF, we will install some/a piece of divert-a-call equipment in a local exchange. (see 5.3.1 Countables and Uncountables)
g If a customer has to wait for a connection, he will hear a pre-recorded announcement.
h If I understood CCS, I would explain it to you.

7.3.2

a This time last year, I was working in Saudi Arabia.
b When the lightning struck, the exchange was operating fine.
c At 14.45 yesterday, I was writing a report.
d He was just making a phone call.
e When he telephoned, we were discussing the project. OR He telephoned while/as we were discussing the project.
f When the power was cut, the engineers were installing the equipment.
OR The power was cut while/as the engineers were installing the equipment.
g At 10 in the evening, the technicians were still replacing the circuits.
h When it started snowing, they were laying the cable. OR It started snowing as/while they were laying the cable.
i On Friday morning, I was waiting for my plane.
j When his car broke down, he was driving to work. OR His car broke down as/while he was driving to work.

7.3.3

a iii) **b** i) **c** ii) **d** iv) **e** That seems fine; Great; That would be fine **f** No problem; Certainly **g** Yes, that's it **h** I think I've got the picture.

7.4.1

a 0 **b** £400 **c** 30 **d** 9 **e** £350 (3 hour meeting) **f** 0 **g** 11 **h** 11 **i** £50 **j** £255 **k** 17 hours.

7.4.2

a Picture transmission **b** 5 **c** 3 **d** ii) **e** No, it depends on the trial **f** January meeting.

7.4.3

1c 2e, **g** **3e** **4d** **5f** **6a** **7g** **8h** **9b**.

7.5 Model answer

Subject: Meeting to discuss use of teleconferencing facilities for inter-branch meetings held in London offices of MITEC Ltd., on 10–11–83.

Present: Mr Cornwall (London Branch)
Mr Mackintosh (Glasgow Branch)

1 Mr Cornwall presented the teleconferencing facilities provided by B.T.
2 Cost savings of approximately £305 per meeting were calculated.
3 A time-saving of 17 man-hours per meeting was calculated.
4 It was agreed that a trial teleconference should take place in either December or January.

Unit 8

8.1.1

Fig 8g **a** Analogue signal in 300–3400 Hz frequency band. **b** PAM sampling **c** bus **d** 125 microseconds **e** 8,000 per subscriber.

8.1.2

a To establish a temporary circuit or link between the caller and the subscriber being called.
b **1b** **2c** **3a**.
c A horizontal and a vertical wire at the intersection of which a relay is installed.
d A physical path is established between two subscribers in a space system. Several conversations use the same circuit in a time division system.
e The sampling frequency must be double the maximum signal frequency.
f 4-wire PCM links and the allocation of time slots at a rate of 64 000 bits per second.
g The fusion of several integrated digital networks.

8.2.1

Fig 8h **1** Area II **2** Operation and Maintenance Centre (OMC) **3** E 10 exchange **4** Analogue link between each subscriber and the remote concentrator **5** Remote subscriber concentrator **6** 2, 3 or 4-wire PCM links.
Fig 8i **1** Block 1 **2** Block 2 **3** Block 3 **4** OMC **5** Subscriber connection units from local and remote subscribers **6** Multiplex unit from trunk circuits **7–9** Multiregisters, translators and metering units **10** PCM links to other exchanges.

8.2.2

a The creation of an integrated network.
b 50 km.
c Because sparsely populated areas with a low telephone density can be served as well as urban areas.
d 120.
e One for every eight subscribers.
f 100,000.
g A minicomputer, magnetic tapes and disks, teleprinters, high-speed printers, VDUs.
h 50%.
i detailed billing.

8.3.1

a The switching matrix consists of a number of connection points which are made up of a horizontal and a vertical wire joined by a relay.
b Two types of switching equipment predominate in Sweden: crossbar equipment and digital systems.
c This technique, in which a lot of money has been invested, has one great drawback.
d The first rotary switch, which is still in use today, was invented by Almon Strowger who was an undertaker in Kansas City.
e The analogue signals, which are in the 300–3400 Hz range, are transmitted to the exchange in which they are sampled using PAM.

8.3.2

a He frequently inspects factories. He inspects factories two or three times a week.
b He often plays tennis. He plays tennis three times a month.
c He sometimes reviews production figures. He reviews production figures once a month/monthly.
d He frequently attends sales meetings. He attends sales meetings once a week/four times a month/every Friday/ weekly.
e He hardly ever attends Board meetings. He attends Board meetings once a year/annually.
f He occasionally prepares financial reports. He prepares financial reports quarterly/four times a year.
g He rarely goes to the dentist. He goes to the dentist twice a year/every six months.
h He occasionally gets his car serviced. He gets his car serviced every 10 000 kilometres.
i He never plays football.

8.3.3

a isn't he? **b** didn't he? **c** hasn't it? **d** did they? **e** won't you? **f** wasn't it? **g** can it? **h** isn't it? **i** could you? **j** doesn't it?

8.4.1

Fig 8j 1 Telecom 1 satellite
2 Earth station
3 and **4** Data switches: 3 Level 1 interface connecting premises at individual network level; 4 Level 2 interface connecting individual networks to each other and to the satellite
5 2 Mbit PCM links.

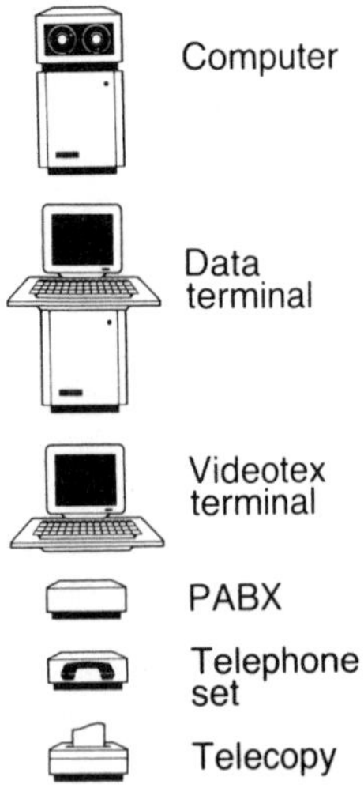

Fig 8k
1 Individual cells **2** Transceiver **3** Radiotelephone switching centre **4** to the PSTN (Public Switched Telephone Network).

8.4.2

a Because he found a brochure on telematics in the same envelope as his telephone bill.
b The association of telecommunications and data processing.
c Applications designed for the ordinary subscriber (videotex) such as Prestel and the electronic directory; companies with large numbers of terminals and other data-processing equipment on their premises (e.g. Telecom 1 system); and specialized users (e.g. cellular radio telephony).
d A network which enables different kinds of data processing machines to be interconnected.

8.4.3

l, **d**, **o**, **a**, **g**, **k**, **n**, **h**, **f**, **b**, **i**, **j**, **e**, **c**, **m**.

8.5

2 The second group is aimed at large companies. The term normally used to describe this application is multiservice network, an example of which is Telecom 1. This consists of a geostationary satellite and an earth station which, in turn, is linked to industrial locations through high-speed data switches. The service enables business users to have access to high-speed data processing networks.
3 The third group is aimed at specialized users. The term normally used to describe this application is specialized services, an example of which is a cellular radiotelephone network. This consists of mobile users with transceivers which, in turn, are linked to the PSTN through a switching centre. This service enables the mobile user to telephone from his car.

Unit 9

9.1.1

Fig 9c **a** Travel industry **b** Homelink **c** Micronet 800 **d** Skytrack **e** Interworking with telex **f** Overseas viewdata systems.

9.1.2

a iii) **b** iii) **c** i), iii) **d** i) Homelink ii) Micronet 800 **e** i), ii), v) **f** i) to specialized information services ii) interactive services **g** travellers **h** ii).

9.2.1

Fig 9d

COUNTRY	NAME OF SYSTEM	TECHNIQUES	DATA BASE CONTROLLER	SPECIAL SERVICES
1. UK	Prestel	alphamosaic	British Telecom	Micronet 800 Homelink
2. France	Télétel	—	Independent companies	Electronic directory/mail
3. Canada	Telidon	alphageometric	Dept. of Communication	—

9.2.2

a i) 'As you would expect . . .' ii) 'As you can see . . .' iii) 'As you'll remember . . .'
b Alphamosaic has a building block appearance; alphageometric has smoother curves and more colours.
c i) companies ii) authorities iii) service agencies
d i) 'Should advertising be allowed on videotex? ii) 'Who has the responsibility for the information provided?'

9.3.1

a In contrast, **b** different **c** unlike **d** on the other hand **e** as opposed to **f** unlike **g** In contrast, **h** different from/to.

9.3.2

b a slow (and/,) complex technique
c a poorly planned scheme
d a simple (and/,) successful strategy
e stringently tested equipment (a stringently tested piece of equipment)
f an efficient (and/,) secure system
g a continuously monitored status
h a cheap (and/,) old-fashioned product
i directly transferred information
j an extremely experienced salesman.

9.3.3

a 'I'd like today to summarize the international developments in videotex.'
b 'I shall confine myself to 3 services.'
c i) 'Let me start with Prestel.'
ii) 'This brings me to the French system.'
iii) 'First, a few words about the Canadian system.'
d 'More about that in a minute.'
e 'As I mentioned.'
f 'Finally, and perhaps most important.'
'These are just some of the questions raised.'

9.4.1

a No, 18 hours a day.
b Payment of bills, direct debiting and crediting, correspondence with banks, applications for mortgages, loan quotations.
c Yes, you can make electronic reservations with Thomas Cook.
d Nothing, it's free.
e Nearly all.
f No, any ordinary colour or black and white TV will do.
g No, it plugs straight into the aerial socket of your TV.
h No, it's as simple to use as a calculator or video.
i There's no need to worry. Homelink uses 10 different security checks to safeguard your account.
j A minimum of £1000.
k Nothing.
l Yes, there's £5 per quarter for use of the Prestel computer network and local telephone charges each time you use Homelink.
m Well, if you use Homelink during the day you will also have to pay Prestel computer charges, currently 5p per minute.

9.4.2

i) **b**, **e** ii) **a** iii) **f**, **i** iv) **d**, **g**, **h** v) **c**, **j**.
NB: Some of these are open to discussion.

9.5 Model answer

Subject Homelink Services

Introduction This report sets out to decide whether it is cost-effective for HITECH Ltd., to join Homelink. It is confined to a cost-benefit analysis of Homelink services.

Findings

A Benefits

Homelink offers 3 useful services to HITECH.

i) Money management: It will enable us to have fast and updated information on account statements, to transfer money easily and correspond with the bank.

ii) Travel Reservations: We will be able to make travel reservations on screen direct with Thomas Cook Ltd.

iii) Prestel Information services: We will have access to 250,000 pages of information dealing with weather, stock market etc.

B Costs

i) Initial costs: It will cost us £1000 to join Homelink. This is the minimum sum which must be deposited with NBS.

ii) Running costs: Based on an annual usage of 100 4-minute calls, running costs will be approx. £100 per year (see attached for more details).

Conclusions Homelink offers HITECH Ltd. considerable savings in secretarial time. It will no longer be necessary to visit the bank in person, to make travel reservations over the phone or write off for information. In addition, it should make financial decision-making more efficient. Budgeting and monitoring of cash-flow will be much easier.

Recommendations On this basis, I recommend that we join Homelink as long as NBS and Bank of Scotland can provide foreign currency services equivalent to our existing bank's.

Unit 10

10.1.1

Fig 10c **1** A low orbit satellite **a** 150–450 kilometres **b** about $1\frac{1}{2}$ hours **c** about 15 minutes **d** remote sensing
2 A medium altitude satellite **a** 9000–18 000 kilometres **b** 5–12 hours **c** 2–4 hours **d** telecommunications
3 A geosynchronous/geostationary satellite **a** 35 800 kilometres **b** 24 hours **c** the satellite's entire life **d** telecommunications **e** over the Equator.

10.1.2

a The launching of the first satellite by the Russians in 1957.
b The American landing on the moon in 1969.
c It receives a signal, amplifies it, changes its frequency and retransmits it.
d A satellite can replace costly terrestrial networks.
e A way of communicating with people who live in isolated areas; a way of broadcasting 'live' TV programmes; and a way of linking computer terminals.
f 1964; 16; 3 billion US$; 109; two thirds.
g It has fallen dramatically.
h Parts of the shuttle launching rocket can be recovered and reused; the shuttle can be reused a hundred times; its payload is greater than any previous rocket's; and it offers greater opportunities for scientists to work in space than rockets do.

10.2.1

Fig 10d **a** Tele-X Steering Committee **b** Co-ordinating Group SSC/ST **c** Swedish Space Corporation (SSC) **d** Contracts **e** Satellite **f** Earth Stations **g** DASAT **h** RASK **i** RATEX **j** Contact Group ST/SBC **k** Swedish Broadcasting Corporation (SBC) **l** Informal Nordic Broadcasting Group.

10.2.2

a Because many aspects of the project are not yet finalized.
b Because his special field is technical organization.
c The Swedish Board of Space Activities.
d The Swedish Space Corporation (SSC), the Swedish Broadcasting Corporation (SBC) and Swedish Telecom.
e One, the SSC.
f Because Swedish Telecom is responsible for operating the earth stations.
g Because it's too long.

10.3.1

a Digital transmission and multiplexing techniques have developed considerably; consequently/therefore/as a result, the capacity of satellites has increased enormously.
b There is a 270 millisecond propagation delay, for/since/as the signal has to travel thousands of kilometres.
c The rockets were lost at sea and, as a result/therefore/consequently, the launches were very expensive.
d The shuttle heralds a new era of space travel for/since/as it can perform at least 100 missions.
e The Kennedy Space Center was fog-bound and, consequently/as a result/therefore, the launch was delayed by 24 hours.
f Mr Leijonflycht is not prepared to answer questions on financial matters as/for/since he is not a financial expert.
g Geosynchronous satellites travel at the same speed as the earth; consequently/therefore/as a result, they are much used for telecommunications.
h The list of private companies involved in the project is long and, therefore/consequently/as a result, Mr Leijonflycht will not give the names of all of them.

10.3.2 Model answer

1 When are you leaving Stockholm?
2 How long are you staying?
3 Which hotel are you staying at?
4 When are you returning?
5 What'll you be reviewing?
6 What'll you be presenting?

7 What'll you be assigning to members of the group?
8 Do you aim to discuss frequency distribution?
9 Are you going to have a meeting with the Nordic delegates?
10 Do you intend to present the latest details of the Tele-X project?

10.4.1

1 low noise amplifier **2** microwave amplifiers **3** downconverter **4** mixer **5** IF amplifier **6** filter **7** VTO **8** satellite receiver **9** amplifier **10** filter **11** discriminator **12** video **13** audio **14** RF modulator **15** channel selector.

10.4.2

a Homearth Mark II **b** two metres across **c** At the focal point of the reflected signal **d** Less than one millionth of a volt **e** We mean a 30 MHz wide band of frequencies centred on 70 MHz. **f** A carrier **g** When there is no cable input. **h** 3: continuously variable; a knob with a number of channels; and an up/down scan system with digital display.

10.4.3

1k **2**j **3**d **4**l **5**e **6**a **7**c **8**b **9**f **10**h **11**i **12**g

10.5 Model answer

Mr Clayton said that it was very kind of Mr Leijonflycht to agree to come and discuss the Tele-X project with him. Mr Leijonflycht answered that it was a pleasure to be there and that he would do his best to answer Mr Clayton's questions. He had to say at the beginning, though, that many aspects of the project were not yet finalized and that he might not be able to give him answers that were as complete as he would wish. Mr Clayton said that was OK and suggested that he should tell Mr Leijonflycht what he knew and that then they could start from there. Tele-X, he said, was an experimental direct broadcasting, video services and high-speed data satellite due to be launched in 1986. Mr Leijonflycht agreed. Mr Clayton continued by saying that the project was a joint one . . .

Revision Unit B

Task 1

Introduction
D I
Needs of individual parts of the Company
—domestic
B H J A
—international
F K
Overall priorities of types of communication
C G
Conclusion
E

Task 2 Model answer

Paul Bailey Esq.
Communications Manager
Reniat (Costerutsi)

Dear Mr Bailey

Thank you for your letter requesting information on the services supplied by the Costerutsi Telecommunications Administration. In reply, I can offer you the following information:
Telephone sets. There are 3 basic types of set, and PABXs range from 1 outside line with 2 extensions to 15 lines and 75 extensions.
Data links. Leased lines will shortly be available offering speeds of 9600 b/s. C.T.A. is responsible for the network up to the modem, the customer is responsible for terminating equipment.
Teletex. At the moment Teletex is only in the experimental stage. The question of who is to supply equipment has not yet been decided.
Facsimile. At the moment Group II equipment is used for private customers, and Bureaufax is also available for members of the public.
Mobile Radio Telephone. This is available in most large towns.
Radiopaging. This is not yet available.
Business Telephone Rental. At the moment this is on average approximately $C 700 per annum.
International links. Although occasional delays are experienced at the moment, the new undersea cable to be completed in 9 months' time will mean the virtual elimination of delay.
Equipment suppliers. At the moment all equipment is supplied by C.T.A. However, the situation is being reviewed and some change is likely in the near future.

I trust this answers your questions. Please do not hesitate to contact me again if you have any further questions.

Yours sincerely

Bill Wallace (International Accounts Manager C.T.A.)

Task 3

Minutes of a Meeting held between Paul Bailey (Communications Manager—Reniat) and Bill Wallace (International Accounts Manager—C.T.A.).

Equipment

Mr Wallace informed Mr Bailey that at the moment all equipment is supplied by C.T.A., but that within 3 years it would be possible for private manufacturers to sell telephone sets, data terminals and facsimile transceivers. A new PABX with 25 lines and up to 150 extensions would shortly be on the market.

Services

In answer to Mr Bailey's enquiry about the availability of certain facilities Mr Wallace explained that Teletex services would be delayed by difficulties with the software, but that full radiopaging services would be available within 6 months, and MRT was available widely enough to cause no problems for Reniat.

Costs

Mr Wallace explained that the average telephone rental cost for businesses was about $C 700 p.a. but that this might be reduced, depending on the amount of traffic.

Training

Mr Bailey expressed interest in training facilities. Mr Wallace explained that these are provided free with all equipment.

Contacts

Finally it was agreed at Mr Wallace's suggestion that regular meetings would be held (about every 6 weeks) to discuss matters of mutual interest.

Unit 11

11.1

Fig 11b **1** High **2** Low **3** Average/Medium

Fig 11c **a** Vélizy, Versailles and Val de Bièvre **b** 84·4% **c** Terminal (display and keyboard) **d** 2 500 **e** $0.1 per 5 minutes **f** Access to data banks, booking flights, ordering goods etc. **g** 18 months.

11.2

Fig 11d **a** First crossbar exchanges installed **b** Research into electronic switching **c** World's first electronic switching centre handling real calls connected to the public network **d** 7th economic plan (No. one priority is telecoms) **e** Vélizy **f** Electronic directory **g** Téléfax **h** Télécom 1 **i** Optical fibre pilot scheme in Biarritz.

Fig 11e **1954** 1.75/4% **1965** 3 **1970** 4 **1974** 6.2 **1976** 8.4/16% **1978 (Jan)** 10 **1978 (Dec)** 12 **1982** 19.3/35% **1983** 21/38.5%.

11.3.1

a about/around/some **b** far more . . . than **c** just over **d** nearly/almost/just under **e** less than **f** precisely/exactly **g** less than **h** around/about/some **i** many fewer . . . than **j** much less than.

11.3.2 Model answer

a enormous **b** slowly **c** sharply **d** dramatic **e** marked . . . slow **f** rapidly **g** gradually **h** significant.

11.4

Fig 11f **a** user **b** public telephone network **c** Télétel computer centre **d** leased line **e** local computer **f** TRANSPAC **g** remote computer **h** remote computer.

11.5

1 54%, 16%, 30% **2** Senior office executives **3** 40–49 **4** 25,000 **5** 15 minutes, 3.3 services **6** Saturday, Wednesday **7** 5–11p.m., 3p.m. and 5p.m. **8** local info, media info.

Unit 12

12.1.1

Fig 12a

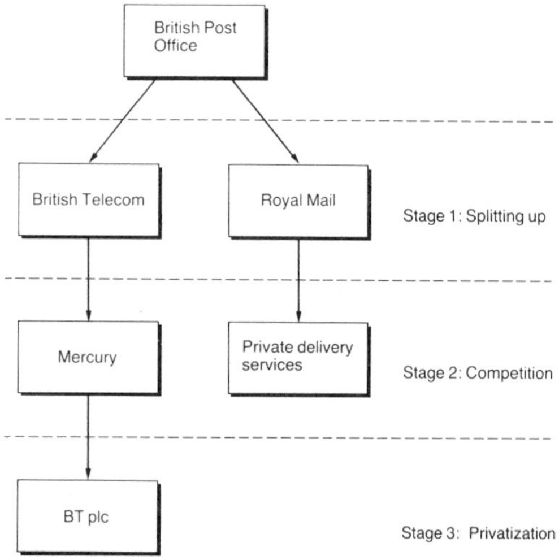

12.1.2

Article **A 1, 2, 4, 7**

Article **B 3, 5, 6, 8**

12.2.1

Fig 12b	GOVERNMENT	TEMA
a	√	0
b	√	√
c	√	√
d	×	√
e	√	√
f	0	√

12.2.2

a liberal, privatized
b value-added
c red-tape
d body
e fees
f appreciate
g hard
h massive
i open the floodgates
j up to
k sit back

12.3.1

a competitor
b emergence
c to liberalize liberal
d to privatize privatization
e politician political
f installation
g to profit/to make a profit profitable
h subsidy
i legislation
j approval
k reliability reliable
l to regulate regulation

12.3.2

a doubled
b trebled
c rose/increased/went up
d slowed down
e fell/dropped/decreased
f declined/decreased/fell/dropped
g speeded up, slowed down
h increase . . . decrease

12.4.1

Fig 12c

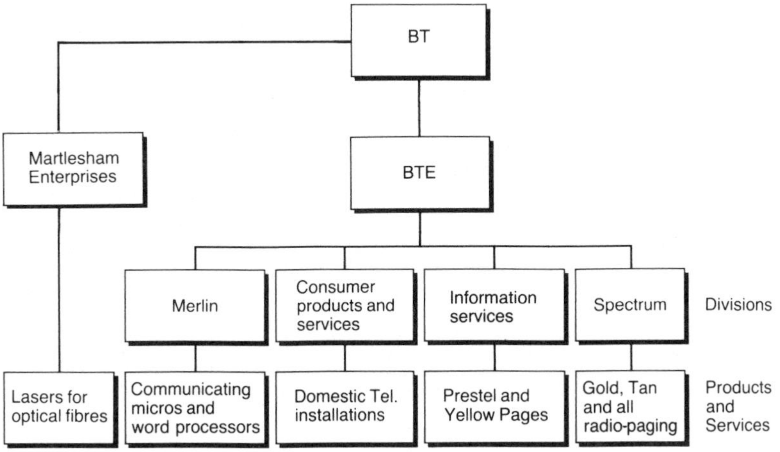

12.4.2

a to grab a chunk of the market
b to launch
c to keep quiet about what you've got up your sleeve
d our new competitive arm
e to face competition
f commercial off-shoot
g spin-off ideas

12.5.1

Fig 12e **a** Birmingham **b** London **c** Bristol **d** Stoke-on-Trent **e** Manchester **f** Intelsat V or Telecom I **g** Oxford Ground Station **h** monomode optical fibre **i** microwave link **j** optical fibre ring.

12.5.2

a London, Bristol, Birmingham, Stoke-on-Trent, Manchester and Leeds **b** monomode optical fibre (565 Mbit/s) **c** concrete ducts **d** cellular radio **e** mid-1985.

Unit 13

13.1.1

Fig 13a

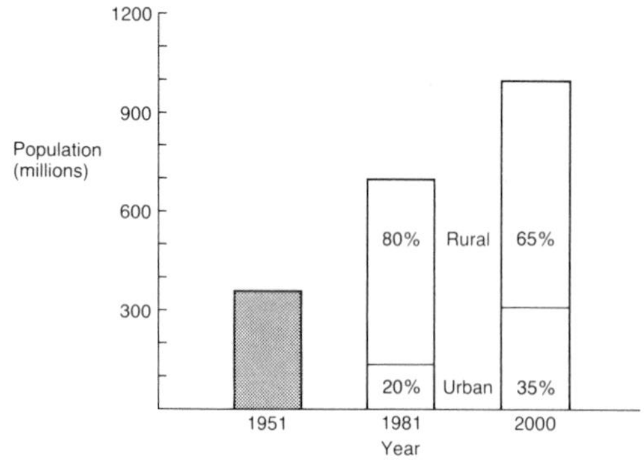

Fig 13b **a** most densely populated state **b** 1300 villages with two to ten thousand inhabitants each **c** Varying population density **d** 80% villages with population of less than one thousand.
Primary Switching Centres: Madras, Calcutta, Bombay, Delhi.
Fig 13c

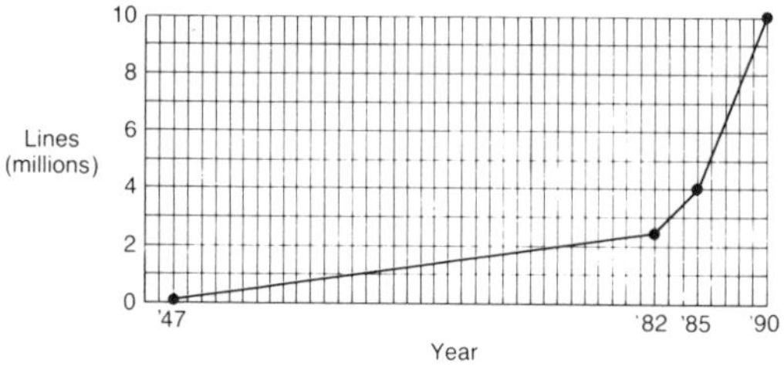

13.1.2

a 1, 2, 8 **b** 4 **c** 5, 9, 11 **d** 3, 6, 7, 10, 12.

13.2

Fig 13d **a** B.Sc. in Maths/Physics **b** Junior Supervisory Staff **c** ALTTC (Advanced Level Telecom Training Centre) **d** TTC (Telecom Training Centre) (13) **e** Circle or District Training Centre (26) **f** Directorate **g** Divisional Engineer **h** Assistant Divisional Engineer **i** Assistant Engineer **j** Junior Engineer **k** Technician **l** Operative Staff.

13.3.1

1 agreement **2** allocation **3** benefit **4** collaboration **5** completion **6** co-operate **7** development **8** elimination **9** estimate **10** extension **11** implementation **12** improvement **13** investment **14** maintain **15** product/production **16** promotion **17** provision **18** recruit **19** expense **20** train.
a allocated **b** improve **c** improvement **d** agreement **e** allocation **f** spent **g** investment **h** maintenance **i** extend **j** provide **k** recruited.

13.3.2

a We will have . . . **b** We have signed agreements . . . **c** We only had about . . . **d** We/The Indian Government found this situation unacceptable and . . . **e** We have made an effort . . . **f** We hope to have/We will have . . . **g** We have outlined our objectives and they are: **h** We aim to/must implement . . . **i** We aim to/must eliminate . . . **j** We aim to/must provide . . . **k** We aim to/must extend . . .

13.4

Fig 13e **1** TRC/Delhi/Adapting equipment and developing systems/Rs. 50 Crores
2 TDC/Jabalpur/Equipment testing and development and design work/Rs. 14 Crores.
Fig 13f **1** Telecommunications, meteorology, TV broadcasting **2** 31 **3** Delhi, Madras, Bombay, Calcutta, Shillong **4** 8 **5** 15 **6** 3 **7** Rs. 120 Crores **8** More routes become available.

13.5

Fig 13g 1 Manufacturing of E10 under licence in India **2** Building factory (full production 500,000 lines per year) at Gonda, Uttar Pradesh for sale to ITI **3** Development of new time-division switching system **4** Delivery and installation of 23 E10 exchanges
Fig 13h **c** Ahmedabad/10 000/1 **d** Bombay/60 000/7 **e** Hyderabad/10 000/1 **f** Madras/12 000/2 **g** Calcutta/32 000/4 **h** Kanpur/10 000/1 **i** Delhi/50 000/5.

Unit 14

14.1.1

Fig 14a **a** Ministry of Transport and Communications **b** ELLEMTEL **c** Teleinvest AB **d** Management Services **e** Long-term planning **f** Internal auditing **g** Financial **h** Technical **i** National Network Dept. **j** Marketing **k** Material Services **l** Telecommunication Areas **m** Teli **n** Radio.

14.1.2

1a 2b 3f 4e 5d 6i 7g 8j 9h 10c.

14.2.1

1c 2e 3g 4f 5i 6d 7a 8h 9b.

14.2.2

h, d, a, e, g, b, i, f, c, j.

14.3.1

a 6/six **b** report to **c** are split **d** responsibility for **e** are broken down **f** in charge **g** Below/Under **h** responsibility **i** supported by/backed up by **j** supported by/backed up by **k** (matrix) responsibility for **l** are supported by/backed up by **m** is involved/engaged **n** in charge of/in control of.

14.3.2

a I'm very pleased to welcome you to . . .
b Can I suggest we take a look around . . .
c Shall we move on . . .
d Here you can see . . .
e This you might find interesting . . .
f Sorry to hurry you . . .

14.4.1

Fig 14d after paragraph **1** 14e after para. **7** 14f after para. **2** 14g after para. **9** 14h after para. **8** 14i after para. **6**.

14.4.2

1 a, e, g 2 c, i, f, j 3 d, l, b 4 h, k.

14.5.1

Title of course	Location	Length of course	Course Dates (84)	Type of participant	Course objective & content
1 IPTM	Teleskolan (Kalmar)	9 weeks	mid-Aug. start	Senior mgrs.	Analysis of methods & approaches to telecom mgt. Future planning/ purchasing
2 Digital networks	Teleskolan (Kalmar)	4 weeks	June	Senior engineers & mgt.	Understanding of digital techniques; network structure; costs & distribution; equipment; route planning; transmission media.
3 Opman	Teleskolan (local area)	12 weeks (7 in local area)	mid-Aug. start	Middle mgrs.	To clarify & demonstrate operational mgt. control system—implementation in own networks.

14.5.2 Model Report

Introduction

The benefits of using Swedish Telecom's international training derive principally from their extensive experience of telecommunication administration and technology. In addition they offer a broader base of experience than most TAs in that they are also involved in manufacturing equipment.

The advantage of sending personnel on courses rather than study-visits is that the more formalized arrangements and programming of a course lead to better results.

Courses

They offer three types of course. Two at a senior management level, one for middle managers.

The first course—The International Programme for Telecommunication Management (IPTM)—lasts 9 weeks and starts in August. It principally covers analysis of methods and approaches to telecommunications management, future planning and purchasing (please see attached documentation for more detail).

The second course—Digital Networks—is aimed at senior engineers and managers and lasts 4 weeks beginning in June. It is designed to promote an understanding of digital techniques. It looks at areas such as network structure, costs and distribution; equipment; route-planning and transmission media.

The last course—Operational Management—lasts 12 weeks, running concurrently with the IPTM course. This one is designed for middle managers and aims to clarify and demonstrate an operational management control system in order for the participants to implement a system in their own networks. Seven of the twelve weeks are spent working in a local area.

Conclusions

1. The IPTM course seems to be pitched at too high a level for our administration.
2. The Digital Networks course looks useful, but is held at a difficult time of year for us since most employees will be on holiday.
3. The Operational Management course seems very useful, particularly because of its practical nature (7 weeks in the field).

Recommendation

I recommend that we send 2 middle managers on Opman this August.

Unit 15

15.1

Fig 15a **a** North America/199/38.1% **b** Central and South America/24/4.4% **c** Europe/203/39% **d** Asia/81/15.5% **e** Oceania/10/1.8% **f** Africa/6.5/1.2%.
Fig 15b Model Answer **a** 3/expensive, consequently limited to commercial government use—will combine with data network **b** 1/affects every aspect of life—soon a telephone in every village—allows free circulation of news **c** 4 **d** 2/necessary for spreading information—helps to establish a national consciousness—solar cells will replace batteries—perfect reception will come from direct broadcasting satellites.

15.2

1 Tuckerton, New Jersey **2** Widemouth Bay, England **3** Penmarc'h, France **4** 140 Mbits/s **5** $335 million **6** $250 million, $52 million, $33 million **7** 9 **8** British Telecom (16%)
Fig 15c **a** 850 **b** 3 **c** LW-MM **d** multimode **e** 0.8 **f** 25 **g** 1300 **h** single mode **i** 35.

15.3.1

a Their Teletex service is about to be launched.
b The country's first long-distance optical fibre link has just been taken into service.
c They have just gone over from a manual to an automatic mobile radio service.
d The capital city's tenth teleshop is about to be opened.
e Their fourth communications satellite is about to be put into geostationary orbit.
f The maintenance supervisors had just returned before the opening of the exchange.

15.3.2

Fig 15d **1** Swedish; a Swede; the Swedes **2** Finland; Finnish; the Finns **3** France; a Frenchman/woman; the French **4** China; Chinese; a Chinaman **5** Italian; an Italian; the Italians **6** Greece; Greek; a Greek **7** Japan; Japanese; the Japanese **8** Germany; a German; the Germans **9** Spanish; a Spaniard; the Spanish
10 Norway; a Norwegian; the Norwegians **11** Russia; Russian; the Russians **12** The Netherlands; Dutch; a Dutchman/woman **13** English; an Englishman/woman; the English **14** English; British; a Briton; the British
15 Australia; English; an Australian; the Australians
16 (The United States of) America; English; American; an American **17** Algeria; Arabic; Algerian; the Algerians
18 German; Austrian; an Austrian; the Austrians
19 New Zealand; English; a New Zealander; the New Zealanders **20** French/Italian/German/Romansh; Swiss; a Swiss; the Swiss.

15.4.1

Fig 15f **a** Northern Telecom Ltd; Mitel Corp. **b** Rolm; MCI Communications; GTE; AT&T (Western Electric Co); IBM; Stromberg-Carlsson Corp; ITT **c** Italtel
d CIT-Alcatel; Thomson; Jeumont-Schneider **e** Plessey; STC; GEC **f** Philips **g** Ericsson **h** Siemens **i** NEC; Fujitsu Ltd.
Fig 15g **a** Western Electric Co. **b** ITT **c** Thomson **d** CIT-Alcatel.

15.4.2

1g 2c, f 3a 4b 5d 6e.

15.5

Fig 15h **a** Ford; worldwide communications; England; co-ordination of manufacturing and sales/strategic means of effective competition **b** First National Bank of Boston; data communications network; Boston (New York, London, Hong Kong); speed of approving loan applications **c** Atlantic Richfield (Arco); videoconferencing system; Los Angeles (Philadelphia, Denver, Houston, Dallas, Washington); $10 million annual saving in travel costs **d** American Express; worldwide network; Phoenix; speed and security of credit card transactions lead to lower costs.